BIDS, TENDERS & PROPOSALS

BIDS, TENDERS& PROPOSALS

Winning Business Through Best Practice

2nd edition

Harold Lewis

RECOMMENDED BY
INSTITUTE OF DIRECTORS

KOGAN
PAGE

London and Sterling, VA

The views expressed in this book are those of the author and are not necessarily the same as those of the Institute of Directors.

Publisher's note
Every possible effort has been made to ensure that the information contained in this book is accurate at the time of going to press, and the publishers and authors cannot accept responsibility for any errors or omissions, however caused. No responsibility for loss or damage occasioned to any person acting, or refraining from action, as a result of the material in this publication can be accepted by the editor, the publisher or any of the authors.

First published in Great Britain and the United States in 2002 by Kogan Page Limited
Second edition 2005

120 Pentonville Road
London N1 9JN
United Kingdom
www.kogan-page.co.uk

22883 Quicksilver Drive
Sterling VA 20166-2012
USA

© Harold Lewis, 2002, 2005

The right of Harold Lewis to be identified as the author of this work has been asserted by him in accordance with the Copyright, Designs and Patents Act 1988.

ISBN 0 7494 4369 3

British Library Cataloguing-in-Publication Data

A CIP record for this book is available from the British Library.

Library of Congress Cataloging-in-Publication Data

Lewis, Harold, 1933–
    Bids, tenders, and proposals : winning business through best practice / Harold Lewis.—2nd ed.,
        p. cm.
    ISBN 0-7494-4369-3
    1. Proposal writing in business. 2. Proposal writing in public contracting. 3. Letting of contracts. I. Title.
HF5718.5.L49 2005
658.15′224—dc22

2004029043

Typeset by JS Typesetting Ltd, Porthcawl, Mid Glamorgan
Printed and bound in Great Britain by Creative Print and Design (Wales), Ebbw Vale

Contents

Contents _____

Contents _____

List of figures

Preface to the second edition

This new edition extends the scope of the book in several ways. Chapter 1 now includes a section on the processes of business development and market intelligence that precede the stage of writing a bid. The discussion of bid management in Chapter 8 has been expanded to give more advice on document collaboration and version control. In most sections of the text, points of detail have been added with the aim of making the book even more useful as a practical guide to successful bidding.

Information on the EU procurement framework (Chapter 2) and EU research funding (Chapter 4) has been brought up to date, along with other references throughout the book. Some of the examples of proposal material and other figures have been refreshed, while in places the text has been restructured to improve its flow.

1

A bid to succeed

ABOUT THIS BOOK

If you are engaged in professional services, consultancy or research, you will find guidance here on every step in the process of writing bids, tenders and proposals for contracts and project funding. The book puts at your disposal techniques that the author has perfected as a specialist writer in this field and insights gained from his experience as a tender evaluator with client organizations in the public and private sectors. Those who are new to bid writing will learn how to build the confidence to start producing successful bids. Those who are more experienced will, it is hoped, be shown new ideas that extend and reinforce their skills.

There are points of definition to be made at the outset. Though the type of document that is the subject of this book – a formal written offer to undertake work or provide services for a stated price – is called a 'tender' in services procurement, consultants are more likely to refer to it as a 'proposal' or 'bid', while research bodies may talk about an 'application for funding'. Since the book is relevant to all these fields, the words 'bid', 'tender' and 'proposal' are used here without distinction as inclusive and generic terms. Similarly, the term 'contractor' should be understood to mean any individual, firm or organization putting in a bid, whatever their background.

The scope of the book includes a broad range of procurement and funding. The text aims to deal comprehensively with its subject matter, but it does not cover tendering for supplies or works contracts or 'design, build and operate' schemes and similar contracts. Much of the material will be relevant to public–private partnerships, though procurement issues related specifically to these initiatives are not addressed directly in the book.

This introductory section is followed by chapters highlighting aspects of bidding in three broad environments: public sector procurement, particularly within the EU framework (Chapter 2); contracts for private sector clients (Chapter 3); and research funding (Chapter 4). Pre-qualification procedures are the subject of Chapter 5. The process is then traced out step by step from the decision to put in a bid (Chapter 6) through the task of managing its preparation and development to the construction of the text (Chapters 7 to 12). The categories of information normally included in a bid, from technical analyses to cost estimates, are discussed in Chapters 13 to 20. The concluding sections (Chapters 21 to 25) follow the bid through the stages of submission and evaluation as well as outlining a procedure to assist in the continuous improvement of bid quality.

The techniques described in the book are within the reach of everyone, whether firms of consultants or individuals working on their own: they can be put to use in bidding for small projects as much as large contracts, in writing short proposals as much as multi-volume tenders. Chapter 12 contains a complete bid – a letter of just a few pages – as a practical and small-scale example of the approach set out in the book.

That example shows the process of bidding at its simplest: a fairly short letter in response to a direct approach from a client. At the other extreme, the process can go through a number of stages, involving a sequence of documentation on the part of clients and consultants. The choice of process is determined principally by the context of the bid and the scale of the contract: clients in the private sector tend to prefer a direct and uncomplicated approach, while public sector authorities are generally required to adopt more formal procedures and have less flexibility in the way they select consultants and award contracts. Figure 1.1 summarizes these two approaches, indicating the types of document that are commonly associated with each stage in a formal process of bidding.

In most sectors of procurement, competitive bidding is the norm for all except small, low-value and low-risk assignments. Single sourcing is generally considered acceptable only if the work is a logical extension of a previous or existing contract and continuity is required, or if only one contractor is qualified or trusted to undertake the work, or if a contract has to be awarded quickly in an emergency. But even in these situations it makes good sense for the client to ask the contractor for what is to all intents and purposes a bid, stating how the work will be performed, when it will be completed, what the outputs and deliverables will be and what the work will cost.

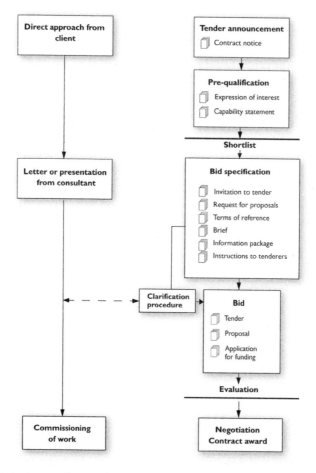

Figure 1.1 *Approaches to the bidding process*

GUIDELINES TO SET YOU ON COURSE

Focus on the client's needs

The prime function of a bid can be seen from the standpoint of the contractor as winning business through a competitive response to the client's requirements. But it is important to view bidding also from the client's perspective. For the client, the purpose of the process is to help identify accurately and reliably the contractor likely to deliver the best value and achieve the best results. Following the client's instructions and supplying the information the client needs to reach this decision are matters of common sense; yet it is surprising how many bids fail in this respect.

The procurement activity in which the bid plays a central role is 'owned' by the client: it is the client who sets up the competition, invites contractors to bid and judges the strengths of each competitor. So the client's priorities, not those of the contractor, have to take centre stage. A bid that shares with the client an identity of understanding and commitment is more likely to succeed than one presenting only the contractor's point of view. This is why it is so important to try to gain in-depth knowledge about a client's business environment, strategies and objectives before starting to prepare the bid. And it is the reason why an effort has been made throughout the guidance offered in this book to reflect the views and preferences expressed by clients.

Do not misunderstand the point of writing a proposal. It is not meant to set out a solution to the client's problems. That would amount to dispensing free advice, not winning business! What a proposal is meant to do is convince the client organization that you have the skills, resources and experience to work out the right solution, and that it will gain unique added value and achieve its objectives best by awarding the work to you.

Match the bid to the opportunity

Knowing how to develop bids efficiently and communicate them powerfully is a key business skill, essential for survival and growth. Bids are first and foremost business documents. To succeed they need to exhibit businesslike qualities both in the way they address the work to be done and in the way they speak to the client.

The bid has to show that the person or people who wrote it thought hard about the client's requirements, interpreted them accurately, developed the bid specifically for that opportunity and exercised care in its preparation, and that it was not just patched together using copy-and-paste commands. Some contractors seem to have a production-line attitude to bids. They think they have found an easy solution: all that is necessary is to splice and recycle the same material, adding a touch of local flavouring here and there. This is because they see bid preparation as a chore to be despatched with as little effort on their part as possible. It is a frame of mind that wins few marks from clients. They can instantly detect a standard, off-the-shelf formula dusted down for one more appearance.

Few contractors manage to win work by half-heartedly going through the motions of tendering. There is little point in submitting a bid unless it has distinctive benefits to offer the client, and unless it is designed to be as competitive as it can be in terms of both technical quality and value for money. The aim should be to establish an invincible case for the superiority of the bid, working hard to get its content right and communicating its strengths as convincingly as possible.

Be honest and realistic about what you can achieve

Don't oversell or inflate the bid with unrealizable promises. The only result of that will be flocks of chickens coming home to roost. Once clients come to believe that they cannot rely on you to deliver what you promise, you will have your work cut out to regain their confidence. This point is important to bear in mind when you are bidding for further work from them, especially if there are aspects of your past performance that ran into problems or failed to meet their expectations. You will have to address those failings directly in the bid and show that you have taken action to put things right. Blithe assurances about your commitment to developing a new relationship and delivering fully in future are not enough. If your bid is to have credibility, clients will want to see hard and convincing evidence that you mean to do what you say.

When seeking work from new clients, you are unlikely to get far if you just make generalized assertions about the strength of your expertise or the breadth of your experience. As observed in Chapter 18, you need to validate your claims with solid facts and credentials that you can prove.

Readability makes a difference

No amount of slick phrasing can disguise a lack of technical substance. But a bid needs to be written in a way that conveys energy and enthusiasm, and it should be interesting and easy to read. There is a consensus among evaluators that the bids most likely to win are those that make their case straightforwardly, concisely and vividly. Once in a while an evaluator will be fortunate enough to come across one that is really outstanding: it may have an imaginative and compelling structure; its content may project a sense of value in a way unmatched by any other bid; it may have examples that bring the text to life; it may communicate an intense commitment to the challenges of the assignment; its use of graphics may be unusually creative; it may have a hands-on feel and a clear sense of having done the job before. All these qualities give the bid a directness and personality that heighten its competitive impact.

Keep calm and in control

If they were willing to admit it, there are many contractors who greet the arrival of an invitation to tender not with eagerness but with feelings close to panic. This reaction is understandable when you are faced with a complex and stressful intellectual challenge and an unforgiving deadline, particularly if you have relatively little experience of bid writing. But don't let fear last for more than about five minutes: you need to get down to work! The best antidote is to know that you have to hand a structured procedure that will enable you to develop the bid methodically and that will quickly yield positive results. That is what the guidance in this book is intended to provide.

DEVELOPING SKILLS IN BID WRITING

The more experience you gain in writing bids, the less intimidating the task seems and the easier it becomes to find the most effective means of communicating your message. For people who are on the staff of a firm one useful route into the process is to start by contributing technical input to bids and pre-qualification material, working with bid managers and proposal specialists. If you are a manager looking to develop good bid writers, you need first to identify people with the right qualities and then help them build up a bank of skills not just in business communication and the logistics of bid preparation, but also in the strategic aspects of tendering:

- gauging a practicable response to the scale of contract requirements;

- analysing contract issues, options and approaches;

- seeing contracts from the client's side of the table;

- viewing the work as a service delivered to the client, not a technical exercise;

- matching work procedures with their cost implications;

- applying project management techniques in developing work programmes;

- researching markets and projects;

- understanding client needs and priorities;

- applying first-hand project experience to bid development;

- acquiring an attitude of mind that looks into the mechanics of a project, sees what problems might occur and how to prevent them, and builds these measures into an effective partnership between client and contractor.

Successful bid writers:

- are bright technically;

- know how to write clearly and directly;

- work conscientiously and methodically;

- do what the client asks;

- care about detail;

- perform well in a team;

- understand outputs and meet deadlines.

MARKET RESEARCH AND INTELLIGENCE

Opportunities to bid for work can come through any number of channels: from a client who knows the services you provide and approaches you directly; from a referral by someone in your profession or in a related field of consultancy; from a contract notice in the EC *Official Journal*; from information you read in the technical press, or from your own initiative in detecting a requirement on the part of a client and structuring a possible solution. An invitation to bid may be the reward for nursing a project over a period of months or even years in which you have built a relationship with a client and established the value of your skills and experience. Or it may arrive quite out of the blue, simply because a person you worked with in the past remembered your name and gave it to someone else who happened to know a client in need of your type of expertise. Whatever the route, your success in capturing these opportunities will depend on the information clients have about your services and the information you have about them and the environment in which they operate.

There are three general points that apply to all types of market intelligence. First, it has to be up to date and dependable or else it is useless – which means that it needs to be maintained as part of an efficient management information system. Second, it has to be structured in a form that relates to your competitive strengths and business objectives. Third, you should never underestimate the time, effort and money that may have to be invested in researching a market, getting to know clients and gaining an inside track before you see positive results.

If you have built a good relationship with your existing clients, delivered value for money and earned their trust, you should get an early lead into opportunities while they are in the process of being defined by management. You may be able to help managers develop their ideas about the work and shape the content of a bid specification. You may learn the budget available for the work and the client's priorities for allocating the budget. At the very least you should gain a sense of how client managers view the scale and scope of the work and what they will look for in terms of added value from consultants.

Maintain contact with clients between assignments, but don't do this just to advertise your availability. Try to develop a genuinely professional relationship with counterparts and managers in the client organization, so that you build up a dialogue in which you can discuss their needs and problems as one professional talking to another, rather than as a seller talking to a buyer. Be careful not to take this relationship for granted or to assume that the client will from now on turn to you as a matter of course: a new manager may arrive who is unacquainted with your work or takes a different view of consultants. Keep track of the situation and change your approach if necessary.

Records of personal contacts may be no more extensive than a file of business cards or an index listing job titles, phone numbers and e-mail addresses; but they are an essential part of every consultant's marketing network. If you have been in practice for some time, you will know that it is not uncommon for professionals to migrate from consultancy firms to client organizations and vice versa. People whom you knew as colleagues in the past and perhaps worked with on consultancy assignments may now have senior management posts with clients and may be in a position to put work your way, or at least arrange for you to meet other managers in their organization. The relationship is not necessarily one-sided; they may well be glad to have you available as a known and dependable source of specialist advice whom they can recommend to their employers. Keep your professional contacts in good repair: the quality and strength of these relationships are all important. Help from one's friends can make all the difference when times are hard and jobs are scarce, but a phone call after 10 years of silence just because you are desperate for work is hardly likely to produce results.

Though potential clients may not be so forthcoming as existing ones, it is possible with the right approach to gain a substantial amount of information about their structure and operations, their expectations of consultancy performance and the way they perceive their requirements. The principal medium is the face-to-face meeting, the technical dialogue that establishes your claim to be considered a professional resource that can deliver what they value more satisfactorily than anyone else.

Adopt a policy of researching as much as possible about a potential client before a first meeting:

▪ Does the client use consultants on a regular basis? Do any of your competitors have close relationships with the client? Conversely, even though you may be facing an entrenched competitor, is there evidence that the client may want to take on new advisers who can offer a fresh approach?

9

- How are consultancy services bought in? Is this arranged through a central procurement department, following a set procedure, or do individual units have discretion in the way they engage advisers?

- In many organizations your 'client' will be a group of managers and other decision-makers and stakeholders in the work whose support may be essential to success. Who are the people with most influence in the process? Is there one individual on whom you should focus your marketing efforts, or are responsibilities divided between several people in various offices? Do consultancy appointments require endorsement by a board of directors, and will it be enough to convince the managing director about your merits?

- What is the organization's management style? Is it run in an authoritarian manner by executives who are defensive about their sectors of responsibility, or does it encourage an open, participatory style of working? Do you have an initial sense of how the chemistry between you and the client might develop? Are there aspects of the way the client works that can offer you a competitive advantage?

- What messages does the organization project to its own customers? How much can you learn from its business publications? Annual reviews or reports and accounts often contain useful material about key management personnel and their responsibilities as well as strategic issues such as business restructuring and investment programming. Company newsletters and in-house journals will offer useful pointers to business plans and projects.

One common-sense though sometimes forgotten point: you have to make that first meeting an interesting and professionally worthwhile experience for the client! You want the client to see you as a potential colleague not as someone pitching for business. If the client manager feels that he or she is gaining value from the meeting in terms of information or insight, it is likely to prove rewarding for you as well.

As we will see in Chapters 6 and 7, there may be a large number of questions to answer in deciding whether or not to put in a bid, and even more issues to consider when you are analysing a bid specification. The more thorough your market research, and the more information you are able to acquire about possible work opportunities, the better equipped you will be to address those questions and develop a confident, competitive bid.

Registration

In both the public and private sectors it is common for clients to maintain registers or lists of approved suppliers or preferred contractors. Entry to these registers is generally obtained through the completion of forms and questionnaires covering the size and structure of a firm, its personnel, specialist skills, experience, financial standing and related matters, as well as quality management and 'business excellence' issues.

- Pursue a systematic approach to registration. Obtain accurate information on the individual requirements of client organizations: there are often wide variations even within a single administration or business group.

- Complete all the client's requirements in full detail.

- Review your firm's registrations and update them regularly. What was the date of the last set of documents, and to whom were they sent? Does the client organization still exist in that shape, or has it been superseded by another authority or taken over by another business? It is easy to lose track of developments and then find that registrations have lapsed or become obsolete.

- If and when you visit a client's offices, check on the status of your registration and replace any out-of-date documents with new material.

- On its own, registration simply brings you eligibility for selection and places your firm in the database or filing cabinet. In some instances it may succeed in getting you on an extended list with an invitation to express interest; but the mere fact of being registered with a client or funding institution is not in itself an endorsement or a credential and should not be portrayed as such on your website or in your proposals.

2

Bidding for public sector contracts

THE EU PROCUREMENT FRAMEWORK

The term 'public sector' as used in EU member states covers central government, regional and local authorities, utilities, European institutions such as the European Commission and its related programmes and other bodies governed by public law. The Commission estimates that public sector procurement in the EU in 2003 had a potential value of more than 1,500 billion euros, equivalent to about 16 per cent of EU gross domestic product. Across the individual member states its value ranged between 11 per cent and 20 per cent of gross domestic product.

All public sector authorities are subject to European public procurement rules, intended to secure open and fair competition, transparent and auditable contracting procedures and equal access to contract opportunities for all EU suppliers. Utilities (defined as entities operating in the water, energy, transport and telecommunications sectors) are required to comply with procurement rules that differ in some points of detail from those applying to other parts of the public sector.

Public procurement rules are defined in a series of EU directives implemented at a national level through regulations and other forms of legislation. In February 2004 the EU adopted a new public sector procurement directive that consolidated the existing public works, services and supplies directives into a single text. The broad aim of the new directive is to simplify and coordinate procedures for the award of public contracts, updating them to reflect the advent of new technologies such as e-communication, removing elements of ambiguity and rigidity and increasing the transparency of contract award procedures. The directive introduces a new procedure termed 'competitive dialogue', which can be used in awarding contracts for complex projects and is intended to help public authorities identify the best means of meeting their requirements through negotiation and the progressive refinement of technical solutions.

The public sector procurement directive is accompanied by another new directive that consolidates the rules applying to utilities. New regulations implementing the consolidated directives have to be in place by the end of January 2006. In the meantime the existing regulations apply.

The purpose of the procurement rules is not so much to establish consistent procedures across the EU member states as to eliminate discriminatory and uncompetitive practices counter to the public interest, and to ensure public money is spent in a way that achieves best value. Authorities in the UK are able to apply their own procedures for tendering and contract award on the basis of standing orders, provided these do not infringe EU rules or the requirements of UK legislation and government accounting principles.

Public sector contracts for services and consultancy in the UK are governed principally by the following regulations:

■ The Public Services Contracts Regulations 1993;

■ The Public Contracts (Works, Services and Supply) (Amendment) Regulations 2000;

■ The Utilities Contracts Regulations 1996;

■ The Utilities Contracts (Amendment) Regulations 2001;

■ The Public Contracts (Works, Services and Supply) and Utilities Contracts (Amendment) Regulations 2003. These largely implement an

EC directive on the use of standard forms for contract notices as part of the introduction of electronic procurement.

KEY ASPECTS OF THE PROCUREMENT REGULATIONS

Financial thresholds

Specific rules apply to contracts with values at or exceeding financial thresholds set out in the regulations; contracts with lower values are subject to less stringent requirements. The regulations include formulae for calculating values for a series of contracts and for framework agreements.

In January 2004 new threshold values came into effect, which will remain unchanged for two years in the case of EU member states outside the single currency. The sterling values of these thresholds are calculated on the basis of exchange rates between sterling, euros and special drawing rights (a currency unit devised by the IMF). Contracts with values at or above the following sterling amounts are subject to the procurement rules, with certain exceptions that chiefly affect categories of research and development and telecommunications services:

	Threshold
Services contracts – central government	£99,695
Services contracts – other public sector authorities	£153,376
Services contracts – public sector small lots	£51,785
Utilities services contracts – water, electricity, urban transport, airports and ports sectors	£306,753
Utilities services contracts – oil, gas, coal and railway sectors	£258,923
Utilities services contracts – telecommunications	£388,385

(Source: Office of Government Commerce)

Prior information on procurement programmes

If the total estimated value of the contracts that a public sector authority intends to award during a financial year is equal to or exceeds

750,000 euros (a sterling threshold value of about £525,000 at mid-November 2004 rates of exchange), the authority is required to issue a prior information notice at the start of the year, outlining its procurement intentions for the 12 months ahead. The purpose is to give prospective contractors an early indication of tendering opportunities. So far as authorities other than utilities are concerned, the prior information notice is not a call for tenders and does not require a response from contractors, since it refers to an overall programme rather than giving detailed information about individual contracts. Utilities are able to use an indicative notice to call for competitive tenders for a specific project.

Advertisement and publication of contract notices

Issued five times a week in CD ROM format, Supplement S of the _Official Journal of the European Communities_ (_OJS_) contains notices of all contracts for which public sector authorities are calling for tenders. Its coverage includes principally:

- public contracts for works, supplies and services from all EU member states;

- utilities contracts;

- public contracts from EU institutions;

- European Development Fund contracts;

- projects funded by the European Investment Bank, European Central Bank and European Bank for Reconstruction and Development;

- European Economic Area contracts (Norway, Iceland, Switzerland and Liechtenstein);

- notices about European Economic Interest Groupings.

An online version of the _OJS_, updated each day, is available from the Tenders Electronic Daily (TED) website (http://ted.publications.eu.int). Access to TED is free of charge: the database offers multiple search options and in addition to current notices contains information on contract advertisements over the past five years. Tender opportunities that are part of EC-funded programmes may be notified also through internet announcements on programme websites.

In May 2002 a new European directive came into force, making it mandatory for authorities to use a standard form for contract notices published in the *OJS*: its aims are to facilitate the online interrogation of notices, reinforce the development of electronic procurement and overcome problems caused by the appearance of incomplete and sometimes inaccurate information. The content of the new contract notice form is comprehensive: it covers, among other matters, the purpose and scope of the contract; legal, economic and technical conditions for participation; whether a fee has to be paid to obtain contract documents or bid specifications; whether provision of a service is restricted to a particular profession; the type of procedure to be followed in awarding the contract; the award criteria to be applied, stated so far as possible in descending order of importance; the time limits for the receipt of tenders or requests to participate; the language or languages in which tenders or requests to participate can be drawn up, and related administrative information.

Authorities may also use the standard form to publicize contracts not subject to *OJS* notification requirements. Decisions on how and where to advertise such contracts are left to the discretion of authorities: generally, notices about them may be placed in the national, regional and local press and in technical and trade publications.

A note of caution: before deciding to invest time and effort in following up a contract notice about an opportunity in another country, make sure you are adequately informed about both the technical and commercial context of the assignment and the workings of the local procurement environment.

Use of contract award procedures

Contracting authorities have a choice of four types of contract award procedure:

- **Open procedure.** Any consultant or service provider may submit a tender in response to the contract notice. This procedure can have disadvantages for authorities in terms of the time and resources needed to process what might turn out to be an inordinate number of bids, and may lead service providers to question the likely quality and thoroughness of the tender evaluation. On the other hand, it can provide an opportunity for authorities to learn about sources of expertise and solutions that they might not have considered.

- **Restricted procedure.** A service provider has first to submit an expression of interest or a request to be selected as a candidate for tendering through pre-qualification (Chapter 5). The authority then invites tenders from the pre-qualified candidates. Most contracts with values that make them subject to the public procurement rules are awarded under this procedure. In an urgent and exceptional situation, the process may be accelerated: the reasons justifying acceleration must be explained in the contract notice.

- **Negotiated procedure.** An authority may go directly to one or more service providers and negotiate with them the terms of a contract. This type of procedure is used only in relatively exceptional cases, for example when the nature of the services makes it unfeasible to apply either the open or restricted procedure, or when the services and their inherent risks do not allow prior overall pricing.

- **Competitive dialogue.** This is a development of the negotiated procedure. An authority may pursue a process of dialogue with selected tenderers through successive rounds of negotiation until it has identified the solution most likely to satisfy its needs. The participants are then asked to submit their final tenders on the basis of that solution. The contract is awarded to the participant judged to have submitted the tender that is the most economically advantageous, as defined below.

Under the open and restricted procedures, a contracting authority may ask bidders for further information to help evaluate tenders, and bidders may request clarification on points of fact or procedure, but negotiating about the content of tenders, and in particular about prices, is not permitted. Discussions may take place between bidders and authorities only for the purpose of clarifying or supplementing the content of tenders or the requirements of authorities and provided this involves no element of discrimination or unfair practice. Requests for clarification are discussed in Chapter 7.

Pre-qualification criteria

In pre-qualifying bidders under the restricted procedure, an authority is required to apply objective and non-discriminatory criteria that relate to their legal position and their technical, economic and financial capacity. The contract notice will list the pre-qualification criteria, indicating the references and evidence that are required as proof of the competence and suitability of bidders. Technical capacity is judged on the basis of resources, quality standards and past performance, including references from other clients. So far as financial status is concerned, clients may look for evidence that a bidder is considered likely to remain in business over and beyond the lifetime of the contract. Pre-qualification may involve more than one stage of selection. Approaches to pre-qualification are the subject of Chapter 5.

Utilities may apply a qualification system to register potential service providers in place of contract-specific pre-qualification procedures, on condition that the system meets the requirements for objectivity and even-handedness. The UK utility industry uses a Utilities Vendor Database (UVDB) as a single focus point for pre-qualification information, enabling utility companies to comply with EU procurement requirements without having to place individual calls for tenders in the *OJS*. The option of using a comparable qualification system in sourcing contracts above the EU thresholds is not available to public sector clients outside the utilities sector, though most local authorities maintain lists, registers or databases of approved suppliers for lower-value contracts. Research undertaken in 2000 for the former UK Department for Transport, Local Government and the Regions (DTLR) by its Local and Regional Government Research Unit found that over 90 per cent of local authorities used approved lists for procurement and commissioning.

In order to secure an adequate degree of competition, the shortlist resulting from the pre-qualification process will normally have a minimum of five names and perhaps as many as seven or eight. EU procedures enable contractors to receive an explanation of the reasons for failure to pre-qualify.

Contract award on the basis of either the lowest price or the most economically advantageous tender

In services procurement, lowest price is normally used as the sole criterion only in awarding low-value and relatively low-risk contracts. For other contracts, authorities generally prefer the concept of the most economically advantageous tender. This can be defined as the tender that offers the best value for money taking account of technical merit and quality as well as price and cost-effectiveness. The criteria that authorities apply in identifying this tender are discussed in Chapter

22. They have to be the same criteria as those indicated in the contract notice, but must differ from those used in pre-qualification. Changes in the list of criteria or in their relative importance may indicate that an authority favours a particular bidder: they can be grounds for questioning the fairness of the award procedure.

Publication of contract award notices

Authorities are required to publish in the _OJS_ details of contract awards, including the award criteria, the number of tenders received, the name and address of the successful tenderer(s) and the price or range of prices paid. Unsuccessful tenderers have the right to ask for an explanation of why their tenders were rejected and must receive a response within 15 days of requesting this information.

OUTLINE OF THE PROCUREMENT PROCESS

Figure 2.1 indicates the principal actions that might be taken by a local authority and a contractor respectively in a typical procurement process for services or consultancy: the process is shown as far as, but does not include, the stage of contract negotiation. The figure is presented simply as an example of common practice; as observed at the start of this chapter, procedures as distinct from rules are not applied in an unvarying form across the public sector and authorities are free to follow their own methods so long as they do not conflict with EU rules or UK law.

Keeping abreast of change

In terms of their detailed application, EU procurement procedures are more complex than can be indicated in this brief outline. There are circumstances and conditions that give rise to exceptions from general rules, and aspects of the directives are open to differing interpretations. It is essential for prospective bidders to make a thorough analysis of the information in the contract notice and the bid specification (Chapter 7). And it is important to be up to speed on rules and requirements.

Local authority	Contractor / Service provider
Planning and preparation	
Consultation and market testing to ensure that procurement strategy and contracting practices are conducive to securing an effective competitive response	**Market analyses and business strategy** **Focus on target sectors** **Market intelligence for contract opportunities**
Project definition and design, including initial **drafting of bid specification** or **terms of reference**	**Client and project research**
Decision to adopt the **restricted procedure**	**Contacts with client managers**
Determination of **contract award criteria, weightings** and **quality:price ratio** (Chapter 22)	
Appointment of **assessment and selection panel**	
Review of **supplier database,** registration and pre-qualification information	
Notification and pre-qualification	
Initial advertisement and contract notice, inviting expressions of interest	**Response to contract notice** **Preparation and submission of expression of interest**
First stage of selection: assessment panel filters received expressions of interest and, if necessary, reduces list to a manageable total for second stage of selection	
Second stage of selection: a more detailed assessment of prospective bidders, possibly including interviews and visits	
Definition of **shortlist** – say, four to six selected tenderers	
Tendering	
Finalization of work specification	
Issue of proposal invitations and accompanying documentation	**Acknowledgement of invitation** **Decision to bid** **Confirmation of intention to submit a proposal**
Decisions on **evaluation approach**	**Analysis of work specification** **Preparation of proposal**
Arrangements for dealing with **clarification requests**	**Request for clarification**

Figure 2.1 *Steps in a typical local authority procurement process for services or consultancy*

Formal site visits or briefings, if appropriate	**Briefing or meeting with client, if appropriate**
Receipt of proposals	**Submission of proposal**
Evaluation	
Formal **tender opening** and **checks for compliance**	
Proposal evaluation – quality and price	
Arrangements for **presentations** by lead contenders	
Preparation of format and key questions for presentations	**Preparation of presentation**
Assessment of presentations	**Delivery of presentation**
Further clarification of contract issues, if appropriate, through negotiation	Further clarification of contract issues, if appropriate, through negotiation
Selection of the most economically advantageous tender	
Contract award	
Notification to successful bidder, including any **conditions** to be discussed at a further contract negotiation stage	
Notification to unsuccessful bidders, including placing a reserve or hold on the bidder ranked second in case contract negotiations with the first-ranked bidder fail	

Figure 2.1 *continued*

As well as the main EC portal (http://europa.eu.int), the TED site and Euro Information Centres (www.euro-info.org.uk), the SIMAP website (http://simap.eu.int) offers a useful means of staying up to date with developments in EU procurement and obtaining copies of documentation: it is particularly informative about changes in legislation and procedures. SIMAP (Système d'information pour les marchés publics) was launched by the European Commission as an information resource to help create a more open procurement market and facilitate the development of EU-wide electronic procurement. One interesting feature of its website is a discussion forum carrying views and opinions on public sector procurement issues and best practice advice, including responses from Commission officials to questions raised by contracting authorities.

PRIORITIES FOR THE PUBLIC SECTOR

The introduction in April 2000 of the UK Office of Government Commerce (OGC) as part of the Treasury reflected a concern to achieve greater efficiency in public sector procurement and the delivery of large-scale projects and to secure best value for money through best practice techniques. One of OGC's main strategies is 'to achieve effective competition for government business by simplifying access to the government marketplace'. It provides a flow of procurement guidance and advice to government departments, agencies and local authorities, and has clear messages about the factors that authorities are required to take into account when awarding contracts. These messages are essential considerations for anyone hoping to win contracts in the public sector.

- **The key priority for authorities is to identify the best value for money, not just the lowest price.** The concept of value for money is defined by OGC in general terms as 'the optimum combination of whole life costs and quality to meet the user requirement'. With respect to services and consultancy, the definition can be rephrased as 'meeting the user's requirement with the best quality of service at the right price'. In long-term service contracts, authorities are encouraged to seek continuous improvement in value for money as part of the public sector best value regime, which came into operation at the same time as OGC.

- Like contract specifications, bids are expected to focus on **outputs and outcomes** – ie meeting required levels of quality and performance and delivering the results that the contract is intended to achieve.

- Authorities need to see realistic and convincing proposals for **resourcing the contract, managing its delivery and developing a constructive team working relationship with client personnel**.

- Bids should show an **understanding of the client's business objectives** and an awareness of the importance of **risk management** in contract performance.

- Depending on the nature and scale of the contract, public sector authorities may require service providers to work within the terms of the **best value** regime – challenging activities and services against the preferences and expectations of service users and stakeholders and undertaking programmes of continuous service improvement.

Suppliers should:

- be committed to continuous improvement;

- work closely with local authorities in managing longer-term contracts;

- share the benefits from improvements in efficiency and effectiveness over the life of a contract;

- be prepared to adopt an open-book approach in complex contracts;

- provide managers who are experienced or trained to understand the local authority environment;

- together with local authorities, protect the legitimate interests of staff during transfers and monitor the effects of TUPE (Transfer of Undertakings (Protection of Employment) Regulations) and the local government pension scheme regulations when re-tendering.

(from the Summary of Key Recommendations, *Report of the Local Government Procurement Taskforce*, June 2001 – the taskforce is an independent unit whose members are drawn from across the public and private sectors, set up in 2000 to review local government procurement in England)

Guidance from clients

The guidance that OGC offers public sector authorities can help contractors gain a deeper insight into the view clients take of procurement relationships and their perceptions of quality of service, value for money and public–private partnership. Most of the material produced by OGC is freely downloadable from its website (www.ogc.gov.uk), including *Tendering for Government Contracts: A guide for small businesses*, published by OGC together with the DTI's Small Business Service. This informative booklet contains a comprehensive reference list of government purchasing departments and contact details.

In June 2002, OGC and the Small Business Service jointly published a booklet called *Smaller Supplier. . . Better Value?* aimed at procurement professionals in the public sector and produced in the context of the government's 'Think Small First' initiative. The booklet is intended to raise awareness of the value for money and other advantages that small firms can offer and to explore the issues that can make it difficult for them to win public sector contracts. The EU defines small and medium-size enterprises as independent businesses with fewer than 250 employees, and either an annual turnover of less than about 50 million euros (about £35 million) or a balance sheet total of less than about 43 million euros (about £30 million).

Other recent OGC publications focus on partnering – the development of long-term, collaborative working relationships between public sector authorities and suppliers. Key documents include:

- *Effective Partnering: An overview for customers and providers* (March 2004);

- *Improving the Efficiency and Effectiveness of Procurement to Achieve Faster Delivery* (June 2003);

- *Forming Partnering Relationships with the Private Sector* (December 2002);

- *Risk Allocation in Long-Term Contracts* (December 2002);

- *Contract Management Guidelines* (November 2002).

OGC's *Successful Delivery Toolkit* includes a series of workbooks and other guidance for authorities on best practice in procurement and contract management, including business justification, procurement strategy, investment decisions and effective partnering. This emphasis on efficient management, performance and delivery is normally reflected in the bid specifications for high-value public sector contracts by a requirement to provide plans for progress measurement, performance monitoring, quality control and the management of risk and change.

The older guidance notes produced by the Treasury's Central Unit on Procurement (CUP) are now being revised and brought up to date by OGC. *Procurement Guidance No. 3 (Appointment of Consultants and Contractors)* was issued in April 2002 (Version 2), superseding earlier

CUP material, and is essential reading. Contractors will find it useful to acquaint themselves also with the principles behind the OGC Gateway process, which reviews delivery programmes and procurement projects at key decision points in their life cycle, and the PRINCE 2 project management method. In addition to material published by central government, individual authorities may produce guidance to inform prospective bidders about their procurement policies and contracting procedures.

BIDDING FOR PROJECT FUNDING

'Challenge funds', 'partnership funds', 'new opportunities funds' and similar schemes are some of the funding streams used by government departments to support local authority projects and business initiatives. The funds are normally distributed on a selective basis following the submission of bids in a process analogous to bidding for research funding. Applicants prepare their bids in response to guidance from the department; panels of experts assess the bids and recommend which projects should be accepted for funding and how much they should receive; the final decisions on funding are taken by the department.

Points to remember

- Departments may set a limit on the funding available to an individual bid, or they may indicate that bids over a certain threshold will need to put forward robust and convincing arguments. In any event, it is important to be realistic about the amount of money you are asking for.

- Your bid will have a better chance of success if you can show that the project will not go ahead without the support of the fund. At the same time, it can be useful to indicate that you have finance committed to the project from other sources of funding that recognize the value of what it is trying to achieve and are prepared to invest in it.

- Departments like bids that are linked to the fulfilment of government strategies, programmes and targets, that can add value to other initiatives and that can mobilize jointly the efforts and resources of different sectors of the community.

- They will expect you to set the elements of the bid in a logical order of priority and to show the extent to which particular elements are dependent on the scale of fund support: in other words, if you were to receive only, say, 50 per cent of the funds you are seeking, what would you be able to achieve and would this damage the viability and value for money of the project?

- Proposals for pilot or demonstration projects must show that what they are seeking to demonstrate is genuinely innovative, and that the results are likely to be useful to others.

- Departments will want to see a breakdown of total estimated costs and will assess whether the expected outputs of the project represent good value for money. Set out in the bid your plans for monitoring, measuring and reporting progress. Departments need information about the benefits achieved through the use of funding so as to be able to make a case for the fund schemes to continue in the future. You may be asked to provide a business case in support of your figures.

- Will the work of the project carry on after funding support comes to an end? If so, you will need to explain how you intend to make the project sustainable.

- Show that you have made a realistic assessment of the required funding profile and the risks to the success of the project, and that you understand the need to manage risks (Chapter 11). How far will the outcome of the project depend on factors outside the control of the applicants? If there are substantial risks, are they justified by the potentially high value of the outputs?

- There appears to be a positive relationship between bids that win project funding and bids that open with an eye-catching statement. ('A place where people succeed. This is Middletown. An area of achievement but also an area with problems that can be tackled only through a strategic approach to regeneration.')

- Never forget that you are in a contest. Your job is to stake an undeniable claim for funding support. To do this, you need to make sure that your bid stands out among all the dozens of competing claims. It has to be technically sound, well thought through and businesslike. It has to show how your project will make a difference. And in an environment where so much writing is bland and characterless, it has to be presented in a way that seizes the attention of the people charged with assessing its merits and wins their enthusiasm.

3

Tendering for the private sector

EQUAL CONCERN FOR VALUE FOR MONEY

The procedures outlined in the preceding chapter reflect the need to demonstrate even-handedness and transparency in the award of public contracts. Because contracting in the private sector is normally free from these considerations, clients have more flexibility about the way they manage procurement and let contracts.

Though only large corporate clients may choose to emulate the formalities of public sector procurement, most businesses recognize the merits of competitive bidding as a means of identifying not just the contractors with the lowest price but those who can provide the best all-round response to their needs. Competitive bidding offers several benefits: a consistent and methodical basis for selecting contractors; access to different ideas, approaches and solutions; an opportunity to learn how well contractors understand the client's requirements; and the chance to assess the quality of the working relationship likely to develop once the contract is awarded. Most important of all, there is probably no more direct or reliable way to learn who represents the best value for money; in this respect the private sector's priorities are not so far removed from the public sector concept of the most economically advantageous tender.

Private sector clients are generally less prescriptive about the format and structure of bids, giving contractors more scope to devise an individual approach tailored to the requirements of the contract. They are also more forthcoming about meeting contractors and talking to them about the context of the work.

When evaluating bids, business clients ask much the same questions as clients in the public sector. The messages that go out to public sector authorities from the Office of Government Commerce (Chapter 2) are derived essentially from best practice in the private sector. Just as public sector authorities are advised not to think in terms of lowest cost, business clients appreciate that in working with contractors they get what they pay for, and that contractors who offer services at rates cut to the bone may be offering also low quality, poor performance and minimal standards of professionalism.

Their first concern will be to identify the bid that offers the best overall value for money, displays the most businesslike approach to meeting their objectives and responds best to the bid specification. Like their counterparts in the public sector, they will want to see prices that are realistic in relation to the scale of the contract; they will look for quality in the inputs and resources proposed for the work; they will need to have outcomes and deliverables clearly defined; and they will seek evidence of distinctive added value and reliable performance. But there are other factors that come into play particularly in a business context, and these can influence decisively their views about the bid that is right for them:

- **Insight into the client's operating environment:** Does the bidder appear informed about the sectors of activity in which the business is engaged and the factors that influence its market environment and profitability?

- **Partnering and synergy:** Is there a sense that this bidder is the one best placed to work with the client in a productive team effort? Are the corporate values and policies of the business understood and supported?

■ **Risk and professional accountability:** Has the bid addressed these concepts? Does it indicate an understanding of their significance for successful contract performance?

■ **Innovation:** New ideas, fresh thinking and solutions that competitors will find it hard to match are ingredients that can win the day, but innovation needs to be dependable. Has the bidder taken account of the risks associated with innovation?

■ **Flexibility and responsiveness:** Does the bid communicate a willingness to adapt methods and procedures in response to unforeseen changes in the requirements of the contract?

Business clients will expect their existing contractors to be able to offer cost and efficiency savings as well as continuity of personnel, and to have the capacity to get up to speed rapidly on a new contract so as to start producing useful output without mobilization delays or steep learning curves. To this extent clients may find that there is a comfort factor in giving work to people with whom they have reliable working relationships, provided they still offer good value for money. But existing contractors must not imagine they have security of tenure! The need for them to defend their position by offering extra added value is emphasized in Chapter 16.

If you have managed to develop a good professional relationship with the client – for example, as a result of your marketing efforts and previous contracts – you may be able to gain an indication of how the evaluation team will be structured. Figure 3.1 shows a decision-making structure that is characteristic of services and consultancy procurement in large businesses. There are three main participants: 1) the manager responsible for the bidding process, for commissioning the work, running the client's side of the contract and maintaining the day-to-day relationship with the contractor; 2) a procurement manager who assists the business unit manager in dealing with contractual and commercial issues; and 3) technical specialists who can advise on detailed aspects of the work such as health and safety or quality assurance.

Some business clients adopt a practice of skimming through bids quickly to gain an overall idea of their quality before subjecting them to a more thorough analysis. First impressions can be decisive – which is a further reason why contractors need to make sure that bids are seen immediately to be organized efficiently, structured logically and presented in a competent professional manner. The length of time that

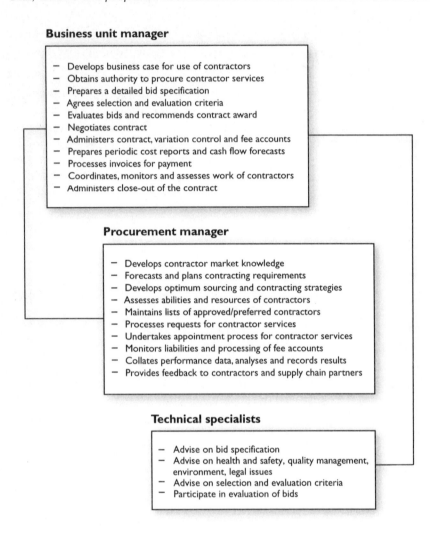

Business unit manager

- Develops business case for use of contractors
- Obtains authority to procure contractor services
- Prepares a detailed bid specification
- Agrees selection and evaluation criteria
- Evaluates bids and recommends contract award
- Negotiates contract
- Administers contract, variation control and fee accounts
- Prepares periodic cost reports and cash flow forecasts
- Processes invoices for payment
- Coordinates, monitors and assesses work of contractors
- Administers close-out of the contract

Procurement manager

- Develops contractor market knowledge
- Forecasts and plans contracting requirements
- Develops optimum sourcing and contracting strategies
- Assesses abilities and resources of contractors
- Maintains lists of approved/preferred contractors
- Processes requests for contractor services
- Undertakes appointment process for contractor services
- Monitors liabilities and processing of fee accounts
- Collates performance data, analyses and records results
- Provides feedback to contractors and supply chain partners

Technical specialists

- Advise on bid specification
- Advise on health and safety, quality management, environment, legal issues
- Advise on selection and evaluation criteria
- Participate in evaluation of bids

Figure 3.1 *Typical decision-making structure in corporate procurement*

a client can devote to the task of evaluation will be governed, as one would expect, by pressures of work and the specific circumstances of the contract. The process is often more intensive and concentrated than bidders may imagine: you may have taken a month to write a bid but the client may be able to spend only an hour or so evaluating it.

TAKING ON CONTRACTORS

Our divisional managers use their commercial judgement in appointing consultants and other advisers. When they take these decisions they have a lot at stake professionally. Their futures in the group can depend on the way their contracts work out. Managers like contractors who make their life easier, not contractors who cause them problems. No one wants to be seen as a manager who lets contracts run out of control. So we look for contractors who understand the way we work and the importance we attach to efficient delivery. The worst thing contractors can do is to fill their bids with nice words and brave promises but then fail to deliver. It's bad for us and for them – we won't use them any more.

When we read bids, we are looking for hard facts about people's experience and signs that they will fit in with our business style and team up well with our own personnel. It's also good to see evidence that consultants realize that the work we are paying them for isn't a technical exercise but something that has value only if it helps us in our business strategy. They need to have this practical focus if they are to gain the respect of our people. If they seem to offer genuine potential for a long-term partnership relationship, so much the better.

We are sometimes disappointed with bids from existing contractors. They can go through the formalities of competing for the work without any real spark of energy or commitment. It's a complacent attitude, as if they are assuming that no one else can know enough about the job to put in a credible bid. We are also unimpressed when they fail to acknowledge problems and failures on their part. If contractors have made mistakes in the past, they should have the courage to admit them and show how they have learnt from errors so as to improve their performance.

(Chief executive of a banking and financial services group)

4

Bidding for research funding

Organizations that fund research almost invariably define the form in which funding applications or proposals are to be structured, the type of information they need to see and the way they want it set out. Applications may have to be submitted in two stages – first as an outline proposal or 'concept note' and then as a final bid or full proposal; a call for proposals may be preceded by an invitation to submit expressions of interest to help in preparing work programmes and lists of research topics; or funding applications may take the form of a 'main bid' – providing information on the research unit or partnership, the proposed implementation plan and team, methodology, project control and start date – and a cost bid that includes a financial analysis of the project. Clients may also use proposal structures that focus on a statement of the work programme and its deliverables, the benefits and innovations expected to result from the work and the mechanisms to be used in disseminating and transferring the knowledge gained.

In calling for bids, many bodies either require or favour the formation of partnerships and associations among researchers. Factors to be considered when selecting research partners include their level of knowledge and experience, the complementarity of their research activities, their status in terms of scientific or technological excellence, their capacity to perform successfully a substantive role in the research, the degree to which they share a common approach and perspective and the technical and management credibility of the partnership. In contexts such as EU-funded work, the choice of team partners will be influenced also by concepts such as 'transnationality' – cooperation across borders through consortia of research organizations from different member countries.

TENDERING FOR EU-FUNDED RESEARCH

EU-funded research projects are undertaken largely in the context of multi-annual research, technological development and demonstration (RTD) framework programmes. The Sixth Framework Programme 2002–2006 (FP6) has a budget of 17.5 billion euros, which represents about 5 per cent of the total expenditure on RTD in EU member states. Detailed information on the programme is available from its website at www.cordis.lu/fp6, and from the EU research portal at http://europa.eu.int/comm/research/, which provides access to a comprehensive set of FAQ pages about all aspects of FP6. Two key documents that can be downloaded from the FP6 site are _The 6th Framework Programme in Brief_ (33 pages, December 2002) and _Guidelines on Proposal Evaluation and Selection Procedures_ (48 pages, May 2004).

This chapter can offer only a broad outline of FP6. Its essential features may be summarized as follows:

■ The key objectives are to integrate resources and activities into a coordinated European research effort and to strengthen the European Research Area, reinforcing the scientific and technological bases of European industry and encouraging its international competitiveness. New funding instruments such as integrated projects and networks of excellence have been developed to achieve these objectives.

■ The programme is designed to address a clearly defined range of priority themes, which include, for example, life sciences, genomics and biotechnology for health; Information Society technologies; sustainable development, global change and ecosystems; and citizens and governance in a knowledge-based society.

■ Each theme has its work programme, set out in detail in calls for proposals. Researchers who want to take part in the programme have to check that their ideas for research projects fit within the scope of the priority themes. They are able to submit multidisciplinary proposals addressing several topics.

■ Proposals may be submitted only in response to a call for proposals published in the EU *Official Journal*. Each call is accompanied by a specific information package containing documents, a Guide for Proposers and forms needed in the preparation of a proposal.

■ For certain types of project, a short outline proposal is submitted and evaluated against a limited set of core evaluation criteria, defined in the work programme. Researchers whose proposals pass all thresholds in the first-stage evaluation are then invited to submit a full proposal, which is evaluated against the full set of criteria.

■ As in previous framework programmes, the costs of a project will be shared between the EU and the research participants, but the extent of EU funding will depend on the specific work programme and the type of research activity.

■ Some 15 per cent of the research funding related to priority themes has been reserved for SMEs. They have two special types of scheme available: 1) cooperative research projects, in which a group of SMEs from different countries commission external research organizations such as research institutes or universities to do research work for them; and 2) collective research projects, in which industrial associations or groupings commission external researchers to undertake research on behalf of communities of SMEs.

■ Constructing a strong and cohesive partnership of complementary organizations is one of the keys to success in winning FP6 funding as in other areas of bidding (Chapter 10). Research partners are expected to manage their own contractual relationships through a consortium agreement.

- There is a preference for partnerships that integrate research institutions and industry since these are thought likely to facilitate the implementation of research findings. Proposals have to contain a 'plan for use and dissemination' to show how the knowledge generated will be taken through to practical application.

- In developing their proposals, researchers will need to show an awareness of ethical and gender issues and the potential effects of scientific and technological research on society.

- FP6 proposals have a two-part structure. Part A is a set of administrative forms with basic information on the proposal and the participants, which will be encoded in a database for computer processing. Part B is a text file describing the research project and the consortium.

- Though proposals may be prepared and sent in on paper, the preferred method of submission is by electronic transmission (Figure 4.1), using the EC's web-based EPSS (Electronic Proposal Submission System), which works through a standard web browser rather like an internet banking application.

- Researchers can obtain assistance in preparing proposals from the national contact points established in all EU member states and in other countries associated with FP6. The EC also operates 'info-desks' for the various priorities and activities of FP6.

Procedures for proposal submission

Proposals may be prepared and submitted by the following methods:

1. Preparation and submission using the online Electronic Proposal Submission System (EPSS)

The proposal coordinator must register his/her intention to prepare a proposal by visiting the web page set up for this purpose. In return, he/she receives a coordinator login and password as well as a partner login and password. The coordinator may now access the EPSS system in order to fill in administrative forms and upload files containing the contents of the proposal. On upload, the EPSS performs a check for computer viruses. If any virus is detected, the coordinator is informed of the fact and that the upload has been refused. It is

---

Figure 4.1 _Procedures for proposal submission, FP6_

the proposal coordinator's responsibility to ensure that infected files are deleted or that viruses are removed before the file can be uploaded.

Once they have received their login and password from the coordinator, proposal partners may access and edit their individual administrative forms and view all other parts of the proposal. Only the coordinator may compile and edit the proposal contents.

The only file format accepted by the Commission for the proposal contents is PDF ('portable document format', compatible with Adobe version 3 or higher with embedded fonts). Compressed ('zipped') files will not be accepted.

Once the proposal is complete, the coordinator must submit it by entering his/her login and password. On submission, the EPSS performs an initial check on eligibility and informs the coordinator of any apparent eligibility problems with the proposal. This check does not replace the eligibility check carried out by the Commission and the coordinator may decide to submit the proposal even when apparent eligibility problems have been indicated by the EPSS. Annexes (eg video presentations, brochures, etc) other than these specifically allowed for in the call text are refused.

Once successfully submitted, the coordinator receives a message that indicates that his/her proposal has been received and accepted for submission. The coordinator may continue to modify his/her proposal and submit revised versions overwriting the previously submitted one up until the call closure, but will not be able to modify the proposal after call closure. Proposal files successfully submitted, but which later turn out to contain computer viruses or which are unreadable or unprintable, will be excluded.

2. Preparation using the offline proposal submission tool

The EPSS also comprises a software tool for preparing proposals offline. The coordinator may download this tool to fill in forms and attach the proposal content file(s). The same restrictions on file format apply as for the online submission method. Submission may then be carried out in two ways:

■ by registering as set out above to use the online submission system and then uploading and submitting the files via the online system;
■ if paper submission has not been excluded by the Commission, a paper copy can be prepared by using the offline tool, which is then delivered before the call closure to the address given in the call for proposals.

3. Preparation on the forms distributed with the Guides for Proposers, followed by delivery to the address given in the call for proposals

Proposals submitted on paper must be submitted in a single package. If proposers wish to submit changes to a proposal or additional information, they must clearly indicate which parts of the proposal have changed and the changes/extra parts must be submitted and received before the call closure.

Figure 4.1 *continued*

Additional or amended proposal contents received after the call closure (or intermediate closure date for continuously open calls) will not be treated or evaluated. Delivery of packages containing proposals on paper may be carried out using normal post, private courier service or by hand. Versions of proposals for indirect RTD actions submitted on a removable electronic storage medium (eg CD ROM, diskette), by e-mail or by fax will be excluded.

The Commission intends to move progressively to fully electronic proposal submission. Therefore the Commission reserves the right to restrict submission for particular individual calls to electronic proposals alone. For these 'paper-free' calls, paper submission will be allowed only in very exceptional cases where a coordinator can demonstrate to the Commission's satisfaction that he/she is unable to submit via the online EPSS. Such an exemption has to be requested and requires the explicit approval of the Commission. The Commission will reply to such a request within five working days and, if the request is accepted, will provide in the reply the necessary materials needed to prepare the paper proposal providing that the call is still open.

The Commission takes no responsibility for delays caused by the postal system or couriers in the transmission of the material to prepare the paper proposal. Proposers wanting to use paper submission take the responsibility to ensure that the requests for exemption and the associated procedures are completed in due time for them to meet the call deadline.

(Reproduced from *Guidelines on Proposal Evaluation and Selection Procedures*, Sixth Framework Programme, EC, May 2004)

Figure 4.1 *continued*

Careful advance preparation will not only ensure a proposal with the best chance of success, but will save time and rushing to meet call deadlines. Broadly you could think of the preparation in three stages:

▪ Study the general documents to understand the objectives of the FP6 and see if you are able and willing to contribute to them.

▪ Study the relevant Work Programmes (and calls for proposals if published) to find out if your particular subject area is applicable to FP6 and to see what instruments and evaluation criteria are to be used so that you can select the type of project you are going to propose.

> ■ Form a partnership with complementary organizations and create an outline of your proposal including basic principles of contractual relationship, project management and intellectual property rights issues.
>
> All these stages can be substantially completed before a call for proposals is issued. Then the call with its associated deadline will simply be the trigger to finalize the details and submit the proposal.
>
> (from CORDIS guidance on 'FP6 step by step' – a structured walkthrough of what FP6 participation entails)

The evaluation of proposals under FP6 is discussed in Chapter 22. Figure 4.2, reproduced from *The 6th Framework Programme in Brief*, outlines the bidding process from the initial call for proposals to contract signature.

ESSENTIAL DOS AND DON'TS

The contents of this book offer detailed points of advice on the means of developing a convincing and competitive proposal that are as relevant to research applications as to bids for consultancy and services contracts. Though the chapters that follow do not have the word 'research' in their titles, they include guidance that will be endorsed by all research administrators:

■ Read carefully the information from the funding organization, as well as its instructions about the submission of applications. If the organization provides a standard application form or template, you must use it and complete all the relevant parts. If you neglect to do that, you risk disqualification.

■ Applicants often fail to respond adequately to the guidance they are given. Ask yourself why the organization wants information presented in a particular way, why it attaches importance to a particular aspect of the research. Just repeating phrases from the guidance will not be sufficient: you have to put flesh on your ideas and communicate depth not superficiality.

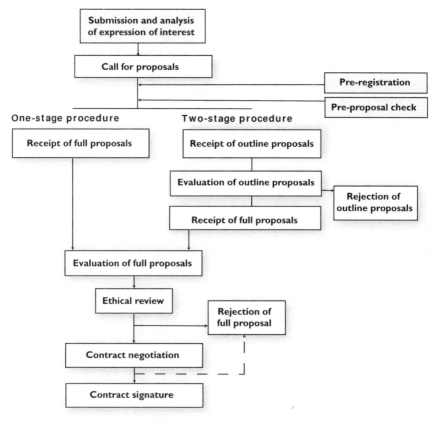

Shaded boxes indicate activities that are not applied in all calls for proposals.

Figure 4.2 *Outline of the bidding process for FP6 funding*

- Remember that you are competing for funding, not simply apply-ing to do the research. Think about the strategic priorities of the organization, and explain why its involvement is necessary.

- Check that you and your partners in the research team meet the eligibility criteria for funding: for example, researchers who already hold grants awarded under a related call for tenders may be ineligible to participate in certain contracts.

- Make it clear which of you is taking the lead in submitting the bid. Ensure that all the necessary letters of commitment and intention to collaborate are included.

- Don't just list the research partners. Explain the rationale of the partnership – why you have formed that association; what its joint and distinctive strengths are; how these strengths complement each other and add value to the proposal; and what each member of the team will contribute to the research in terms of time and resource inputs.

- Give a sharply focused statement of the objectives of the research and the significance of your work. Describe its context and its links and connections with other work in the field.

- The application has to show balance, practicality and realism: it cannot afford to be over-ambitious. Set out a clear, uncomplicated path through the research programme, with a sound methodology.

- Make a realistic assessment of the resources that the project will require.

- When developing your proposal, you need to project forcefully your competitive strengths and eliminate any weak points.

- The way the application is written can have a decisive impact on how evaluators judge your quality and professionalism. Opaque writing is viewed as a sign of opaque thinking, and no one is keen to fund that. If you cannot communicate clearly and concisely to your peers evaluating your ideas, how will you communicate your results to the wider community?

- Your ideas about disseminating the results of the research have to be properly thought through. For example, posting research reports on the internet may seem a straightforward solution to you, but will not necessarily be an effective means of reaching the people who stand to benefit most from your work.

- If you are resubmitting a previously unsuccessful proposal, explain how you have amended and improved its content in the light of its initial evaluation.

- Bear in mind that a significant proportion of research proposals fall at the first compliance hurdle because they do not fulfil all the submission requirements. Quality management is essential.

RESEARCH COUNCIL AND GOVERNMENT FUNDING

Together the research and development procurement programmes of the research councils and government departments in the UK are estimated to have an annual value of over £1 billion. The UK research councils' website (www.rcuk.ac.uk) is the portal for information about the opportunities and types of funding available from these organizations. Each has its set of application procedures and information requirements, supported by handbooks and other detailed guidance information for applicants.

Most government departments and agencies fund research projects, which are normally subject to open competitive tendering procedures and may form components of research programmes or appear as discrete pieces of work. Websites include news about calls for tenders and proposals, links to overviews of research strategies, summaries of research programmes, funding arrangements, application requirements and contact points.

Bidders normally receive a guidance package about the research requirement. A typical package contains the following information:

- **topic details:** a description of the work to be funded;

- **competition guidance and criteria:** instructions or preferences about the information to be included in the bid, how it is to be structured, how the information should be presented to give the best chance of success and the criteria that will be used in assessing the bid;

- **contractual terms and conditions:** these are not normally negotiable;

- **an application form, together with forms for CVs and cost information;**

- **production and submission details:** the number of copies needed by the department; instructions about presentation of an 'original' signed copy; envelope marking and packaging requirements; electronic submission and so forth (Chapter 21);

- **contact details** for the purpose of clarifying the formal bid requirements.

Bids are expected to include detailed information about at least the following aspects of the research:

- **Purpose:** a statement of the problem to be addressed by the research and its technical context.

- **Objectives:** the aims to which the research is meant to contribute, expressed so far as possible in verifiable and quantitative terms.

- **Approach, implementation plan and methodology:** the structural logic of the research and plan of action, with analysis of options.

- **Milestones** related to the achievement of research objectives, against which to monitor performance and measure the progress of the work.

- **Resource inputs**, with bar chart information showing who will be involved in the research, what their responsibilities will be and how much time they will spend on the work, supported by CVs of key personnel.

- **Total estimated costs**, specified exactly as defined in the guidance or application form.

- **Management arrangements:** explaining how participants will coordinate their inputs and activities, how day-to-day work will be managed, how responsibilities will be assigned within the research team and what the proposals are for team communication, quality control and related procedures. You will need to convince the funding body that your programme of work can realistically be delivered within the required timescale.

- **Outputs and results** expected from the research and the deliverables to be produced, including progress and management reports (Chapter 15).

- **Plans for communicating and applying the results of the research**, including, for example, an outreach strategy focused on key sectors, groups and organizations.

- Names and contact details of **external referees**, if these are required.

Application forms may include a section on **small business** information. In April 2001 the UK government's Small Business Service launched an initiative to help smaller firms as well as charities and other independent organizations gain more research and development contracts from government departments and research councils. This is a counterpart to the small business scheme for public sector contracts noted in Chapter 2. The target is to source at least 2.5 per cent of government research work, worth about £50 million, from smaller firms.

The evaluation of research proposals is discussed in Chapter 22. For the research councils, the prime criteria are scientific merit and the presence of a strong and convincing research partnership. Government departments also seek best value for money and direct relevance to their policies and programmes.

5

Pre-qualifying for tender opportunities

Pre-qualification helps clients secure an effective degree of competition by identifying the people whose skills and experience most closely match the requirements of the work. It is a way of narrowing down the field to arrive at a select group of contractors, chosen on the basis of their ability to satisfy a defined set of criteria. It means that ostensibly every contractor starts with the same degree of opportunity and no one reaches the stage of submitting a tender without getting through the preliminary rounds. In the EU framework outlined in Chapter 2 the process offers an objective and auditable basis on which to determine the professional, technical and financial status of potential bidders. It also makes competitive tendering a more manageable procedure for clients and a more focused one for contractors, since only those who can substantiate their place on a shortlist need commit resources to the development of a tender.

The process of formal pre-qualification related to individual contract opportunities is normally applied only by public sector authorities and is associated with contracts that have values at or above the thresholds defined in public procurement legislation, as noted in Chapter 2.

Though procurement legislation has laid down the ground rules for pre-qualification, methods and approaches vary across the public sector. Individual authorities, government departments, utility companies and EC-funded programmes may each define the form in which they apply the process. EC rules do not preclude contracting authorities from discussing forthcoming opportunities with potential bidders even before a contract notice appears and encouraging them to express interest, provided there is no element of discrimination in these contacts. As a general principle, the starting point is the tender notice, which will advise prospective contractors about pre-qualification procedures and the information required from them in this initial stage.

Contractors may be asked to complete a **pre-qualification application form**, which may accompany an internet announcement of the contract, or to submit an **expression of interest** or a **pre-tender submission**, which may consist in part of forms covering corporate and administrative data, technical information and responses to questions about quality assurance, management practice and policies, as well as details of existing and previous contracts and clients and trade/credit references. Clients prefer by and large to use standardized forms so as to obtain a consistent basis for the comparison and assessment of information. Where expressions of interest are requested, the structure and content of the document will normally be defined by the client, who may also set a limit on its length – eg '10 pages of A4 with a minimum font size of 11pt'.

The criteria applied in pre-qualifying contractors generally relate to their personal or corporate repute, technical capacity and ability and financial status. Contractors who have been found guilty of professional misconduct can be excluded from tendering. Technical capacity is judged on the basis of skills and resources, quality standards and past performance on comparable work, including references from other clients. So far as financial status is concerned, clients may look for evidence that a contractor is considered likely to remain in business over and beyond the lifetime of the contract.

PRE-QUALIFICATION INFORMATION

The categories of information to be supplied will vary from client to client and will usually reflect the scale of the contract. Contractors may be asked to provide material on the following points, as appropriate:

Corporate data

▪ Name, ownership, nationality and structure of the organization; details of company registration; year of establishment; identity of parent company, directors, partners, key personnel, associated companies, retained subconsultants.

▪ Name of the responsible contact person.

▪ Office locations (head and regional), with phone, fax and e-mail details.

Experience, skills and performance

▪ Experience and past performance (similar contracts, relevant expertise, work in comparable environments, related technologies and so forth), indicating roles and contract values plus the names and addresses of client officials or managers responsible for the work. Clients may stipulate a minimum or maximum number of contracts to be listed. They may require evidence of successful team working and partnering arrangements, quality management and experience of coordinating the activities of subcontractors and specialist consultants.

▪ Evidence of areas of specialist skills and competence.

▪ Evidence of quality accreditation and quality management systems in use.

▪ Current project commitments, with names of clients.

▪ Evidence of breadth and quality of recent project performance: eg the past two years' work in list form.

▪ Contract performance record – specifically any failure to complete a contract or termination by a client, with an explanation of the reasons.

- Statements on professional conduct issues and experience, including any history of arbitration, litigation or industrial disputes.

Resources

- Strength, quality and availability of staff, including CVs of key personnel.

- Charge rate information for key personnel.

- Specialist resources and facilities, eg IT, laboratories, training.

- Copies of policies on professional development and training, equal opportunities, health and safety, environmental issues, industrial relations and so forth.

- Information on insurances and professional indemnities.

- Staff turnover for the last two/three years.

Financial status

- A banker's reference.

- Published or certified accounts for the last two/three years of trading, plus a copy of the latest management accounts or other evidence of financial status. In line with its policy of helping small firms to gain access to the public sector marketplace, the UK government advises authorities to request only two years of accounts and to accept other appropriate information if accounts are not available.

In addition, contractors may be required to include statements declaring their intention to submit a bid if invited to do so (this is intended to reduce the incidence of abortive shortlists), and confirming that neither they nor any individual or organization associated in the pre-qualification request are liable to be faced with a conflict of interest if selected to undertake the contract. If the pre-qualification request is being put forward by a consortium or group of contractors, information will normally be required from each member of the group.

GUIDANCE TO GET YOU AHEAD

- Pay strict attention to the client's **instructions** about the information to be supplied. You will not pre-qualify unless you comply fully and exactly.

- Procurement rules normally state that pre-qualification can be achieved only on the basis of the **information** provided in the context of each individual contract. The best experts can fail to pre-qualify if they assume that the contracting authority must already know about the quality and breadth of their experience, without needing to have this substantiated in the expression of interest.

- Contracting authorities need to see evidence of achievements in the form of **facts, client references, dates and contract values**. Glossy phrases ('unique record of experience', 'unparalleled expertise' and the like) will not suffice.

- If the client asks for details of five **comparable assignments** you have undertaken, that is precisely the number you must provide, no more and no less. It doesn't matter that your experience may extend to 30 or more such contracts: listing them all will gain you nothing. The right course is to select the five that have most points of similarity with the contract for which you want to pre-qualify and describe them in a way that underlines their relevance and the results you achieved.

- In many instances, contractors' responses will be assessed through a **scoring procedure** to arrive at a shortlist drawn up on a quantitative basis. Expressions of interest may be marked against weighted criteria reflecting key aspects of professional status, technical suitability and financial standing. The client may rule that all contractors achieving or exceeding a defined proportion (normally 65 or 70 per cent) of the total available points will be eligible to be invited to submit a tender. Clients may also require contractors to reach at least a minimum score on each criterion as well as an overall quality threshold.

- While you are preparing your response, check through the **background material** provided by the client. Does it indicate, for instance, the conditions of contract that are to be used, or whether participation by consortia and joint ventures will be acceptable?

- It pays to think about what the phrase **'expression of interest'** means. Interest is often the last thing expressed by many such documents, which merely replicate a tired formula instead of actually demonstrating keenness to work for the client and undertake the contract. What the client perceives is a contractor attempting to pre-qualify without being prepared to put much effort into the process – a waste of time for both parties. Express interest only when you have the evidence to justify the submission of a bid and you are serious about wanting to win the work.

- Remember, there are five key requirements for successful pre-qualification:

  - **full compliance with the client's instructions;**

  - **strict attention to each detail of the specification;**

  - **data focused sharply on relevant areas of expertise and experience;**

  - **information presented in a way that is directly accessible;**

  - **the expression of real interest and enthusiasm.**

- If you are a **newly established** firm without a large amount of business experience, you have to make the strongest case you can, presenting the facts of the situation honestly and not attempting to talk yourself up. Perhaps your work background shows evidence of specialist expertise, innovative approaches or challenging responsibilities. These should be emphasized in pre-qualification material, making it clear if the experience was gained in a personal capacity before you set up on your own.

- Failing to pre-qualify may leave you disappointed, even aggrieved. In many areas of public procurement there are formal mechanisms that enable you to receive an explanation of the reasons for not being selected. But when you are successful, it pays to **ask the reason why** – 'What has earned us our place on the list?', 'How does the client perceive our strengths and capabilities?' and, most important of all, 'What type of approach does the client expect to see in our bid?' It would be a shame if in this case the client were the one to be disappointed.

CAPABILITY STATEMENTS

Clients sometimes ask for pre-qualification evidence to be produced in the form of a capability statement. There are no hard-and-fast rules about how this differs from an expression of interest, though a capability statement generally focuses on market sectors and fields of expertise rather than addressing a particular contract opportunity, and the structure of the document is usually left for the individual contractor to decide. Capability statements are meant to answer the following questions:

- Can you perform satisfactorily the services we need?

- What special qualities do you bring to your work?

- What professional resources do you have available?

They typically include the following material:

- information about the contractor (or group) putting forward the statement;

- an outline of the contractor's or group's fields of activity;

- details of specialist skills and the availability of professional resources;

- short profiles of key personnel;

- a brief analysis to indicate familiarity with the context in which the client operates;

- a summary of relevant contract experience.

Evidence of financial status may be required, as well as the names of existing and recent clients who can vouch for the contractor's performance.

If your firm has several strings to its bow, you can gain points by offering a picture of a consultancy that takes an integrated view of its activities and knows how to apply its skills in a unified effort. Another useful thing you can do is disarm the sort of assumptions that may be keeping your name off shortlists. Clients may for one reason or another associate your name with a particular line of activity that represents only part of what you offer. They may see only stereotypes – viewing large firms as poor value for money, monolithic and unable to provide the small teams and close relationships they would expect from small specialist firms, or believing that a small firm would be no match for the responsibility of a large contract. They may have preconceived opinions about particular professions or career backgrounds, or any of a host of factors all of which may be reducing your opportunities to bid for work. None of these assumptions may be justified, but until you address them directly you cannot begin to limit the damage they may cause.

6

Deciding to bid

Contractors often talk about their success in terms of 'hit rates' – one in four, say, or one in three. The question is which one in four, which one in three? What you ought to be winning is the contracts that will do most to help you achieve your marketing objectives, gain sustained income and add professional value to your services.

Writing a tender can entail a substantial commitment of time, money and other resources that might well be spent more productively in other ways or on other possibilities. The decision to bid needs to be based on a realistic and carefully weighed assessment of the opportunity, its potential benefits and its costs.

The basis of this decision will depend on an array of factors that include the financial situation, operational capacity and technical resources of your business; the strategic direction in which you see it moving; the professional demands of the contract; the nature, scale and duration of the work; the identity and status of the client organization; and the strength of any professional relationship you may have established with client personnel, among other matters. If the decision is positive, some of the aspects examined at this stage will need to be explored later in more detail as part of the technical analysis of the bid specification (Chapter 7); but this initial assessment involves a different set of considerations, aimed at determining the merit of a bid rather than defining its content.

ISSUES TO CONSIDER

The issues can be expressed as a set of checklists relating to:

- the competitive situation;

- the relationship of the contract to your business strategy;

- bid preparation costs;

- project costs and revenues;

- the characteristics of the client;

- the professional value of the contract;

- its implications for your workload, management and personnel;

- the skills and experience you can offer.

It is now that the work you put into researching the opportunity (Chapter 1) starts to pay off. Some of the questions listed here may be readily answerable from information that you gained at the research stage or from the bid documentation, or they may have been raised initially during pre-qualification. Other questions may need to be explored through further research.

If you are seeking clarification on a factual point, you should be able to talk to the managers or technical officers responsible for the tender announcement. Make sure your interpretation of the situation and the information you use are reliable.

The key issues influencing your decision will seldom be clear cut. In many instances the outcome will reflect a balance of commercial judgement and technical considerations. You must try to reach a decision as quickly as possible. If it is 'yes', you cannot afford to lose time; if it is 'no', you will want to target your efforts at other prospects.

Don't be dismayed by the length of these checklists. Not every question will need to be asked in every case. The lists are detailed because they aim to cover points that can be relevant to a broad range of bid opportunities, whether for the public or the private sector, in the UK or overseas.

The competitive situation

- Is there a real prospect of a contract? Do you have reason to believe that the client may not award a contract but intends to do the work in-house, taking advantage of whatever good ideas the bids may contain? Clients sometimes put out an invitation to tender just to test the market, to keep their existing contractors on their toes or to keep themselves up to date with business processes and technologies.

- Does the bid specification point to a hidden agenda behind the invitation? Is the client using the bid process as a front for efforts to secure financing for a project, or in an attempt to give professional respectability to political aims? There are occasions when clients seek consultancy advice only as a form of technical collateral to gain credibility for a predetermined strategy. They may want external advisers who will put the gloss of their name and reputation on a scheme without questioning too sharply its justification. Bid specifications that are biased toward obtaining a favourable outcome from a 'feasibility study' are a clear warning sign. Would you be comfortable in the role the client has in mind?

- If the information that comes with the tender invitation appears cursory or the bid specification imposes unusually restrictive conditions or the timetable seems rushed, this may indicate that the client has a particular firm in mind: the specification may have been drafted by an existing contractor and the client may be going through the formalities of a competition for procedural reasons.

- Do you know how many others you will be competing with and who they are? Is the procedure open to all and sundry, or has a shortlist been selected? If invitations have gone out to a large number of firms, it must be doubtful whether the client has the time and resources to evaluate each bid in detail. There will then be the temptation for the client to look at price not quality.

- Has the client said how the bids will be evaluated? Will the client use an evaluation procedure with which you are familiar?

- If you know the identity of your competitors, how do your strengths and weaknesses compare with theirs? Are you or is anyone else a clear front-runner? Does a competitor have a particularly close relationship with the client?

- Is there any form of 'mystery shopping' that you can undertake to check how your competitors go about the delivery of their services?

- Is the work a continuation of an existing contract? If it is, can you realistically hope to put in a bid that is sufficiently strong in terms of quality and price to offer better value for money than the present contractor?

- How good was the last bid you produced for that client or for that type of work? What was its fate, and what does that tell you about your competitive position for this contract?

- On bids for work overseas, can you seek your government's support or endorsement for your bid? Are any of your competitors state-funded agencies rather than genuinely independent businesses? Are they able to offer the contract services as part of a programme of technical assistance? Do your competitors include firms that have a reputation for 'buying' contracts?

- In certain overseas markets, procurement is characterized by a nexus of interests in which contract decisions are made on the basis of financial links between politicians, administrators and developers, rather than on technical or value-for-money grounds. It is often large business groups and enterprises that hold the real levers of power and make the key decisions, because it is they that drive the mechanism of what may be termed 'patronage' in some contexts and 'corruption' in others.

You may be able to find answers to some of the questions in this list from people in your personal and professional network of contacts, or even colleagues in your firm. Do they know the client and its business practices? Have any of them worked with a competitor firm? What can they tell you about the way they are likely to approach the project?

Relationship to business strategy

- Is the contract in line with your business objectives and marketing strategy? Is it in a target sector of your market and a core field of activity or does it have only peripheral relevance?

- Is it likely to bring you sustained and reliable income? Will it take you into new markets with good prospects for long-term growth and profitability? Does it involve an area of expertise where there is an unsatisfied demand for services? Will it help you develop a new and distinctive package of benefits for clients?

- Will the contract give you the opportunity to form a valuable strategic alliance with other companies?

- Will it help lock your competitors out of a niche market?

- Might the contract involve a conflict of interest with your work for other clients?

- Do the procurement terms mean that winning this contract will disqualify or exclude you from bidding for other work such as related or downstream contracts?

Bid preparation costs

- What will be the costs of preparing the bid and then negotiating a contract, with all the delays and difficulties that may arise? Will an effective bid require an intensive programme of research and analysis? Can you afford to sustain these costs? Will a conscientious and committed bid be feasible if the fee value of the work is low?

- How do these costs compare with the profit you might realistically expect from the job?

- If the contract involves a large-scale project, do you have associates with whom you can divide the costs in proportion to your share of the expected fee income?

- Have you already invested large amounts of time, money and other resources in the process of pre-qualifying or in marketing to the client? Are your chances good enough to expect an adequate return on that investment, or might you simply be throwing good money after bad? These questions become particularly critical when cash flow problems arise, when resources are stretched and overdraft facilities are under pressure. There are rules of thumb that you can apply to help determine the viability of bids and control bid costs. The rules may be expressed in various forms: for example, spending on bid preparation up to a set percentage of the expected gross fee income from the job – say up to 5 per cent in the case of small or medium contracts or up to 1.5 per cent for large contracts; or spending up to a set amount per staff-month of expected input, defined in relation to the total available marketing budget and the firm's overall success rate in competitive bidding.

- Does the client organization require the submission of a bid bond or tender bond as part of the tendering procedure? This is a form of surety for the client (and financial risk for the contractor) that you are likely to encounter only in the context of large-scale international tenders, where it may amount to as much as 5 per cent of the expected contract value.

- Even within the EU procurement framework, clients may insist that bids are written in their own language. If you do not have appropriate language skills in-house you may need to use a translation service, which can be expensive as well as risking quality problems if the translators are not experienced in the terminology of your sector.

Project costs and revenues

- Is it clear what the type of contract will be – fixed price, time-based fees plus expenses or some hybrid form? Does the client documentation include a draft or specimen contract, and are its terms acceptable? Conditions of contract that are unfamiliar may require you to obtain legal advice before going ahead with the bid.

- What is the total fee income and profit you can expect from the contract? How does it match your estimate of the professional effort required?

- Do you have sufficient information to prepare a cash flow profile for the contract?

- Is there a risk that winning the contract might strain your financial resources? Will the requirements for working capital be manageably even throughout the contract or will you be faced with sharp peaks? What effect is the contract likely to have on your cash flow, particularly in the event of late payment?

- What do your provisional costings tell you about the lowest price at which it will be feasible for you to undertake the work? What is the highest price you can put in while remaining competitive?

■ Are there reasons to bid low or even take on the work at a marginal price – for example, if it will keep your staff employed or reinforce your position in a particular sector of expertise?

■ Are competitors likely to undercut your bid through some form of overt or hidden subsidy from their parent companies or governments?

■ Would the assignment be expensive to start or hard to support logistically?

■ Is the assignment likely to require your taking on contractual responsibilities for a large consortium, perhaps receiving a minor share of the fee but shouldering the financial risks and ultimate accountability for the work of the consortium? Or is there scope for you to limit your exposure to risk by working as a subcontractor to a larger firm?

■ Is the client organization likely to require the winning tenderer to provide a performance bond at the start of the contract, to cover the risk of failing to meet contractual obligations?

■ If the bid is for an overseas client:

  – In what currency will you receive payment?

  – Will you require special financial services such as foreign currency loans and overdrafts, short-term finance and export funding or risk management services to guard against transaction exposure? The effects of swings in exchange rates can dwarf the scale of profits or losses from the contract itself.

  – If the contract involves a long-term assignment in an economy prone to inflation, is there a credible local index to which you can link contract prices?

  – Are there specific insurance costs that you will incur?

  – How dependent will you be on local associates to facilitate the receipt of payments, remittance of fees or repatriation of profits (Chapter 10)?

  – Is a third party such as a donor agency or funding institution involved? If so, how will its participation affect your costings and the conditions of payment? Will the contract be with the agency or the client? Some agencies apply standard rates of remuneration in particular countries and regions.

Client characteristics

▪ Is the client a single entity or a group of organizations with different responsibilities? If it is a multiple client, what will be the contracting authority? Is it a form of public–private partnership? These points will have a material influence on many aspects of the working relationship.

▪ Do you have past experience of the client's operational procedures? Is it a good client to work for? Has it paid on time or argued about invoices? Have you got on well with its managers and other personnel? Do you know what client managers think of you? Has the client had occasion to criticize the way your business has performed on previous contracts – for example, your capacity to deliver on schedule or the effectiveness of your team management? If so, what impact is your past record likely to have on your chances of success?

▪ How well do you understand the business needs and attitudes of decision-makers in the client organization? Where does this contract sit in relation to their overall procurement plan?

▪ Would you feel unhappy about turning down an invitation from that client? Do you believe a 'no' decision is likely to prejudice your chances of receiving further invitations?

▪ Are there discriminatory or politically questionable aspects of the client or work environment?

▪ Is the client or the contract located in a place that you would find particularly congenial or particularly unpleasant? Are there unusual risks involved, such as working in areas affected by political unrest, security problems or health risks?

▪ Do you have information about the type of people the client prefers for this contract – known quantities or new faces?

▪ Are there unusual features of the work specification or problems that are unlikely to be resolved either by discussions with the client or in negotiations?

▪ On projects overseas, does the client have a reputation for seldom or never awarding a contract to an expatriate firm, or for habitual late payment? Will the work be paid for entirely from the client's own resources or will an international financing institution or donor agency provide counterpart funds? Is there a contractual requirement to associate with a local firm?

Professional value

- Will the contract offer a particularly interesting or stimulating professional challenge?

- Will it have social, developmental or environmental benefits that you regard as professionally important? Is it in a good cause – for example, helping a local community to save an environmental resource or combating disease?

- Will the contract bring you useful political or business contacts, enhance your professional standing and raise your profile in the market?

Workload, management and personnel implications

- Is the contract likely to involve you in risks that you are unable to accept, manage or transfer to the client? Does the client's view of the work rest on dubious assumptions?

- How does the proposed time-frame relate to your existing work and other business opportunities? What impact would it have on the performance of your other contracts and your ability to field key staff?

- What is the current state of your workload? Do you need the contract to keep your staff not just employed but chargeable, or are they fully committed to other work? Would the contract overextend your personnel resources?

- Do you have enough time to prepare an adequately competitive bid? Are there other bids on the drawing board? Do you have someone available who can manage the bid effectively, along the lines suggested in Chapter 8?

- Do you have on your staff an appropriately qualified manager or team leader for the contract? If not, can you obtain the right sort of person?

- Does the bid specification call for a team formed of permanent in-house staff? Can you meet this requirement? Would the contract mean that you have to take on specialist staff whom you might have difficulty in employing on other work?

- Would the contract necessitate a change in the management structure of your company – for example, if you need to give the team leader the status (and rewards) of a senior manager, might that become a source of tension within your staff?

Skills and experience

- Will the contract mean a steep learning curve or do you have all the necessary competencies? Are particular non-technical skills required, such as an aptitude for motivating people and facilitating change or interpersonal and communications skills? Can you bring in additional competencies, for example from associates?

- How does the contract relate to your mainstream activities? Will it give greater breadth and depth to your capabilities, or is it an unfamiliar area of expertise that might put your reputation at risk?

- Does your experience match the demands of the job? Identify with the client: ask yourself, 'If I were the client, would I hire me?'

- Does the bid specification indicate requirements for quality accreditation and indemnity insurance cover, statements on matters such as equal opportunities policy, health and safety matters, or declarations about professional conduct, TUPE issues, industrial relations and so forth that you might have difficulty in complying with? Does the client require a level of indemnity insurance cover that is out of proportion to the value of the contract?

- Does past experience of working in a similar contract environment suggest any likely problems?

- Projects overseas may need the collaboration of local associates. Are they available or have they been signed up by competitors? If there is a requirement for foreign language skills, do people in your team possess them?

RISK ASSESSMENT

Despite the length of these checklists, deciding whether or not to bid can at times be straightforward! If the contract is in a target sector of the market or for a key client, the answer is likely to be positive. But it often involves balancing a complex set of points for and against. Some businesses require a risk assessment to be undertaken if the cost of preparing a bid is likely to exceed a defined proportion, say 5 per cent, of the contract price, or where a substantial amount of working capital will be needed if the bid is successful. Thresholds may be defined at which progressively more demanding criteria are applied – for example, where contract values are above £1 million or where peak working capital needed during the contract will exceed £500,000 and so forth. At these high levels there may also be a requirement to obtain the approval of the chief executive officer or board of directors.

Factors likely to have a particular influence on the risk assessment include:

- the value of the contract;

- the average working capital and peak working capital required;

- the length of the payback period;

- bid preparation costs;

- the expected profit margin;

- whether the contract will require long-term partnership or consortium arrangements;

- whether the client requires a bid bond or performance bond;

- whether payment will be related to performance;

- whether the contract will involve penalty clauses, and the possible level of loss resulting from termination;

- the staffing implications and resource costs of the contract;

- whether exceptional risks are involved – for example, in terms of political, security, taxation or legal issues;

- aspects that may have particular implications for professional indemnity insurance cover.

A wide choice of management software is available to assist in risk assessment, including spreadsheets that allow the application of multiple criteria and weightings. Risk assessment necessarily includes both objective and subjective considerations: some items may be quantifiable in monetary terms; others will be matters of professional judgement. Each business has to determine for itself the questions to be answered. The important point is to have in place a consistent procedure that can ensure time and money are not spent wastefully on contract opportunities with little economic sense or professional merit.

If you have to decline the invitation, tell the client as soon as possible of your intention not to put in a bid. Unless you really want to have nothing more to do with the client, try to explain your decision in a way that indicates a conscientious assessment of the situation and does not prejudice your chances of being invited to bid for other work in the future.

7

Analysing the bid specification

In this book the term **'bid specification'** is used to mean the documentation that the client supplies to bidders about the tendering procedure and the contract. The documentation may be called 'request for proposals', 'invitation to tender' or simply 'tender documents'. Information about the services required under the contract may be referred to as an 'information package', 'tender package', 'tender dossier', 'terms of reference', 'brief for consultancy services', 'project brief' or a similar title. The client's requirements for bid submission are often presented as 'instructions to tenderers', particularly in public sector procurement. Clients may also convey their requirements in the form of guidance notes indicating the approach they expect bidders to follow, listing the information to be provided in each part of the bid and explaining the criteria that will be used in assessing bids. Where a client gives instructions, these must be taken seriously and followed strictly. Contractors who prepare bids in ways that suit them rather than the client do themselves no favours.

Read through the bid specification thoroughly, point by point – it will almost always contain more information than can be absorbed at a first examination. Keep it to hand at every stage of preparing the bid, and check your work against it to make sure you are going about things in the right way. Do not neglect any material the client may have attached by way of supplementary information, lists of publications, technical data and so forth: the reason for including it was to help you gain a correct understanding of the demands of the contract. You will have to take it on trust that the information supplied by the client is accurate; but clients may include a clause of limitation to the effect that the information is provided for the convenience of bidders and that bidders are expected to make their own investigations to determine the facts of the situation.

Your analysis will be a matter of interpretation, of trying to grasp what the project implies in terms of professional effort and what the client expects in terms of results. Guard against making hasty assumptions on the basis of an initial scanning of the document, reading into it things that are not there. Note down your first thoughts about the work requirements, the client's objectives and priorities, the points you will want to emphasize in the bid and the ideas that may give you a competitive edge. If you are an experienced bid writer, you will quickly get a feel for the essentials of a job; but take care not to let your first reactions fix your whole approach to the bid.

Don't fail the client's test

The bid specification ought to be the outcome of a structured process of project design, through which the client organization defines its requirements correctly, identifies the objectives of the contract unambiguously and gauges the practical demands of the work accurately. You will not need reminding that this is not always the case, and at times you may be justified in complaining that the information coming from the client is vague, imprecise and incomplete. But contractors often fail to appreciate that when clients invite them to prepare a competitive bid, they are not just asking for a list of services and personnel and a price quotation: they are also setting up **a test of approaches and ideas**.

An essential part of this test is seeing which if any of the bidders has a really perceptive understanding of the client's situation and requirements, and can offer fresh ideas and creativity. In a competitive arena it is not in the client's interests to do the bidders' thinking for them. It is unreasonable to expect the client to tell you everything there is to know about the context of the work: you have to contribute research and intelligence of your own. The client's specification should be regarded as the minimum that bidders are expected to know. Marks are never awarded simply for quoting the client's words verbatim, which after all does no more than show that the people who prepared the bid can read. The challenge lies in applying your insight, ideas and experience in a distinctive way that establishes the benefits that you and only you can bring the client.

Check for information

Hard copies of bid specifications are sometimes sent out with lines, paragraphs or even pages missing or repeated. Look through the document straight away to spot any errors of that sort.

See whether items you would expect to be told about are included, and identify points that may need to be clarified directly with the client or through further research about the contract environment. Background material such as policy documents and statistical information is sometimes made available to bidders through a client's website.

Turn the client's instructions or guidance into checklists to help guide the preparation and production of the bid. These checklists can form the basis of the bid development worksheet (Chapter 8) and the bid response matrix (Chapter 12).

POINTS FOR CHECKLISTS

As you read through the documentation, look for information on the following topics:

- requirements for bid submission;

- the background and objectives of the contract;

- the scope of services covered by the contract;

- issues and priorities identified as important by the client;

- factors likely to favour or detract from the competitiveness of your bid;

- emphasis on particular competencies, qualifications, experience, team composition or logistic capabilities;

- the acceptability of consortia and subcontracting;

- evidence of either a predisposition toward a certain approach and method or receptivity to alternatives and variant solutions;

- the client's attitude to risk management;

- the time-frame for the work and the delivery of results;

- the outputs and deliverables of the contract;

- any indication of the available budget for the work and financial constraints;

- the client's perception of its responsibilities and inputs;

- the information and material to be included in the bid;

- the required treatment of price information;

- the criteria for evaluating bids;

- any further stages in the procurement process;

- clarification procedures;

- contractual matters and conditions;

- any unusual aspects of the work or requirements about bid style and presentation.

Bid submission

Pay special attention to the text of the tender notice or invitation: it probably will set out requirements for submitting the bid that are not repeated elsewhere in the documentation. In particular, note the following points:

- the precise wording used in the title of the notice to denote the contract: use the same form of words in communicating with the client and in titling the bid;

- the client's contract reference, if stated;

- the date of publication of the notice: an urgent response may be necessary if there has been a delay in seeing the notice or receiving the invitation; moreover the deadlines for procedures such as obtaining detailed tender documents, requests for clarification and the submission of bids may be expressed in terms of numbers of days after the date of publication;

- any requirement to acknowledge receipt of the invitation, to inform the client whether or not you will be submitting a bid, and to give prior notice of the date and mode of delivery;

- any details of enclosures or attachments: check that you have received all the material referred to in the invitation to tender; look in particular for forms that have to be completed and returned with the bid;

- the details of your address, if an invitation has arrived by post, fax or e-mail, and the person for whose attention the invitation is addressed: has the client got the details right?

- the name and post of the signatory of the notice or invitation: is this the person to whom you should address the bid?

- information on whether the bid is to be produced as hard copy or in digital form – for example, on CD ROM – or both;

- instructions for submission of the bid, including date, time and location and the number of copies required; instructions about packaging and labelling and whether you need to obtain an official receipt: clients may specify how bids can be delivered – for example, by hand, registered post or recorded delivery courier – and they may veto submissions by fax or e-mail;

- instructions on identification of bids: some clients require that the sealed package in which the tender is delivered must give no indication of the identity of the bidder; others want this information to appear on the package; clients may also provide a reference label to be attached to the package.

Depending on the procurement context and the approach taken by the client, the notice or invitation may also include information on other matters:

- the contracting procedures under which the proposed contract is to be awarded;

- rules governing the eligibility of tenderers, consortium bids and use of subcontractors;

- requirements for tenderers to provide a bid bond, performance bond or both;

- whether a tendering certificate declaring that the tenderer has not colluded with any other bidder has to be completed;

- whether bidders are required or expected to have quality accreditation – for example, to ISO 9000 series or comparable quality management standards;

- required period of validity of tenders;

- specific requirements that have to be met if the bid is to be accepted as compliant;

- admissibility of variant or qualified solutions;

- whether there is any provision to modify the tender before the formal submission date;

- a contact in the client organization to whom bidders can refer for factual information;

- whether bidders are forbidden to have any contact with the client, other than in writing or in the context of a formal clarification meeting, before submitting their tender;

- arrangements for briefing or clarification meetings, visits to project locations or explanatory presentations by the client;

- the required format of the tender – for example, a set of forms and cost schedules that bidders have to complete;

- whether there is a limit on the page length of the bid, eg 'no more than 25 A4 sides';

- whether price information has to be submitted in a separate financial bid (Chapter 20);

- the date, hour and place of the tender opening;

- names of other firms invited to tender.

Background and objectives of the contract

- Is it clear exactly who the client is – the organization itself or one of its departments?

- Is the client a multiple entity or partnership – for example, combining public and private sector interests?

- Is the structure of responsibilities on the client's side explained?

- Do you get a consistent picture of the background of the contract and the developments that have led to the present situation?

- Are the client's objectives stated clearly and convincingly?

- Do you sense that the client really knows what it wants from the project?

The way objectives are phrased may be the product of a committee system embracing different viewpoints – ie there may be items that do not properly cohere – but the particular form of words will almost certainly have the endorsement of senior decision-makers or directors. Whatever else your bid does, it has to respond to the client's statement of the intended outputs of the contract.

Scope of services

- Are the technical requirements of the work clearly defined?

- Is the contract part of a continuing programme of work or a one-off initiative?

- Will there be an even and continuous flow of work throughout the contract or will the work be subject to intervals and interruptions?

- What data have been supplied with the bid specification, and why?

- What level of professional effort will be needed to undertake the contract? Is most of the work routine or are there particularly demanding requirements?

- Are there tasks and activities that will clearly have a decisive influence on the outcome of the work and deserve a high priority of effort, but are given only a passing mention in the bid specification?

▪ Does the specification refer to mandatory procedures, methods or standards with which contractors must comply?

▪ If the client intends several contractors to have a role in the work, what are the client's proposed arrangements for coordinating their services? Do there appear to be overlaps or gaps in their work responsibilities?

An exhaustively detailed specification may be the mark of a practical, carefully thought-out approach and a consistent sense of professional direction; or it may reveal a rigid attitude to the contract, restricting your freedom of choice as a contractor and perhaps indicating that the client has a certain bidder in mind for the work. Particular constraints may lead the client to specify features of the brief in detail – for example, statutory requirements or timetables imposed externally, health and safety factors or audit trail procedures on which the client has little or no room for negotiation.

At the other extreme you may receive just the barest outline of the services you are expected to provide. A key indicator of the adequacy of a specification is the clarity with which it defines the questions to be answered and the outputs to be produced. Clients should be able to say where they want the contract to lead, even if they are not certain how to get there.

Specifications and terms of reference prepared by international financing institutions and development agencies may include a logical framework or 'logframe' – a hierarchical matrix that sets out the logic on which the project is based. This will state the purpose of the assignment, indicate immediate and longer-term objectives and identify the required inputs and outputs, as well as quantifiable indicators of success. Where a logframe is provided, take account of its structure and content in shaping the text of the bid.

Issues and priorities

Issues are questions that need to be decided, matters that need to be resolved: they are not necessarily the same as problems. The bid specification may sometimes not reveal all the issues underlying the contract or the real priorities of the client. As noted earlier, there may be good business reasons or political considerations that dictate what is said in the specification. You have to search for clues that will tell you what is in the client's mind, why some points are mentioned and others not. Insight into this information can put you on an inside track. Where the client has identified the issues that are central to the contract, your response has to address them clearly and perceptively to stand a chance of winning.

Competitiveness factors

What aspects of the bid specification offer you competitive strength? Among the detailed information are there items you can use to your advantage or that suggest key messages you should develop in the text of the bid? Are there other items that hint at possible weaknesses on your part and disadvantages that you need to counter?

Competencies, qualifications, experience, team composition and logistics

- Are there pointers to the professional strengths and competencies that the client regards as essential to the success of the work?

- Do you have an indication of the number of people the client would expect to do the work and their professional backgrounds?

- Has the client expressed a preference for personnel who are part of the bidder's in-house staff?

- Is there a requirement to work in a joint team with the client's staff or to liaise with outside bodies such as research and development units, institutes of technology or university departments?

- Are there particular logistic requirements, such as a field office, laboratory facilities and online software documentation?

- Does the client say where the work is to be undertaken?

Consortia and subcontracting

Where subcontracting is acceptable, the client may ask bidders to indicate the parts of the contract that they propose to assign to third parties. The bid specification may define the maximum proportion of the total services that subcontracted firms are allowed to provide, and may require signed declarations from intending subcontractors (Chapter 10).

Approach and method

▪ Does the specification show preference for a particular approach or procedure?

▪ If variant solutions are allowed, does a bidder who wants to put one forward also have to submit a conforming solution?

▪ Are options excluded that you think should be considered?

▪ Are there other methodological points that need to be questioned and debated in the bid?

Risk management

▪ Does the bid specification refer to processes for managing project risk such as delays and cost overruns or failure to deliver the intended outcomes of the contract?

▪ Are you asked to propose mechanisms and actions for mitigating risks?

▪ To what extent are bidders required to share or accept responsibility for risks?

Time-frame

▪ Has the client stated the expected duration of the contract? If the bid specification includes a timetable, does this look realistic in terms of the expected deliverables?

▪ Are starting and completion dates clearly defined?

▪ Are there indications of how quickly a contract award is likely to be made?

Outputs and deliverables

▪ Is there a clear statement of the expected outputs of the contract?

▪ Does the bid specification include a schedule of deliverables?

- Has the client set performance targets related to outputs and deliverables?

- Does the schedule allow sufficient time for reports and other material to be reviewed and if necessary amended before approval?

- Is an inception report required?

- What are the client's requirements in terms of management reporting?

- Is the final deliverable that will mark completion of the contract identified?

Inclusion of budget information

In most contexts where cost is a key criterion in the selection of contractors, clients do not indicate the budget available for the work. But there are sectors of procurement in which contracting authorities do provide this information. It is standard practice in certain areas of EC-funded work, and is an option sometimes taken by other development agencies and international financing institutions in contracting for assignments that are simple, capable of precise definition and subject to a fixed budget.

- If you are told the budget, does it match your perception of the scale of the professional effort required?

- How is the available budget likely to be structured over the duration of the contract?

- How will these points need to be reflected in your cost estimates?

Client responsibilities and inputs

- What can you learn about the client's degree of commitment to the success of the project?

- How does the client organization perceive its role and responsibilities?

- What data, resources, facilities and logistic support is it offering to make available to the contractors?

Required content of the bid

■ Has the client indicated how the bid is to be structured and the information it needs to contain?

■ Does the documentation include items such as a form of tender or provider agreement that you are required to sign and return with the bid?

■ Are there forms or templates that you must use to supply particular categories of information such as delivery plans, contract experience and CVs?

■ Are you given the opportunity to include additional material explaining your approach?

■ Has the client invited comments on the bid specification or ideas on aspects of the work programme that might be enhanced?

■ Have limits been set on the length of the bid as a whole or parts of the bid?

Price information

■ Has the client given instructions about the way price information is to be structured?

■ Does it have to be set out in a particular format defined by the client – for example, by completing a schedule of prices included in the client documentation?

■ Are there optional services for which the client requires separate stand-alone prices?

■ Does the client require detailed information about the elements that make up your costs (Chapter 20)?

■ Is the contract to be operated on an open-book basis?

■ Does the documentation include the client's proposed payment terms?

Evaluation procedure and criteria

- Does the bid specification identify the evaluation procedure and criteria to be used in deciding the winning bid and the weighting to be assigned to individual criteria?

- Will the evaluation be undertaken in stages – for example, an initial review followed by a full evaluation? If so, will the initial review assess the whole of the bid or just part of it? The implications of a multi-stage evaluation are discussed in Chapter 22.

- Is the award of contract to be made on the basis of the most economically advantageous tender?

- What part is price likely to play in the evaluation?

- Will the quality of the technical approach be decisive?

- Are there indications of the factors that represent added value and multiplier benefits to the client?

- Has the client emphasized points such as value for money, management capability, technological experience, innovation and creativity?

Procurement process

Is this the decisive stage in the procurement process, or will there be a further stage in which selected bidders are asked to prepare more detailed solutions to the client's requirements while taking part in technical and commercial negotiations?

Clarification procedures

In the context of public procurement, clients normally apply a formal procedure for dealing with requests for further information on factual points. Requests usually have to be made in writing, and there is a cut-off time for their receipt – for example, a certain number of working days before the deadline for the submission of bids. To ensure even-handedness and avoid any suggestion of treating some bidders more favourably than others, clients will communicate the reply to a request for clarification simultaneously to all bidders, not just the one that raised the query. Where the technical aspects of a contract are particularly complex and demanding, they may arrange a formal briefing session or clarification meeting to which all the bidders are invited.

You will compromise your position and risk disqualification if you contact the client in the hope of floating ideas and fishing for pointers about items other than matters of fact. It's your tender and you must use your own judgement about what you say in it. Don't feel you have to take part in the clarification procedure just to show that you are a serious contender. If you are astute enough to see points in the specification that can help you develop a more effective bid, you will not want to share these insights with your competitors. Bids are no place for altruism.

As you read through the bid specification, identify the items that appear to require clarification and any points you think are missing. Check back to the document to make sure you have not simply failed to spot the information and that it is not implicit in some other part of the text or in the instructions to tenderers or letter of invitation. Make sure any question you do ask is sensible and worth asking: you don't want to appear foolish by showing that you have not read the specification properly.

Contractual matters

- Does the client's documentation include a draft contract? Are there items that are at variance with the conditions of contract under which you normally work?

- Are there contractual points that call for detailed treatment in the bid?

Overseas contracts

There are additional points relevant to tenders for clients overseas:

- If any part of the client documentation is in a language in which you are not fluent, have it translated reliably by someone who is and who understands the technical basis of the contract. Commercial or legal translation agencies may not have the means or procedures to ensure that a translation makes technical sense.

- Are there instructions or recommendations about working jointly with a local firm or making a visit to the overseas client? In the latter case, does the client name an official or manager for you to contact?

- Do not risk leaving it to local associates to inform the client that you have received the invitation to tender or are intending to submit a bid: confirm this yourself in writing.

- Does the client require the bid to be in a language other than English, or to be submitted in the client's language as well as English?

- The client may supplement the bid specification with statistics and other data related to the contract. From your knowledge of the client or the country, how reliable and current do the data appear? Will your work programme need to provide for additional surveys and research?

- Are there issues of contract law, taxation, foreign exchange, industrial relations and so forth that will need to be defined?

Extension of submission date

In some circumstances, you may feel that the deadline set by the client allows an unreasonably short time to write a satisfactory bid, and you may think of asking for the submission date to be extended. Before making this move, you need to be certain that it really is not feasible to meet the deadline and confident that other bidders too are likely to ask for an extension. You will not want to weaken your competitive position by appearing ill prepared to meet the client's requirements, however demanding these may be.

Clients will generally put back the submission date only in the following situations:

- when all or most of the bidders request an extension on grounds that the client can accept;

- when the client organization has management problems or disagreements on policy that make it difficult to handle the submission process on the initial timetable;

- when one firm that has a favoured relationship with the client needs more time to prepare its bid;

- when the programme is disrupted by unforeseen political, social or other factors outside the client's control.

8

Managing the bid

As soon as you have decided to compete for a contract, you need to organize yourself to produce a bid that does justice to your abilities. If you work on your own and write straightforward bids that mostly take the form of a letter, the task of bid management may involve only keeping a clear head about the way you use your time, structure information and deal with business documents. Your chief concerns will be to make sure that:

■ your assumptions about the effort the work will require and the price that will make your bid competitive are correct;

■ the bid appears a presentable document;

■ it is submitted by the deadline.

When you have to coordinate material from other professionals as well as writing your own input and at the same time keeping fee-earning work going, or if the bid is likely to be a complex document, it becomes clear that bid preparation is a procedure needing to be managed as strategically as any other business activity. How you go about this procedure can be critical to success.

The key is to have it planned out well beforehand and to follow an approach that is **systematic** – leaving nothing to chance; **cohesive** – bringing the document together as an integrated effort; and **deliberate** – progressing in a confident and fully considered direction. Bid management on these lines enables you to make the best use of resources and improve quality and consistency while cutting preparation costs. In short, it brings higher productivity and greater success.

PLANNING AND COORDINATION

Defining management and writing responsibilities

Bids fall flat and get out of control when it is uncertain who is supposed to be managing what or writing what. **Defining these responsibilities clearly and rapidly is an essential first step.** In the majority of firms bid writing is a task undertaken by technical experts or senior managers, while promotional material, CVs and so forth are produced and maintained by technical or secretarial staff. Some firms bring in specialist writers and consultants to mastermind bids and facilitate the production of technical input. Others may have no system at all either for managing the necessary resources or for allocating bid responsibilities: in some cases, the work of preparing a bid will be given to any staff member who happens to be around or has downtime between contracts – not a recipe for success.

In large contracting organizations, bid skills are often recognized as a specialist resource supplied by staff who spend most of their time writing and developing bids. A multi-skill firm may support a group of bid specialists sufficiently versed in the technical background of its activity to be able to draft sections of text and edit material from other experts and senior managers. They may also have the job of keeping promotional material, CVs and project records up to date and fine-tuning this material to the requirements of each bid. This type of unit is found most commonly in firms where large-scale contracts tend to overlap divisional boundaries, though an aversion to central overheads has reduced its incidence.

One proviso that has to be made about using bid-writing specialists is the need for them to keep in touch with the practical realities of managing projects and the challenges of meeting deadlines, especially in difficult work environments. If bid writers grow isolated from the day-to-day mechanics of contracts, they risk making poor judgements about time schedules and staff inputs, which can put in jeopardy both the professional results of the assignment and its financial outcome. The bid writer has a responsibility to be realistic about what can be achieved in the time available. Bid writing should alternate with project work, and practical experience needs to be fed back into bids.

The use of a **bid manager** provides the structured approach required by businesses that have to deal with a continual flow of invitations to tender. Bid management may be a full-time job or a role taken by the person best suited to match the particular requirements of each bid – for example, the proposed team leader or project director, or the individual who knows most about the technical demands of the work. The bid manager may serve the firm as a whole or one or more of its constituent parts: his or her time may be devoted exclusively to bids, pre-qualification documents and marketing activities or it may include participation in project work. Precisely how the responsibilities of bid management are best handled is a matter that each firm has to determine for itself.

The bid manager's role has four main priorities:

- **structuring, coordinating and motivating the bid team;**
- **driving the work forward and ensuring that input is developed on time and to the required standard;**
- **organizing the content and presentation of the document;**
- **applying the document management controls that are needed to produce an efficient business offer.**

Figure 8.1 lists the key responsibilities the job may entail, covering the structure and content of the bid as well as its administration and production. Checking the text for internal consistency is an essential management function; otherwise there is a risk that the content of one section of the bid may be altered without realizing the effects of the change on other parts of the document. The bid manager should take personal responsibility for seeing that the bid is free of careless errors. Acting as a referee or arbitrator between different technical viewpoints and resolving competing pressures on the time of people asked to contribute material to the bid are further tasks that an experienced bid manager can usefully perform.

☐ Compiling a checklist of the bid requirements specified by the client

☐ Preparing a bid development worksheet

☐ Developing a time schedule for the development and production of the bid

☐ Structuring and organizing the bid team

☐ Setting up a bid planning meeting

☐ Identifying the bid budget

☐ Copying client documentation and other material to people contributing inputs to the bid

Bid planning meeting

☐ Devising a file management structure for input together with version control procedures

☐ Briefing contributors on client requirements, document management and version control principles

☐ Liaison with contributors on input editing and bid design

☐ Securing resource commitment from other offices

☐ Arranging and minuting bid progress meetings

☐ Monitoring the bid budget

☐ Reconciling competing claims on the allocation of bid resources

☐ Obtaining priority for bid activity on computer systems and information networks

☐ Organizing the preparation and production of bid graphics

☐ Monitoring and progress-chasing the bid programme

☐ Ensuring that quality review procedures are applied

☐ Document management and version control

☐ Maintaining a write-protected master text

☐ Ensuring that bid material is securely backed up

☐ Organizing the production and submission of the bid

Figure 8.1 *Bid management responsibilities*

It should go without saying that it is important not to have more than one person managing (or believing that they are managing!) the process overall. Others will need to have their say in deciding the strategy and direction of the bid, but there should be just a single experienced hand on the tiller, steering the process to completion. Regrettably, this rule is sometimes ignored: as a consequence, people in the bid team adopt divergent views of the client's priorities, sail off on their own tack and confuse the message of the bid, which ends up getting nowhere.

In many consultancy firms, the team developing a bid will – depending on the size of the contract and the scale and intricacy of the bid – typically consist of one or more technical specialists and managers, including people from the accounts side of the firm and perhaps specialist proposal writers and document designers. The skills and qualities needed for successful bid writing are outlined in Chapter 1. The bid manager has a key role to play in setting up this team and engaging its commitment and enthusiasm, so that it can work together constructively without wasting time or resources. A combative and competitive spirit is needed, but not inside the bid writing team!

Bid planning meeting

The work of the team should start with a **bid planning meeting**, held as soon as practicable after the decision has been taken to submit a bid. The purpose of the meeting is to ensure that everyone who is available to contribute ideas and experience has the opportunity to do so, as well as helping to assess the best approach to the bid and the inputs required for its development. In some contexts this meeting would be called a 'brainstorming' session – a term that needs to be thought about, since the consequence of a storm can sometimes be a washout.

Ahead of the meeting, you should identify the individuals who would be best equipped to originate material for specific parts or aspects of the bid, and you should send copies of client documentation and related information to everyone taking part.

Points that can usefully be discussed at the meeting include:

- the programme for developing, writing, editing and producing the bid;
- the bid team structure and options for association or partnership;
- assignment of writing and editing responsibilities;

- arrangements for visits and meetings with the client, if appropriate;

- pointers from marketing research, previous bids and other background information;

- implications of the client's evaluation criteria, if these are included in the bid specification;

- the format and structure of the bid;

- strategies for the bid approach;

- basic cost and pricing assumptions for the financial information;

- preparation and coordination of CVs, project experience summaries, policy and method statements and other basic material;

- the preferred style and presentation of inputs to the text;

- reviewing and mark-up conventions;

- design ideas for the bid.

An experienced member of the team should be given the task of checking through the client documentation specifically to detect any devils lurking in the detail – unusual, questionable or surprising requirements – and other matters that may need to be raised with the client as points for clarification.

While the bid is being developed, the team should maintain regular contact to check progress, to confirm that drafts and other material sent to team members have been received, and to resolve any issues that may need to be debated.

DOCUMENT MANAGEMENT AND VERSION CONTROL

Developing the content of the bid into its final form is normally a collaborative process. Individuals may be assigned responsibility for originating parts of the bid, but they need to see what others are writing and their drafts need to be reviewed by the team as a whole. As a result, work on the bid takes the form of a succession of continually changing drafts, accumulating comments and revisions, insertions and deletions as they pass from hand to hand, while observations that might usefully be reflected in the text can easily be lost or ignored. It is a process that quickly leads to confusion unless expertly handled.

The first principle is to have one person managing the flow and review of input to the document. As indicated above, this should be one of the bid manager's responsibilities. The basic procedure can be quite straightforward. Input that the bid manager originates, or that comes in from other members of the team, is sent out for review and comment. Team members mark up their comments and their suggested changes and send the reviewed material back to the bid manager. He or she then has the task of collating this material, reconciling the various points of view and arriving at a definitive version. This will probably entail consultation with team members and other managers to resolve differences or conflicts between individual sets of comments and revisions. The process is an iterative one, but it cannot be allowed to seem an endless loop. As a final step, the bid manager coordinates the production of the final agreed and integrated document.

You must be able to distinguish immediately the latest version of any part of the text from superseded versions. Your colleagues will find it hard to forgive you if you have asked them to work on obsolete drafts. Earlier drafts may be saved on your system – and on occasion you may need to retrieve them – but you cannot afford to misidentify them or to get them out of sequence when the text is being edited since failure to reflect changes can destroy the consistency of the bid (Chapter 12). You have to be able to identify also the person who produced a revision file and the date when it was produced, since the same person may have to review that part of the text more than once.

The simplest approach is for the bid manager to maintain batches of related files in specific folders or sub-directories corresponding to sections of the bid. For example, let us suppose that all the drafts and revision files that have to do with the first section of a bid, the introduction, reside in a folder named 01intro. Each revision file is then identified uniquely by a draft number and the team member's initials: thus 01intro2JS.doc signifies that the file contains JS's comments and changes to the second draft of the introductory section. Each file should also indicate its date in the footer.

As well as the file structure, the rules and conventions for marking up text need to be agreed at the start so as to have everyone working on a consistent basis and to distinguish between firm changes, helpful suggestions and mere observations. The latest version of Word's comment function (in the Insert menu) usefully identifies the person making a comment and the date and time it was made. You may find

TEN STEP PROCEDURE FOR DOCUMENT MANAGEMENT

1. Identify content originator(s) for each section of bid, including graphic elements. Circulate list of content originators to all members of the bid team.
2. Identify reviewers for bid input: some parts of the bid may warrant review by all the members of the bid team; other parts may require only specialist review.
3. Develop timetable for origination, review and finalization of bid input. Circulate timetable, together with guidance and information on mark-up conventions, version control, file naming and so forth.
4. Coordinate a) receipt of input from originators; b) distribution of input to reviewers for comment via e-mail/intranet or CD; c) forwarding of reviewed input to the bid editor for processing. It is essential that input is received at a central bid management point and that drafts are sent out for review from that point.
5. Reviewers mark-up their comments, questions and suggested changes and send the reviewed input back via e-mail/intranet or CD.
6. Monitor progress of the receipt and review of inputs against the timetable.
7. Collate the reviewed drafts for each section, dealing with questions, reconciling points of view and arriving at an updated version of the content.
8. Send out revised drafts for any necessary further review.
9. At the end of each working day, update and back up a protected and controlled text that consolidates the latest versions of the various parts of the bid.
10. Working with the bid editor, produce a definitive version of the bid content, cleaned-up in terms of comments, changes and formatting. Proof-read this version.

the change-tracking function (Tools menu) easier to use. If, like most people, you are using Word, persuade team members to disable automatic bulleted and numbered lists and not to use 'styles', or you may have to spend a lot of time cleaning up messy formatting, particularly when files have to pass through transmission as e-mail attachments.

So far as distributing files is concerned, the easiest way is to use e-mail attachments or CDs. It would be ideal to be able to use a secure internet-accessible or intranet-based document management server that allows people to view and comment on the same document simultaneously. Document management tools with those capabilities tend to be complex and expensive, though they may be the answer if bids have to be produced as joint efforts by teams of people working simultaneously and remotely – for example, in offices located in different time zones.

At the end of each working day, update and back up a protected and controlled text that consolidates the latest versions of the various parts of the bid. The use of this text in the quality management of the bid is discussed below.

If other companies or external advisers are providing input, ask them to supply material in a format consistent with the requirements set by the client and with your preferences. Before people start to write their contributions, give them guidance on the style you want them to follow and the points to observe.

PROGRAMMING PRODUCTION AND DELIVERY

The bid should be treated as an **internal project** that needs to have resources made available and critical tasks scheduled. The same project management techniques that apply to contracts can be used to coordinate the management of bids. MS Project is the most widely used of many project management applications that the bid manager can employ to help assign resources, schedule tasks, track progress and avoid production delays, as well as developing the contract work programme. The printouts from project management software present information through a range of graphics that can be used to reinforce an image of business competence.

Even a simple chart of the bid production schedule can be useful in keeping track of the progress you are making, judging if the pace of work on the bid needs to be boosted and developing a realistic programme to meet the submission deadline with time in hand. The time that is allotted to production and the time discounted from the schedule to allow for delivery must include adequate contingency margins.

CHECKING BID QUALITY

There are clear advantages to be gained from treating the **quality management** of the bid as a continuous procedure built into its development from the start. It is important to check the bid thoroughly for the accuracy of its response to the client's priorities and for its completeness and quality of presentation – and to do this systematically throughout the process of writing the bid, not just at a concluding review stage. Your chances of success may well depend on getting small details right. The production timetable may allocate time at the end of the process for the text and graphics to be reviewed before the definitive version is printed out, but experience shows that if this is left until late the time available can easily be consumed by other pressures: in the worst cases, bids can leave the office unchecked, so that the first person to spot an obvious error is the client.

Quality management has three aspects. The first is **strategic** – ensuring that:

- whatever requirements the client has expressed about the content, structure and submission of the bid are recognized and observed;

- the client's view of the contract has been properly understood and reflected in the bid;

- the information supplied by the client has been used efficiently in constructing the bid;

- the text puts forward a balanced approach to the work;

- the basis on which the price of the work is calculated matches accurately the proposed technical input.

The second aspect is **tactical** – detecting and correcting omissions, factual mistakes, word processing errors, miscalculations, misspellings, inconsistencies in layout and so forth. Search for mistakes, check points of detail fastidiously, and take nothing for granted. For example:

- Is all the material that the client requires in the submission finalized and in place?

- Have the correct templates and schedules been used – for example, in setting out work activities, costs and personnel?

- Is one person shown in the work programme as performing two full-time activities simultaneously?

- Are two people claiming credit in their CVs for identical project responsibilities?

- Are all the CVs in place, and in the order that corresponds to the team listing in the text or CV index?

- If the text includes tables, do the numbers add up correctly and correspond with information given elsewhere in the text?

- Are graphics in the right places and the right order and consistent with the text? Do they have the right captions?

- Is the client's name spelt correctly? Contracts have been lost in situations where it was not.

It is always useful to have the text and graphics looked through by someone who was not involved in preparing the bid but knows its subject and context well enough to spot points that may seem questionable or need clearer explanation or more substantiation, or statements that the client is likely to misunderstand. One critical task is ensuring that the production schedule for the bid graphics is able to accommodate any late changes in the proposed work programme, team composition, time inputs or price schedule.

Thirdly, there is what may be termed the **competitive** aspect of quality management. Does the document have the necessary ingredients to make it a convincing and successfully competitive bid – insight and penetration, creativity and innovation, energy and enthusiasm, in addition to value for money and technical confidence? Does it express the message that your bid offers a distinctive added value that clients will not be able to obtain from your competitors?

If you maintain a protected text of the bid, as advocated above, keep it in a directory or folder accessible to everyone with an interest in the contract. This allows the progress and quality of the bid to be monitored throughout its development, so that managers can read the text at any time, suggest any necessary changes in direction early in the day and reduce the possibility of encountering disagreeable surprises at the last minute.

Some firms use what is termed a 'red team' to review the bid when it is close to a final draft. The job of this team is to read through the bid critically as if they were the client's evaluation panel, checking to see how competently it meets the requirements of the contract and how fully it matches the client's evaluation criteria. They adopt a devil's advocate role, challenging the thinking in the bid, searching for weaknesses and inconsistencies, and suggesting how the shortcomings they find in the text can be put right.

Though one cannot fault the principle of examining the bid from the client's perspective, the red team procedure is no substitute for a continuous quality review. First, if the people making up the team are sufficiently informed about both the client's view of the contract and its technical content to play a red team role effectively, they might be better employed providing original input to the bid rather than commenting at a distance and at a stage when it might be difficult to accommodate their changes coherently. Second, maintaining this review team will probably be cost-effective only on bids for particularly high-value contracts. Third, experience shows that 'us and them' tensions can easily build up between the people writing the bid and the people on the red team, especially if no one on that team takes the trouble to discuss the reasons why a particular approach was taken. Red teams should not just 'red-pen' the text: if they think something is inadequate they have a responsibility to put forward a better solution.

BRINGING TOGETHER RESOURCES AND INPUTS

Time: the resource that is wasted most easily and most often. A common fault is to leave the drafting and writing of the bid text until late in the day, forcing people to work frantically at the last moment. It is pointless blaming the client for not giving you longer to prepare the bid. If you are a professional and the work is worthwhile, you have to make the best effort you can in the time available. No matter how much time you have, it will never be enough unless it is managed properly. Managing time means stretching it to reach all the targets on your schedule.

Money: Do you have a budget for each bid? How much are you able to spend on pre-submission research? Do you monitor how effectively you use your budget? Or are you surprised when you learn just how much a bid has cost? If you don't know what you are spending on bids, they are almost certainly costing more than they should. As noted in Chapter 6, many firms find it reasonable for their bidding costs on small and medium-scale contracts to reach about 5 per cent of the total expected gross fee income.

When there are competing priorities, it is important to use resources in ways that make the best economic sense so as to develop bids as cost-effectively as possible. Each firm will need to identify the method of accounting for bid expenditure that offers the most effective financial control, whether this is worked out on a cost-centre basis or defined in other ways.

The essential requirements for bid budgeting are to:

- decide a budget allocation for the variable costs attached to a bid (for example, travel and production costs): this should be a level of reasonable and affordable costs that is not exceeded without justification and agreement;

- monitor closely expenditure on the bid;

- develop a series of budget yardsticks as an aid to cost control and expenditure forecasts.

Information: If all you have to rely on is the information supplied by the client, you are unlikely to convince anyone that you possess the depth of first-hand knowledge and understanding that makes you the contractor best suited to do the work. The tendency simply to regurgitate information contained in the client documentation – often quoting the client word for word (but without quotation marks!) – is a persistent fault in bids and one that dismays clients. The conclusion they draw is that either you had no intelligence of your own to offer, or you were afraid to put forward any ideas in case you said something wrong.

Bid preparation can be hindered also by an excess of information, for example when experts return from field visits with stacks of notebooks or computer disks crammed with material that is never used simply because its mass is so overwhelming. As a result, ideas that it would be useful to include in the bid are lost. The problem is seen in a different form when you read bids with encyclopedic pretensions, where the bidder's message is submerged beneath a flood of detail. There are no marks to be gained by giving clients tables of information that they are perfectly well aware of. Collect information exhaustively, but apply it selectively when it comes to compiling the text. When you do include background information in the bid, never present it cold or without tying it in with the logic of the text – use it intelligently to explain and reinforce your approach.

The profusion of information on the internet and the ability to access it instantly are factors we take for granted. A search through websites can deliver to your computer far more data than you could obtain in the time by any other means. The range, relevance and quality of this information and your capacity to apply it usefully in the bid are quite different matters. Key points to check before pasting material into your bid are: the source of the information (Is it clearly identified?); the authorship of the material and ownership of the site (Does it come from a recognized organization or authority, and are you confident about its veracity? Are opinions and anecdotes being passed off as research?); and its date (Can you trust web pages that do not indicate when they were last updated?).

Web browsers and search engines are essential tools in background research. See whether the client has a website, examine related sites, print off information relevant to the project and assess its implications for the development of your bid – but, again, be careful not to feed back to clients their own material. Using a scanner will enable you to copy material into a bid, though the OCR software that comes packaged with most scanners will not be able to resolve correctly every character in a text, and you may have to spend a fair amount of time putting things right manually.

Insight: One of the most scarce and valuable bid resources, insight may be defined as an informed perception of the client's priorities, which may or may not be stated explicitly in the bid documentation – in other words, looking at the project from the standpoint of the client, showing that you understand what is really important to the client, and demonstrating an ability to get to the heart of the matter. The way to prove this understanding is through the quality and depth of your analysis, particularly in setting out your approach to the work (Chapter 13).

Communication skills: Possessing insight is one thing; being able to communicate it is another. Because a bid is a specialized business document, its development calls for particular skills in the presentation and projection of technical material. Expert knowledge of the subject is not enough in itself: every bidder can be expected to have that. There are additional ingredients that a bid needs if it is to make its mark with the client. Weak bids read like patchworks of bits and pieces rather than the products of original thought. Strong bids convey a sense of creativity, energy and enthusiasm, as well as displaying a robust technical logic.

Points from bid specification	Place in bid	Points and ideas for bid document	Internal input/ comments from	External input/ comments from	Tables and figures?	Schedule and priorities
Requirement to provide Management Summary, to include:	Section 2		PWE and JS			Must have basic drafts by 20/04; comments by 25/04; editing completed 28/04
(a) summary of overall approach to the scheme	2(a)	(a) key priorities: making sure scheme goes live successfully on time; transparency of operation; securing public support; ensuring minimum risk to the Authority	Input from TS office? Ask them to look at draft by 22/04			
(b) demonstration of level of commitment to the scheme	2(b)	(b) describe pilot technology projects funded by the group; investment in practical and innovative applications		ETE on test project results	Photos from pilot project locations	Speak to ETE 18/04 (PWE)
(c) demonstration of understanding of the Guiding Principles set out in Part A of the bid specification	2(c)	(c) short paragraph on each of the principles	LE to comment			
(d) details of recent contracts, contracts in progress and statement on current and future work commitments	2(d)	(d) tabulate contracts by date and in key categories of experience Cut-off point? Annotate with best practice evidence Focus on inner city projects Contact details for client references	PWE SRB bid JS has up-to-date lists	Get contract records from ABA Liverpool!?	Tables of contract experience: PWE to advise on categories and contract selection	High priority: obtain by 19/04 (JS)

Figure 8.2 *Detail of a bid development worksheet*

USING A BID DEVELOPMENT WORKSHEET

Structuring and developing the bid are discussed in Chapter 12. A **bid development worksheet** along the lines of Figure 8.2 offers a useful means of staying in control of these activities, organizing and coordinating your response to the client's specification and building up ideas for the content of the bid. It enables you to map out every part of the response and serves as a framework to help follow through points set out in the specification and identified from your background research.

The example in Figure 8.2 is taken from a recent procurement and relates to one of the requirements in the bid specification, the inclusion of a management summary. The worksheet indicates who is to be responsible for producing this information and where it might feature in the bid; it provides space to record ideas about how this material might be treated and points that need to be emphasized; it identifies sources of information and comment; it flags up requirements for tables, graphics and appendices; and it displays priorities and shows the target dates when material has to be ready.

Using a worksheet like this means that everyone who has a part to play in developing the bid knows what is expected of them, whom they should talk to and when they have to deliver. Progress can be checked off and items that demand particular attention can be highlighted. As its name implies, it is intended as a working document that is adaptable to revision as ideas about the bid take shape.

MAINTAINING BID RECORDS

Developing even a straightforward bid can mean that you accumulate a mass of disparate information about the client, the contract and its context – faxes and e-mails, documents of all kinds, notes of meetings jotted down on scraps of paper, contact details entered into diaries and organizers, not to mention the knowledge that never gets written down but survives perilously in your memory. All this information may be highly relevant, but the next time you need to prepare a bid for the client, will it be readily to hand to make the task easier? Not unless you have a system for recording and managing the information and a means of storing it conveniently and securely.

Office use	Project log no.
	File reference
	Date project registered
	Date file opened
	Manager responsible
Client data	Country / region
	Client title / department
	Client address and communication data (e-mail / fax / phone)
	Client contacts
	Past ref / file nos.
	Regional / local material held
	Bid invitation: date received / acknowledged
Project data	Project outline (2 lines)
	Funding details (if applicable)
	Estimated duration
	Estimated start date
	Work location(s)
	Revenue assessment
Management data	Partner / Director / Associate responsible
	Bid manager
	Bid planning meeting: date
	Bid development worksheet?
	Bid response matrix?
	Quality management procedure
	Designated team leader
	Bid cost assessment
	Bid cost out-turn
Submission data	Deadline: date / time
	Submission address
	Delivery action: mode and responsibility
	Fallback procedure
Association data	Associate(s) and contact data
	Subconsultants and contact data
	Lead firm
Research and intelligence	Project / client research: personnel
	Contacts /sources

Figure 8.3 *Outline of a bid record, showing principal categories of information*

Visit data	Date(s)
	Personnel on visit
	Visit leader
	Accommodation details and contact data
	Debriefing
	Visit notes received
Team data	Team structure: outline / agreed
	Team inputs and rates: agreed
	CVs: draft, editing, checked, agreed (signature?)
Text data	Transmittal letter – person responsible / draft / review / agreed
	Technical text: person(s) responsible / draft / review / agreed
	Summary: person responsible / draft / review / agreed
	Financial information: person responsible / draft / review / agreed
Graphics data	List of graphics
	Cover graphics: person responsible / draft / review / agreed
	Charts: person responsible / draft / review / agreed
	Photographs
	Graphics printing
	Printing details
Production data	Format: hard copy / electronic
	Word processing and illustration: person responsible / draft / review / agreed
	Design and page layout: person responsible / draft / review / agreed
	Hard copy covers
	Production control check: person responsible
	Binding / disk production
	Print order
	Distribution: client / internal
	Supply for delivery

Figure 8.3 *continued*

Small-scale bids may call for nothing more sophisticated than a box file or card index. Complex tenders may require a database solution such as FileMaker Pro. The important point is to keep bid information in a structured form that allows immediate access and avoids the need to repeat basic research. That is the purpose of the **bid record** shown in

Bid planning	Decision to bid: confirmation to client
	Decisions on bid management
	Analysis of the bid specification
	Additional research into competitive situation and market factors
	Clarification procedure
	Bid resource analysis
	Bid team structure
	Bid planning meeting
	Bid development programme
	Decisions on format and content of bid
	Assignment of writing and editing responsibilities
	Quality management procedures
	Document management and version control procedures
	Initial decisions on contract staffing
Bid coordination	Draft structure of contract programme
	Draft schedule of outputs and deliverables
	Finalization of structure and content of bid
	Definition of bid budget
	Cost and pricing assumptions for contract
	Contacts and meetings
	Design and layout principles for the bid
	Coordination of CVs, contract experience and other material
Bid writing and editing	Technical, financial and management texts and appendices
	Bid graphics
	Definitive review
Production and delivery	Production monitoring
	Translation (if appropriate)
	Proofing and collation of bid documents
	Hard copy cover / CD copy of bid
	Hard copy / electronic submission

Figure 8.4 *Bid development outline*

Figure 8.3. It attempts to be comprehensive and so may look too daunting for everyday use; but it can be pared down to include only essential categories of information. The record can be supplemented by an archive of related information such as material gathered from marketing research and intelligence, plans and statistical reports, corporate documentation and so forth. Records of bids for work overseas may involve the addition of further data entries, eg time zone information and visa requirements.

BID DEVELOPMENT OUTLINE

As a form of summary, Figure 8.4 sets out a list of bid development tasks that apply to many sectors of procurement. The list covers the process in outline from planning to production and includes tasks related both to the bid and to the work of the contract.

In addition to the technical sections of text and graphics, the content of a bid may have to include a large number of documents such as forms, schedules, certificates, declarations, questionnaire responses and so forth, which the client may require to be presented in a specific order. Many firms find it useful to prepare a hard copy mock-up of the bid, in which each part of its content is represented by a blank sheet of paper: as each copy of the bid is assembled for packaging, it is checked against the mock-up to make sure that everything is there and in the right order.

9

Talking to the client

The bid specification will normally tell you whether making contact with the client is expected, encouraged or forbidden on pain of disqualification. In many fields of public sector procurement, direct contacts by the bidder are restricted to the submission of written questions seeking clarification on matters of fact or the meaning of items in the bid specification (Chapter 7): the option of meeting the client to talk about the work is ruled out on the grounds that it might be interpreted as infringing the principles of transparency and even-handedness. But in most other contexts, prospective clients will expect you to want to meet them – provided of course that enough time is available and the contract value makes it seem worthwhile. It is not unusual for a client organization to require bidders to visit its office so as to obtain first-hand information about the project and talk to the people handling the work. There may be a pre-tender briefing presentation that prospective bidders are expected to attend. You have to read the bid specification carefully to see what the client has said on this point, and then make the most of what opportunities you have.

Depending on the nature of the work and the degree to which you are familiar with its background, you may still find it advantageous to do local research for the bid even if you are not allowed to approach the client. Talking to other people and organizations that have interests related to a project may give you insights, ideas and information that you can put to good use in the bid and that you would not have obtained by staying at your desk; and if the work has to be done elsewhere than in your offices, you will want to see the location for yourself.

If the client has arranged a briefing session, confirm your intention to attend. Make a full record of what is said at the meeting, both by the client and by your competitors, and ensure this information is taken adequately into account in developing your bid.

If it is you that is arranging the date rather than the client, give as much advance notice of your visit as possible. The timing of a meeting with the client has to be finely judged: it should not take place too early, before you have enough information to know what questions to ask, or too late, when there is too little time to make effective use of its results. In many instances the right moment will be about a quarter or a third of the way into the time available for preparing the bid: ie if the invitation comes in on a Monday and the bid has to be submitted on Friday, then Tuesday would probably be the best day to see the client.

Most of the following points of guidance may seem common sense; but experience confirms that they are not always put into practice. It's all too easy for contractors to shoot themselves in the foot on these occasions.

- To make the visit, choose someone who can contribute input both to the bid and to the contract and is able to speak knowledgeably about the technical aspects of the work – for example, the person nominated as team leader.

- Before the meeting try to foresee what questions the client may want to ask, as well as preparing your own questions.

- Make notes while information and impressions are still fresh in your mind.

- If you are meeting the client as a team, introduce yourselves; do not assume that the client must know who you are. Exchange business cards. If other people come into the meeting, record their names and posts correctly.

■ Develop a dialogue with the client: don't focus just on what you have to say, or monopolize the conversation. Listen actively to what the client tells you: this means following up the client's remarks with questions that allow you to go into more depth and confirm your understanding, and using body language that reinforces rather than weakens the impact of your words.

■ Remember that you are aiming to impress clients with your professionalism and integrity, to give them the feeling that you are the right people to work with. When talking about your professional experience, do not disclose matters that ought to be kept confidential or comment on the internal affairs of your past or existing clients. The people you are meeting may form the opinion that you are likely to gossip about their business too.

■ Try to get copies of whatever relevant documents are available – for example, corporate policy statements and business plans, reports of studies and statistical data. Among the most useful items you can obtain are internal contact lists with phone and fax numbers and e-mail addresses, and information on how the client organization is structured in terms of departments, units, management posts and responsibilities.

■ An important point to find out is the likely structure of the evaluation panel. Will the bids be assessed just by technical personnel or by a team combining technical experts, managers, procurement specialists, contract administrators and other professionals? Will stakeholder groups be involved? Does the client intend to bring in its own independent expert either to assist in the evaluation or to oversee the procurement process?

■ Be alert to any warning signals about the contract. If client personnel are unwilling to discuss the bid specification or appear hesitant about the work, it may be because matters were arranged hastily and they are not certain what they want. Or perhaps the project you thought was real does not in fact exist, and the request for bids is no more than a trawling exercise.

If the visit takes you overseas

■ When the trip involves a long-haul flight, give yourself time to acclimatize and recover from any effects of jet lag. You cannot afford to perform below your best at the meeting. If you are able to arrive a day or two before you see the client, the time can usefully be spent with local associates (Chapter 10), talking to other sources of information and intelligence and getting a clearer perception of the environment in which you would be working.

- Plan the visit as an intensive work trip that will include developing and drafting sections of the bid. Have an agenda with clear and precise objectives, but build flexibility into the timetable and itinerary so that you can take advantage of opportunities to make contacts and visits that will help you create a more informed bid. Do not count on being able to return home on a predetermined date.

- If you are visiting a non-English-speaking environment, you want people with you who know the local language well enough to talk usefully to contacts and read local documentation. Even on a short visit to an unfamiliar location, it is possible by talking to the right people and keeping one's eyes open to become aware of problems and issues that may affect a contract. In many countries there are counterparts to the *Financial Times* that can be a source of valuable information on current developments in your sector of business.

- Tell your contacts in the client organization where you are staying and how they can get in touch with you. Business and government hours may follow a quite different pattern from that in the UK, and it may not be unusual to receive a call to visit a government department, say, at 9.30 pm.

- You will want to talk to the managers or officials who are most closely involved with the contract, but try also to meet other decision-makers. They will have competing pressures on their time: do not outstay your welcome.

- When you are talking to third parties, be careful not to reveal too much about your intentions for the bid or the information you have discovered about the contract. They may be talking to your competitors as well.

- Let the commercial section of your embassy or consulate-general know about your visit. The staff are only too willing to be helpful, provided you give them enough notice, and you may need their assistance if you run into difficulties.

- Try to bring back data on unit costs for comparable assignments – for example, the costs of accommodation, local travel and support staff: these are items on which local associates can be helpful.

10

Bidding in partnership

Even if you are in business on your own, there are occasions when you may want or need to join forces with others. The bid specification may state that the expertise required for the contract is unlikely to be obtained from a single source; parts of the work may demand skills outside your competence; the contract may be too big to undertake by yourself; or your analysis of the competitive situation may reveal areas where links with organizations in related fields could add credibility to your bid.

Whatever the type and size of the group – whether it combines several firms with complementary expertise as well as, say, public sector authorities and research units, or whether you have just one partner in the bid – do not present it simply as a list of names. As noted in the comments on research partnerships in Chapter 4, the client needs to be told the **reasons for the formation of the group**, the distinctive benefits of its combined strength and the part that each member will play in the contract. You should be able to demonstrate both the cohesiveness of the group as an operational unit, working together in an integrated management structure, and the added value that its joint expertise and resources offer the client.

If your competitors on a shortlist include people whom you know and perhaps have worked with on other contracts, you may sometimes see advantages in making a joint bid and using your united strength to outflank the rest of the opposition. Before committing yourself to this arrangement, it is important to check that the client has no objection: the client's attitude to the formation of consortia and subcontracting will normally be made explicit in the bid specification (Chapter 7). There are probably good reasons why a shortlist is structured as it is, and a change in its size or composition may not suit the client's interests.

The key requirement is to have one firm or individual leading the group and able to act as sole contracting party in a negotiation. Clients do not like to see fuzzy groups with a confused pattern of responsibilities. Who takes the lead may depend on several factors. Usually it is the firm that received the invitation and took the initiative in setting up the group; but this may not be the firm scheduled to put most input into the contract, or the firm whose lead role is most likely to help win the contract, or the one that can supply the best bid manager or the best candidate for team leader. The safest formula is to have the group led by the firm that can best combine team leadership and the ability to perform a major share of the work programme with expertise in bid preparation. The lead firm will generally coordinate and manage the bid as a whole, while other members of the group supply specialist input, CVs, contract experience and price information.

GUIDELINES FOR ASSOCIATION

There are key guidelines to follow if you want to achieve a successful basis for association:

- Don't have more associates than you really need. For clients, the best team is one that is no bigger than necessary to meet their requirements.

- Choose them carefully. They need to be compatible with your approach to the bid, with the client's management culture and with each other. On the face of it, units or departments within the same company or contracting group should make ideal partners, but that will only be the case if they can work productively as a team.

- Identify the roles that each associate will play in preparing the bid, in any subsequent negotiations and in fulfilling the contract, including the extent of your responsibilities for particular deliverables. You need to avoid the risk of things not being done because it is assumed someone else is looking after them.

- Get all parties to agree on the principle of sharing the costs of bid preparation and negotiation and the detailed basis on which costs will be divided. Do this at the start to avoid unpleasant surprises later! Normally these costs are split in proportion to the share of total fee income that each participant expects to receive from the contract.

- Draft a letter of agreement or memorandum of understanding setting down these points as well as defining the form of the association. The agreement can be developed into a more formal document if the bid is successful. Have it signed by an authorized representative of each participant. Contracting authorities will normally want you to include a copy of the agreement in the bid.

- It may take some time to firm up the composition and structure of the association. Make sure the people you talk to understand the need for confidentiality during this process.

So far as the form of association is concerned, you may have a variety of options, from bringing in freelancers who undertake contract work as subconsultants to establishing a formally constituted joint venture partnership with its members sharing joint and several liability. Procurement rules generally do not require you to set up the association in a particular legal form.

The best advice is to avoid anything that involves corporate legal and financial obligations such as a joint venture, unless you intend to commit yourself to a long-term relationship with the other members and are confident that they possess the resources to share in any liabilities that may arise. Choose instead either to manage the work on a subcontract basis, where you control the services of your associates, or to set up an informal association or consortium in which each party maintains its normal trading obligations but has clearly defined and understood professional responsibilities as part of the team. To establish a joint venture at the bid stage is premature: it is better to proceed on the basis of a memorandum of understanding until a call to interview or negotiation is received.

Size of association

Unless there is a clear logical relationship between the character of a group, the scope of work and the complexity of the contract, try not to have groups of more than four or five parties. Multiple associations can succeed if they are integrated through sensible and efficient management and a common approach, and if everyone gives the contract an appropriate degree of priority. But a consortium of, say, seven firms can easily translate into a team of 30 or more professionals. The people evaluating the bid may doubt the control and manageability of a team that will have to be answerable to so many head offices as well as accountable to the client, and they are likely to focus on the increased resource and administrative costs that a large group will entail, as well as the increased scope for disagreement and misunderstanding. It is in your interests to keep the group compact and to define a transparently clear structure of management (Chapter 14).

Choosing associates

The best associates will generally be people you know or people recommended to you by reliable contacts in your profession. There are many attributes that make an effective partner, including complementarity of skills and experience; but the essential requirement is to have a shared understanding of professional responsibility and a commitment to performance and delivery that will extend beyond the bid and into the contract. You need associates who are prepared to roll up their sleeves and invest the time and effort to achieve a winning result.

Remember that in developing the work schedule you may not be able to change and adjust the time inputs of your associates as easily as you can the inputs of your own personnel. Associates with other professional commitments may have narrow margins of availability.

Do not misuse professional relationships by enlisting specialists and advisers into your team, using their names to help win the contract and then pruning down their inputs (or reducing their fee rates) unilaterally when it comes to negotiating a price with the client. Keep your associates informed about the progress of the bid, and tell them about the outcome. To leave people in suspense, uncertain whether the month or so they have offered to you will actually turn out to be a month of income, is not conducive to good relationships.

OVERSEAS BIDS: TEAMING UP WITH LOCAL ASSOCIATES

When the contract is for an overseas client, particularly in the public sector, the bid specification may require or advise bidders from other countries to associate with a local organization. The client may state that the local organization will be expected to act as the lead firm, while expatriates will be used only for services that cannot be provided by local professionals. If the contract involves a substantial resource commitment as well as a significant element of risk, it may make good sense to share the commitment with local partners and limit the extent of your own risk.

If your business works extensively abroad, you may already have in place a network of partners and associates who you know can play an effective role in a project team and add insight and experience to help you produce a competitive bid. If you are new to an overseas market, and the bid specification either demands association or indicates that it would be helpful, you will have the task of selecting suitable local partners and establishing a working relationship with them.

This is one of the jobs that have to be done on a visit to the location. Getting it right calls for time, patience and judgement, as well as detailed research both before and during the visit. Use contacts in your profession and in related fields; talk to people in banking and business sectors; find out what information is available from export promotion services at home and from the commercial section of your embassy overseas. Clients may sometimes include with their documentation a list or selection of local firms who are registered with them and available to work jointly with external contractors.

Before you hear officially that your firm is on an international shortlist, you may receive messages from prospective local partners seeking to associate in your bid and perhaps claiming to have insider knowledge. Don't rush into commitments, unless you are confident that the firm that has contacted you really is the one that you need, and you are afraid of losing them to the competition. If you can, wait until you are on the scene and then make a judgement based on an informed assessment of their quality and capability. Before you decide, confirm that your associates will be working exclusively with you and not with your competitors too.

Even where local association is not an explicit requirement, there are benefits that associates can contribute to the bid and its development:

- detailed knowledge of the client and its preferences, plus an insight into the contract environment;

- a particular rapport with the client or with individual decision-makers, which may derive from previous work for the client, from social and political links, from a shared educational background and similar factors – though you should be cautious about anyone whose strongest credential is political influence;

- the integration of local skills and resources within the contract team;

- language capability, at every step from talking to officials to translating documents and writing text for the bid;

- information about the practical and legal necessities of working in the country, eg professional or commercial registration;

- an awareness of cultural sensitivities and local business usage that steers you clear of possible blunders;

- confirmation, if need be, that you are pursuing a genuine project and that the client does intend to award a contract;

- detailed price information on local services and facilities, as well as ideas about savings and economies in expenses that would not occur to an outsider;

- a means of reducing the total cost of the proposed services, if your local associates have lower payroll costs than you;

- contacts in the banking and financial community;

- logistic support in preparing and producing the bid documents;

- the ability to deal pragmatically with what may discreetly be termed 'facilitation fees'.

It is worth bearing in mind that if you do win an overseas contract, your local associates can have an essential role to play in getting your invoices paid. There are countries where public sector clients will make direct payments only to local firms, and where the receipt of funds as a matter of routine on the date specified in a contract is virtually unknown. Securing the payment due to you depends instead on a tortuous chain of administrative and commercial intermediaries, each of whom expects a cut. Without local associates to handle this situation, you would literally be at a loss.

On the negative side, an unwise choice of associate can put the entire bid at risk:

- The people you link up with may have professional or political enmities that are unknown to you, or may in the past have worked unimpressively for the client.

- They may claim an excessive proportion of the work programme and try to take control of the bid.

- At the worst, they may be interested mainly in the money and want to gain the maximum fee for the minimum work.

- They may have the leverage to undermine your bid if you get on the wrong side of them.

- You may become linked to a particular firm through a previous contract relationship and then discover they are the wrong associates for this opportunity.

The keys to making the right choice of local associate are:

- Consider more than one candidate.

- Narrow the field down to organizations with a good business reputation, recommended by people whose honesty and impartiality you can trust.

- Check that they satisfy any conditions for association identified in the client documentation. Are they engaged on other work that might disqualify them from participating in your bid?

- Make sure you can communicate directly with the head of the organization. In some countries where not all professionals speak English, your dealings may be channelled through a relatively junior member of staff who happens to have a good command of the language, but may not be in the confidence of senior management. You need to establish a solid link at the top.

■ Look for openness, trustworthiness and commitment.

■ Ask yourself which organization offers the strongest prospects of performing a satisfactory role in the contract. Remember that if you are the lead contractor you will be responsible for your associates' technical performance.

When you have made your choice, prepare a short written agreement summarizing your understanding of the relationship. If appropriate, have the document translated into the associate's language.

In many instances, the most productive and lasting links with local associates have developed from ad hoc working relationships. If you discover reliable partners in one country, you and they can gain from the association by collaborating on similar contracts elsewhere, with advantages and cost savings all round.

Overseas bids: production decisions

One decision that has to be made at this stage is where the bid is to be prepared and produced – overseas or back in your home office? If you decide to do the work locally and stay on to help coordinate the process, an overseas visit can become an extended commitment. You need to consider the following questions:

■ Will preparation of the bid require a substantial amount of translation? Does the client want the document in its language? If so and depending on the place, it may make sense to produce the bid locally.

■ Where can the development of the bid be managed more efficiently? Are there critical management decisions that can be taken only on site?

■ What are the quality and dependability of the telecommunications and production facilities that local associates can offer?

■ Are there requirements such as the need to have documents notarized and legalized or to include signatures on forms and CVs that may complicate the logistics of production?

- Which location is likely to offer the better result in terms of the quality and impact of the bid? Local associates will know the kind of document the client expects to see – whether it is a weighty and substantial volume or something concise and economical – and they will be familiar with the standard of design and presentation needed to create an immediately favourable impression. Listen to their advice.

11

Thinking the work through

Your analysis of the bid specification will have given you an insight into the client's view of the contract and the results the work is intended to achieve. Does that mean you can now confidently start writing the text of the bid? Well, no. There is a further piece of analysis to undertake, which can be described as thinking the work through – trying to form as clear an idea as you can at this stage about the resources you will need to put into the work to carry it forward to a successful conclusion, and the steps that can be taken on your part to reduce the risk of things going wrong. By looking ahead, you will make life easier and go at least some way toward avoiding nasty surprises. That sounds obvious, yet bids sometimes show little or no indication that anyone has applied their minds to understanding just what the contract will entail. What the client receives is an idealized picture of how the work might be done, closer to fantasy than reality.

Before you can produce a bid that the client will find convincing, you need to think about the following aspects of the contract:

- the practical demands of fulfilling the contract to the satisfaction of the client;

- the relationship between its technical and financial elements;

- the factors that might put at risk its performance and delivery;

- the means of reducing the risk of contract failure.

GET THE MEASURE OF THE WORK

The bid specification may define the tasks to be undertaken, the inputs to be applied, the way the contract is to be structured into blocks of work or stages, the timetable of the work and the outcomes and deliverables that are expected. Even so, you need to consider whether the client's perception of the work offers the most practical and cost-effective route to the results intended. Clients may underestimate the amount of professional effort that will be required, with implications for the budget, and they may specify a pace of delivery that cannot be sustained either technically or logistically in the particular work environment.

Make sure you feel secure about the structure of the work programme and the resources that will be needed both to administer it and to perform efficiently the technical side of the contract. It is important to think about the detailed requirements of the work, not simply its broad outlines. But remember that these requirements are certain to alter as the contract takes shape: your approach will need to show adaptability and responsiveness to changes in the client's priorities.

Some further questions to consider:

- What are the options for structuring the work programme? If the client has indicated a particular approach and the bid specification allows variant solutions, are there reasons for suggesting an alternative structure – for example, on the grounds that it can achieve results more cost-effectively, rapidly and dependably?

- What range of options do you have in terms of technical methods and procedures? What are their resource implications? Are there aspects of the contract to which you can bring an innovative, distinctive and lower-cost approach?

- What tasks are likely to be central to the success of the project, and what are the critical links between tasks and inputs?

- Can the work be fast-tracked? Are there tasks that can be undertaken simultaneously to achieve early results?

- What assumptions are you making about the validity of the data that will be available or the conditions in which the work will have to be done?

- Are there external constraints that determine the way the contract will have to be performed – for example, environmental requirements or health and safety procedures?

- Will the contract require the input of a team working closely together at a central site, either long-term or in the initial stages? Can parts of the contract be delivered successfully by people working remotely?

- If the client has not indicated where the work is to be done, what are your views on this point? Are there methods or processes that would be hard to apply in a particular location or cause problems of logistics?

MATCH TECHNICAL CONTENT AND PRICE

The assumptions you make about the costs of doing the work have to be well researched and based on information that is accurate and up to date. You must control the proposed work plan and personnel inputs to avoid the risk of pricing your bid out of the competition. This means:

- thinking through the cost implications of your initial ideas about the work;

- keeping the proposed work plan under review as it is being developed, and checking how resources are being assigned in relation to the priorities of the contract;

- considering approaches such as shared risk pricing, where a programme of work that addresses the core requirements of the contract is offered at a fixed price, while other activities are priced on a time plus expenses basis;

- if necessary, revising and restructuring the detailed content of the work plan, the composition of the contract team and the length of their time inputs.

These processes require a careful balance of judgement if the bid is to succeed in both winning you the contract and providing an effective basis for the performance of the work. The technical and financial parts of the bid need to be developed in parallel, with a two-way flow of feedback between their contents. Developing each part in isolation may not ruin your chances of winning, but if the professional effort required by the work turns out to be more than you had assumed and you have pitched your price too low, you will run into problems.

RECOGNIZE AND MANAGE RISK

Many types of project carry high levels of risk for clients and contractors alike. As well as commercial, financial and legal risk, there is political risk for those who take (or fail to take) decisions on projects with impacts on the community, the economy and the environment, and professional risk both for the contractors who take part in the design and implementation of projects and for the client personnel who are responsible for contracting and managing their services.

Clients who know how to prepare effective specifications will have identified and assessed those aspects of the work that will have a critical bearing on its outcome or expose the contract to particular risk, and they are likely to have written safeguards into the specification to minimize, or at least contain within tolerable levels, those risks that can be foreseen and are amenable to control. Questions to keep in mind include the extent to which the client may wish to transfer risk to you, how acceptable you would find this, and the extent to which risk transfer can be reflected in your price for the work. In some instances, the tender documentation will include risk ownership tables in which bidders are required to identify risks for which they are prepared to accept full or partial responsibility. If you are invited to negotiate, signing the contract will mean that you accept the transfer of risk.

No work situation can be made totally proof against disruption: events may well occur that no one could reasonably have foreseen or be able to do anything about. Political or institutional changes may force a shift of emphasis or direction in the work; the project may meet external opposition from pressure groups; if client responsibilities are shared with other organizations or external sources of funding, divergences of view between the parties may slow its progress; complications may arise in the physical environment of the contract that may delay its schedule and incur additional costs. But it should be possible, when the bid is being planned, to think ahead about the problems that might arise and help clients design them out of the contract. So far as your role in the contract is concerned, the circumstances most likely to expose contracts to risk are resource deficiencies and ineffective working relationships.

Resource deficiencies

You and your client will face problems if the personnel assigned to the work are deficient in terms of their number, capability, experience or attitude, or if they are poor at communicating their findings. For all sorts of reasons, individuals whose abilities look good on paper may turn out to deliver work that is below the client's expectations of quality. One person's inadequacies can easily jeopardize the performance of an entire contract. Can you afford to accept that risk? How well do you know the people you are asking to work on the contract? Have you met them and talked to them, or are they just names and qualifications on paper? Have the members of a team worked together before? If they have successfully produced benefits for other clients in comparable assignments, this needs to be substantiated and emphasized in the bid.

Contracts often run into problems simply because people make mistakes. Your bid should, if possible, include evidence that the people named in your team are competent to perform efficiently the tasks for which they are proposed. Include in their CVs precise references to the work they have achieved on similar contracts. If an individual's responsibilities will involve, for instance, survey design and analysis as part of a public consultation programme, think about including in the bid examples of survey forms he or she has developed; if the person is to have essentially a training role, include examples of relevant training materials he or she has prepared.

Another factor that may raise concern is the possibility that the experts who are named in the bid may feature also in bids to other clients or may not become available at the required time or may be subject to competing work demands. To counter this problem, the bid specification may require you to include a statement of commitment to field the nominated personnel, together with a signed undertaking from each team member to accept the work proposed by the firm if it is awarded the contract. Even where the bid specification does not include this requirement, a statement of commitment can reassure the client that your approach to resourcing the work is practical and conscientious.

If you are proposing to feed part of the work to subcontractors, clients may have concerns that the people you take on may prove variable in their output, quality, motivation or availability. Identify firms or individuals to whom you propose to subcontract work that is significant either in terms of its value as a proportion of the total contract fee, or in terms of its criticality for the outcome of the contract. Confirm that their engagement will be on the basis of back-to-back contracts, ie you will be accountable to the client for their performance just as if they were your employees. Include the CVs of the key subcontracted staff who would be involved in the work; and describe the quality management procedures you will apply in monitoring their performance. It can also be useful to make the point that you will ensure they receive adequate guidance on the client's expectations about quality and delivery.

Before you define an arrangement with subcontractors, check who their existing clients are. Conflicts of interest might prejudice your bid.

Ineffective working relationships

When clients believe that contractors have not delivered the results they had hoped for, there often turn out to have been failures in communication on both sides, and a lack of mutual understanding at key stages in the planning and performance of the contract. People may be slow to recognize a problem and reluctant to acknowledge their part in its creation. Responsibilities that are left ill defined or that overlap or fall into gaps between the role of the client and the role of the contractor are a particular source of conflict. The contractors may seem to be learning their job at the client's expense or expecting the client to do the thinking for them. When the job is completed, the results may not appear relevant or practical.

With hindsight one can see that difficulties could have been avoided if contract responsibilities had been delineated more sharply, if the contractors had gained a clearer view of the client's priorities, and if both parties had built a more effective working relationship. It is essential for contractors to approach their work in a spirit of professional partnership aimed at helping the client organization achieve its objectives; and it is important that a bid demonstrates convincingly a commitment to developing and sustaining not merely a constructive relationship, but one that offers the client the maximum benefit, optimum value and minimum risk.

The success of the contract can be put at risk by tensions within your team, as well as poor working relationships with the client's staff. You may believe you have a first-class group of professionals, but as the contract takes shape strains may develop at a personal level between individuals so that they cease to work together efficiently as a team. Your personnel and the client's staff may be ill matched in terms of perceptions of competence. If the staff feel they know much less than the people on your team, they may defer to them on issues that ought to be questioned. If they feel they know more, they may resent their presence and treat them with scepticism. Either way, the outcome will be an unhappy working relationship and a damaged contract.

REDUCE THE RISK OF CONTRACT FAILURE

When you come to write the bid, you need to be able to show the client that:

- you have considered the risk factors on your side of the contract;

- you know how to manage these factors so as to keep the work of the contract on track, reduce the cost of risk for the client and achieve optimum value for money;

- if and when problems do occur, you will act promptly and decisively to stop them getting worse.

The way to do this is to think about contract management as a form of preventative maintenance, designed to protect the contract from situations that may damage its outcome. Build into your management approach (Chapter 14) the controls that clients will recognize as evidence that you understand and respect their business priorities – in particular:

- an unambiguous definition of roles and responsibilities;

- a continuous process of dialogue and review, with clear-cut lines of management accountability and transparency in management information;

- a precise statement of the work to be achieved by each person engaged on the contract, with targets and deadlines;

- monitoring of work against agreed quality, performance and delivery standards;

- procedures to resolve problems rapidly and effectively;

- prompt corrective action if the contract gets out of sync with time and budget markers;

- contingency planning to secure continuity and consistency;

- readiness to implement changes if the course of the contract needs to be adjusted and redirected.

It is not enough just to use these phrases. Clients are not looking for rhetoric: they want actual procedures spelt out in practical and convincing detail. Having risk management procedures in place shows a conscientious approach to your relationship with the client. It is critically important that your bid communicates both the mechanics of this approach and its value.

12

Developing and writing the bid

Clients by and large prefer to receive bids that are businesslike and succinct – which means relatively short. It's the quality of the bid that counts, not the quantity of paper. Bid specifications are often explicit about the need for brevity, and it is a requirement that has to be taken seriously. Clients may try to force contractors to keep things brief by imposing limits on the size of the bid (eg 'no more than six to eight A4 pages, presented in one-and-a-half-line spacing') and on the number of pages that may be devoted to particular categories of information.

These limits help clients apply a consistent approach in assessing the adequacy of the contractor's response, and they contain within manageable proportions the work of examining and evaluating bids. They can be useful also to bidders, by making them concentrate on the essentials of what they have to offer and deterring them from spending undue amounts of time and other resources on overweight presentations.

Where you are faced with tight limits, the best approach is to:

- draft the content of the bid in a way that responds fully but concisely to the client's requirements for information, keeping the limits in mind;

- build the text around the key points that communicate the distinctive value that you offer and that answer the client's evaluation criteria;

- compare your text to the space available;

- if necessary, pare it down by summarizing the less essential material.

STRUCTURING THE CONTENT

The bid specification will normally state how the bid is to be structured and the categories of information that bidders are required to provide within this structure. Some clients may want bidders to set out information in a particular sequence, under standardized section headings; others may instruct bidders to use particular formats or templates in presenting their work plan, cost estimates, contract experience, CVs and so forth.

If the structure of the bid is specified by the client, follow it exactly. This cannot be emphasized too strongly. Do not ignore any instructions the client may give about either structure or information content. Your bid is likely to be rejected if it fails to supply fully the information the client has asked for.

What should you not include in a bid? Brochures and other forms of promotional literature. First, they will be seen as an attempt to pad out the bid. Second, they may make the bid look ready-made instead of purpose-designed for that contract. Third, clients by and large do not bother to read general material but turn instead to what you have to say about the contract. Fourth, brochures confuse the function of the bid, since they are essentially pre-qualification material. Clients may require bids to include an account of the contractor's organization, staff, services, fields of specialist expertise and experience; but a few paragraphs written specially for the occasion, focusing on the benefits that your services offer and explaining how your skills and professional resources help clients meet their objectives, will be more effective than a brochure.

If the structure is left open to your judgement, bear in mind that the bid is a functional document produced not for your benefit but to serve the client's needs. There are categories of information that clients will expect as a minimum to find in every bid:

- a statement of the purpose and origin of the bid;

- a summary of your background as a contractor, your credentials for the assignment and your experience of comparable or related work;

- an outline of your proposed technical approach;

- a work plan and timetable – for example, a bar chart indicating timescale and completion dates for each part of the work;

- outputs and deliverables;

- the personnel to be assigned to the work and their individual responsibilities;

- details of management arrangements;

- an estimate or confirmation of the fees and expenses likely to be incurred.

Structure the bid in sections that correspond to these topics and that meet such other requirements as the client may have about the way the work is to be undertaken and managed – for example, sections about quality procedures or risk management.

Normally the preliminary material at the front of the document will include a **letter of transmittal**. This letter is a counterpart of the client's letter of invitation or other form of approach and should be addressed to the person who signed that letter or made the approach. It can serve the following purposes:

- to signal a key message or theme that has shaped the bid or a salient feature that you hope makes it distinctive or particularly advantageous to the client;

- to draw the client's attention, if appropriate, to the fact that the bid is in more than one volume or that it is accompanied by a financial bid submitted under separate cover.

Keep the letter brief and diplomatic: it is not the place for afterthoughts, apologies, attempts at negotiation or allusions to price. One useful point to make may be an offer to follow up the bid with a face-to-face presentation. If the client has indicated that there will be a round of interviews, confirm your readiness to take part.

The client may also find it helpful to see a glossary of technical terms and acronyms or a 'quick reference' index listing, for example, topics discussed in the bid, issues, items and locations – placed not at the end of the bid but ahead of the text.

Introductory section of the bid

This section can usefully perform two functions:

- **Identifying the purpose and origin of the bid.** Quote the client's reference information and other relevant data. If the bid is in response to a contract notice, letter, fax or e-mail, indicate the date and signatory. If it derives from some other contact, explain what that was. Remember that the bid will not necessarily be evaluated by the person who sent the invitation or whose signature appears formally on a letter. Include this identification material in the text even if it appears also in the letter of transmittal.

- **Emphasizing the professional credentials, resources and experience of the firm, group or individual putting forward the bid.** Write two or three paragraphs about yourself or your organization, with the emphasis on benefits that you achieved for clients on comparable projects and attributes that qualify you for the work. This should be a bid-specific description, not an all-purpose one copied from a brochure. Perhaps include matrices and other graphics to portray the sectors in which you have particular competence, the structure of your organization and the technical resources available to you.

If the work calls for specialized resources, make an effective selling point here by drawing attention to the appropriateness of the facilities you possess or to which you have access – eg databases, archives, training centres, laboratories. Mention also any relevant processes, technologies, software or hardware in which you may have a proprietary interest. Refer to any specialist advisers and authorities whose skills you may be enlisting in the team, particularly if they include nationally or internationally recognized sources of expertise.

Figure 12.1 shows an example of the opening paragraphs of a bid. It portrays a possible approach to the introductory section, rather than serving as a model.

If you are associating with other contractors in a group or consortium, present information on each organization in turn. Explain their respective roles and responsibilities in the contract and what each partner contributes to the team and its work. Tell the client who the contracting party will be if the group is awarded the contract. Put forward a convincing image of an integrated group, identifying the strengths that justify its formation and stressing its unity and balance.

It may be useful to include a **matrix of team or contractor experience** (Figure 12.2). This might highlight recent work for the client or related authorities, together with specialized work in relevant sectors of expertise. If there are individuals in the team who are known to the client from previous successful work, bring this point out. To be really effective, the matrix needs to look brimful of relevance, with every one of its spaces filled.

Some of the information in this introductory section will be developed in detail in subsequent parts of the bid. Here and now your aim is to present the essential points up front so as to fix key messages in the client's mind, messages that will resonate through the bid as its distinctive benefits are set out.

Technical approach and methodology

This area of information, which covers your insight into the client's objectives, the methodology to be applied and the tasks and activities needed to achieve the required outcomes of the contract, can form the next section of the bid and is discussed in Chapter 13.

Resources and management

Describe in this section the personnel resources to be applied to the work, the composition of the contract team, the responsibilities and tasks assigned to each team member, the timing of professional inputs and your proposed arrangements for managing the work (Chapter 14).

1 The ABC tender

This tender to provide consultancy services for First Commercial Bank (FCB) is submitted by ABC International Ltd, in response to the letter of invitation (ref. KR/13560/HR/E) dated ...... from ......

The tender complies with both the specification and the Instructions to Tenderers attached to the letter of invitation. ABC International Ltd confirms its acceptance without qualification of the Conditions of Contract enclosed with the Instructions to Tenderers, and its receipt of a copy of the Contract Quality Conditions.

1.1 Structure of the tender document

This introduction is followed by an account of ABC's approach to the concept of partnership, including a statement of its service commitment and an outline of the ways in which ABC will help FCB to maximise the benefits and added value to be gained from a partnership relationship (**Section 2**).

Section 3 sets out ABC's proposals for developing a programme of continuous improvement, quality management and performance measurement during the course of the contract period. **Section 4** presents a company profile, while ABC's experience in similar projects, including comparable partnership relationships with corporate organisations in the financial community, is described in **Section 5**. Proposed resourcing levels and organisational arrangements for management of the partnership are the subject of **Section 6**. **Section 7** provides CVs of the team members nominated for positions within the FCB support group.

1.2 ABC credentials for this project

- As an integrated consultancy specialising in information services for the banking sector, ABC International Ltd is able to meet the skill requirements of the tender in full from its own in-house professional resources, which include experts highly qualified by their background and experience to fulfil the roles specified by FCB.
- Since its launch in 1992, ABC has become one of the most successful and fastest growing consultancies in the EC financial information sector. ABC's success is based entirely on its ability to meet the requirements of its customers dependably and cost-effectively. These are marketing strengths which it can contribute to a partnership with FCB so as to help FCB enhance its commercial performance and achieve its corporate objectives.
- ABC has proven experience of partnership relationships both through its previous and current work for FCB and other clients in the European financial community and through its continuing work with leading banks and funding institutions such as the European Bank for Technological Development, Second Chemical Bank, Mercantile Investment Corporation and the European Carnegie Fund.
- This experience means that ABC can bring to the proposed partnership both an extensive, up-to-date knowledge of trading environments and an international perspective of innovative and affordable information management solutions, developed through its work with other financial institutions, which can in turn help FCB to reduce the costs of information systems development.
- ABC's existing record of work in information consultancy for FCB means that partnership will ensure continuity of service and the maintenance of proven working relationships, freeing FCB from the costs of delays or learning curves.

Figure 12.1 _Example of a bid introduction_

Team member	Years of professional experience	Key competencies	Previous work with client
John Andrew	15	Design and maintenance of track structures Rail development engineering	Development of track geometry and condition standards
George Brown	12	Track maintenance and renewal Coordination of maintenance operations	Maintenance Management Service Contract
James Davis	10	Dynamic track inspection Application of track recording technology	Senior Infrastructure Engineer
Henry Smith	15	Track design, construction and maintenance	Maintenance Management Service Contract
Alan White	10	Track strengthening and renewal Contract management and supervision	Track Renewal Contract, Southern Area

Figure 12.2 *Detail of a matrix of team experience*

Outputs and deliverables

Information about the results of the work and the items or services that the contractor will provide to the client is discussed in Chapter 15.

Team and contract experience

This information includes CVs of team members (Chapter 17) and summaries of experience on similar contracts (Chapter 18).

Price information

Estimates of costs (Chapter 20) will be set out in this section unless the client requires a separate financial bid.

Appendices

These help to meet requirements for detailed information while keeping the main body of the bid trim. Possible material for appendices includes formal documentation such as letters of commitment; extended CVs, particularly when the work involves a large team; detailed contract experience; material published by the contractors; statistics; data processing facilities and software. The bid specification may be reproduced as an appendix if this is practicable.

THINKING DIFFERENT

Where the bid structure is not specified by the client, you may see this as an opportunity to organize the material in a framework that makes a distinctive point about your approach to the contract. Whatever structure you devise, it must not detract from the functionality of the document or from the client's perception of you as the contractor best suited to undertake the assignment.

An unconventional and imaginative structure can work to your advantage, provided that:

- it is a structure that the client will not regard as incompatible with an effective professional response;

- the content of the bid has genuine technical strength: in other words, the structure must not look like an attempt to hide a lack of substance;

- it does not suggest elements of risk to the client;

- the information that the client needs for the purpose of evaluation remains directly accessible. Never lose sight of this point. The easier you make it for clients to access key information, the more you are likely to gain from the bid.

If you choose a structure of your own, include a page explaining how the bid is organized, ie what each part does and how its material links into the following section. Signposting in this way is helpful to the people using the bid, provides an opportunity to demonstrate its logic and thrust and can act as an essential route map through the document.

BID LETTERS

There are many situations that call for nothing more formal or elaborate than a short letter in response to the client's approach. Generally in these circumstances the structure and content of the letter will be left to your judgement.

Start the letter by showing that you understand the client's objectives – perhaps as a result of a meeting to assess the scope of the advice that the client really needs: you may have to help the client identify problems and issues, which may not always correspond with his or her initial view of a situation. Then explain your proposed approach, programme of work and timetable, with an estimate of the expected costs. Conclude with an offer to provide any further information the client may request. Background information about your credentials and experience can be included in the body of the letter, following the opening statement or in an appendix.

Like all business correspondence, bid letters must be clear, precise and to the point. The aim is to avoid a situation in which there can be any misunderstanding or difference of view about either what the client wants you to achieve or what you would expect to do for the client.

To illustrate one possible approach, Figure 12.4 (at the end of this chapter) reproduces in full the text of a successful bid letter, amended only to protect the identity of the client and the bidder. Though the work was for a public sector authority, its fee value exempted it from formal tendering requirements. In this instance, the representative of the client knew the work of the bidder and had requested a proposal. For this reason, material about professional experience did not appear in the body of the letter but was included as an appendix in case the letter had to be copied to other officials. No one else was competing for the assignment: even so, the letter needed to give a precise and clearly structured statement of the services offered and the estimated costs of the work. Having a potential client who is disposed to give you work is helpful, but this does not absolve you from the need to spell out a systematic framework for performing the work, with a realistic timetable and acceptable costs. You can still lose the job through a complacent or sloppy bid!

The qualities that give impact and credibility to a more formal bid apply equally to a letter. The structural principles of logical order and coherent organization, the importance of knowing your strengths and keeping them visible to the client, the need to build client perception of an alert, innovative and dependable source of professional advice – these considerations are central to every bid, whatever its length. And, of course, the content of the letter has to be backed up by the quality of its presentation.

TWO ITEMS THAT ADD VALUE TO THE BID – A SUMMARY AND A RESPONSE MATRIX

Summarizing the bid

The purpose of the **summary** is to give decision-makers an immediate message that communicates the benefits offered by your bid. Though it is probably one of the parts of the bid that are written last, when the document can be viewed as a whole, it ought to be one of the first items to appear in the bid, ahead of the main technical sections, and it must be a convincing statement in itself, with its own logical flow and structure. It should not simply present a section-by-section précis of the full text.

- **Brevity.** The summary has to be brief because decision-makers – the people who will be approving or endorsing the choice of the number one bid – have (or like to think they have) intense pressures on their time. If you want their attention, you have to offer a statement they can read quickly. It may be the only part of the bid that some of them may read, so its effect can be crucial. Make the summary no longer than is necessary to say what is essential and short enough to carry impact. Four pages in total should be sufficient for any bid, however detailed or intricate, but a one-page summary is best.

- **Benefits.** Creating a 'summary of benefits' rather than a 'summary of the bid' is a useful approach some firms adopt. Beside directing attention to the outputs the client will achieve, it demonstrates that you are able to view the contract from the client's standpoint and identify with their priorities.

  For example, your client research may have revealed a particular concern about the way changes in project requirements can affect timetables and budgets: if you can offer monitoring and control procedures that minimize the risk of overruns and delays, you will want to emphasize this benefit. Take account of the information you have about the bid evaluation procedure. If you know that a high proportion of marks will be awarded on the quality of the team, make their strengths and the benefits of their experience salient points in the summary.

■ **Logic.** The summary can also be phrased to emphasize the closeness of fit between your offer and the client's requirements, stating the reasoning behind the bid and reflecting the progression of logic leading from an understanding of client needs to the structuring of the team and delivery of the work programme.

■ **Essentials.** Start to write the summary by listing the essential points that come out of each section of the bid, so that you have a set of points corresponding to the bid structure. Then decide which need to stay and which can go. Include only strong supporting points: there is no place in a summary for details or discussions of issues. Leave those for the main text of the proposal.

Each point has to earn its keep by adding weight to the impact. Every statement has to be consistent with the key message, building an image of clear purpose and direction.

■ **Emphasis.** Give the summary an emphatic style of presentation. Set it out in a way that makes it easy to read. The most effective summaries are often sets of bullet points, written in a crisp and punchy style. Headings and graphics may be appropriate within the summary: think about including a matrix of benefits, for example, bringing together specialist expertise, local experience, outputs and deliverables and other key features.

■ **Make the summary unmissable.** Locate it in front of everything else except the title page and letter of transmittal. Print it on a different coloured paper from the rest of the document.

■ **Basis for presentation.** The summary offers a framework on which to base a presentation to the client, if this is part of the bid procedure (Chapter 23). Use points from the summary to headline the content of the presentation.

Displaying your response

If you have prepared a bid development worksheet as advocated in Chapter 8, you will find it easy to use as the basis for a **response matrix**. This is a counterpart of the compliance matrix widely used in procurement for goods and supplies. The matrix itemizes the requirements defined in the bid specification, as well as other matters raised by the client, and indicates where these points are addressed in the bid (Figure 12.3). Its inclusion at the front of the bid offers benefits for both the client and yourself:

- It guides the client directly to specific items of information, provides a checklist against which the content of the bid can be assessed and makes the task of evaluation easier.

- The inventory of client requirements (the left-hand column in Figure 12.3) gives you a list of the items that have to be addressed in the bid.

- It enables you to demonstrate your coverage of the client's requirements in full.

- It looks businesslike and communicates a sense of practicality and helpfulness.

- It can put your bid in a better light than competing offers in which the client has to hunt down information.

CREATING THE TEXT

- Past bids, perhaps for the same client, can provide a base from which to start building ideas. It is tempting to use as a model a bid that brought success on a previous occasion and even to recycle bids that were unsuccessful but include renewable technical material. Try to understand why a particular approach may have worked in your favour and how it might be developed in the future. Retrieve useful material and adapt bids to a new lease of life. Be careful though not to become dependent on a stock formula. Do not reproduce the same headings and the same paragraphs in every bid without questioning whether they are the best way to address the particular needs of each contract. Even though a new client may not

Item in bid specification	Clause reference	Paragraph(s) in bid	Page(s) in bid
Scope of services	1.2–1.5	1.2–1.6 Section 2	1–2 3–6
Approach guidelines	1.6–1.8	1.7–1.10 Section 2	2 3–6
Key components	1.9	2.3–2.25	7–11
Extension of Youth Training Schemes	1.9(a)	2.5–2.9	7
Vocational qualification programmes	1.9(b)	2.10–2.13	8
Development of multilingual business advice	1.9(c)	2.14–2.17	9
Mentoring and support for new businesses	1.9(d)	2.18–2.20	10
Improving local access to new job opportunities	1.9(e)	2.21–2.25	11
Specialist team	1.10	Section 3	2, 12–20
Experienced team leader	1.11	3.3–3.4	12–13
CVs	3.4	Annex A	40–52
Letters of commitment	3.5	Annex A	40–52
Detailed work plan and programme	1.12–1.13	Section 4	21–26
Schedule of deliverables	1.14	4.4 Table 4.1	22 23
Proposals for monitoring and performance measurement	1.15–1.16	4.5–4.8	24–25

Figure 12.3 *Detail of a bid response matrix*

have seen your style before, ideas that are repeated too often become stale and your thinking grows stale with them. **Treat previous bids as a platform from which to strengthen and sharpen your approach with an innovative response to each new work opportunity.**

- A useful function of the bid development worksheet (Chapter 8) is that it prompts you at the start to prepare a draft structure and assign responsibilities for input to the text. Your ideas about the structure may change as the bid begins to take shape; **the important point is to have from the outset at least a provisional framework on which to organize the material, altering and adapting the structure as you gain new information and insights.**

- **Map out the content of each section and identify key points.** Don't worry at first about getting things in the right order or the right words. The draft is meant to help you decide the items that you need to include in each section. Check through the notes for overlaps and inconsistencies. Make sure you are not repeating points unnecessarily from one section to another.

- Tight deadlines and professional commitments mean that bids generally have to be written under intense pressure; but it is not always easy to sustain a focused effort. **Pace the work so as to make the best use of the times of day when your mind is at its freshest.** Set a target completion date for each section of the bid, taking account of word processing, checking and editing stages. Work out how long you might spend on the more straightforward parts and then try to cut down this amount to allow more time for sections requiring detailed analysis. Make sure the easiest work is done quickly. Contract experience, corporate information and CVs can often be prepared in draft ahead of the rest of the document.

- Do not try to determine in advance the number of pages of typescript to be filled by each section, unless the bid specification, as noted earlier, sets limits on the size of the bid or on the length of a particular section. **It is better to base targets on the timetable for completion than on amounts of paper.** The time to assess relative brevity and prolixity is when the bid is in a more advanced state and you are gauging the internal balance of the text: you can then see which sections appear overlong and which may need expanding.

- Keep in mind how the material you or your colleagues are writing in one part of the bid may affect the content of other sections.

- **Cross-referencing within the bid** will help tie together the logic of the text, projecting an image of consistency and cohesion. But don't raise an issue in one part of the bid and then redirect the client to some other part to learn your response. Having to search backward and forward for information irritates clients.

- In setting out the text, it is advisable to **state a conclusion first and then present the substantiating reasons** – ie:

x (the conclusion) because $y1 \ y2 \ y3. . .$ (the data),

rather than

$y1 \ y2 \ y3. . .$ therefore x.

This is the reverse of conventional practice in research papers, but it works better in bids and technical reports and makes practical sense.

- The word '**indicative**' tends to make clients uneasy. In particular they dislike it when consultants describe cost figures as 'indicative'. Clients read this as implying a host of extras that are likely to upset their budget. Similarly, an 'indicative starting date' suggests the probability of delay. Avoid the word. Instead, state clearly those points about which you are confident, and explain the assumptions you are making about the rest.

- Do your best to get the draft right first time; but always be ready to revise it if there are ways of improving and simplifying it. **Read your text more than once;** if possible, **get a colleague to look it through**, to see if any point doesn't make sense, sounds unconvincing, contradicts something you've written somewhere else or needs more detail or explanation.

- If you are bidding for work from an overseas client whose first language is not English, word the text carefully to avoid intricate sentence constructions, unusual turns of phrase and colloquial expressions that the client might easily misunderstand. If the bid is to be translated, bear in mind that some languages do not possess the wealth of nuances and shades of meaning found in English, while others may apply a variety of expressions to replace one word in English. Don't make the translator's job unnecessarily hard.

Guidelines on technical writing

Sections

- Be clear about the purpose of each section of text – what is its function in the document?

- Put down a statement of this purpose and use it at the start of the section.

- Use sub-headings to identify and manage areas of information.

Paragraphs

- Keep paragraphs short – no longer than about 10 lines.

- Do not crowd too many ideas into one paragraph.

- Make each paragraph a distinct and consistent step in the sequence of information.

- Link paragraphs to each other, to bring out the logic of the text.

- Would bullet points work better than a paragraph? Often, the answer is yes.

Sentences

- Know how each sentence is going to end before you write it down or key it in.

- Keep sentences short – a sentence should be either one statement making a single precise point, or a group of related statements linked as clauses.

- Long sentences work only if their structure is clear. You will have fewer problems if you limit sentences to 20–25 words. Don't let sentences ramble on or become convoluted.

- Every sentence has a part to play in reinforcing the logic of the text. Write as precisely as you can. Don't leave the client wondering what you mean or writing 'so what?' in the margin.

- If you don't state clearly what you mean, clients will assume you don't know what you want to say. If what you write is obscure, they will suspect you have not thought it out clearly.

If they have to read a sentence two or three times to work out what you mean, you have failed to communicate.

Choosing and using words

- There is never just one way of saying something. Think how you could make the point more straightforwardly. Look away from the words; focus on the sense of what you want to say. The more you clarify and simplify, the more value you add to the bid.

- Grammar, spelling and sentence structure must all be correct in a document intended to express professional quality.

- Vary the sentence structure. Don't write in a monotonous drone.

- Don't write hesitantly or vaguely: clients do not want contractors who are insecure. Write positively, using 'will' rather than 'would' – avoid using the conditional to excess.

- Make important points strongly and clearly. Emphasize not by saying 'It should be emphasized that. . .' but by using the right emphatic phrasing.

- Your bid is unlikely to get a good reception if it contains remarks and wording that the client will view as insensitive.

- Make sure that what is shown in a table and what is said in the text are fully consistent, and that each table and graph has a text reference. Never leave tables, graphs or diagrams unnumbered.

EDITING THE BID

Bids often combine material from a variety of sources, but it is important to avoid the impression of a mass of bits and pieces stitched together clumsily with abrupt changes of style. The image you need to create is quite the opposite: an integrated, seamless texture like a single voice.

Before people start to write their contributions, give them guidance on the style they should follow. If necessary, provide a template or example of what you want. This procedure can save you a lot of work rewriting material.

The person editing the bid must make sure he or she really comprehends what is being said, particularly when the text concerns a highly specialized field of expertise. What is the central point being argued? Do you understand it fully? Can you express it in simpler terms to help the client grasp its meaning? If you don't understand the point, go back to the specialist and ask for an explanation. Be diplomatic about this: people can be territorially defensive about the way they write.

Bid editing is often a matter of translation – conveying complex technical issues in language that non-technical people can understand. But editors must be careful not to deprive the text of technical precision, distort its meaning or insert their own ideas.

There are five Cs that are essentials in bid editing: correctness, consistency, conciseness, continuity and coordination:

- **Correctness** means more than eliminating faults in grammar, sentence construction, spelling and punctuation. It covers the use of every type of data and numbers, the way the client and the contract are referred to, the referencing of sections and paragraphs and all other categories of information. Getting the details right does count: slipshod phrasing erodes both the confidence and the tolerance of the client.

- **Consistency** in style and phrasing will reinforce the client's perception of the quality of the bid and by extension your performance as a contractor. A bid that seems the work of one person suggests a team that will work together as one individual.

- **Conciseness** means giving information clearly and comprehensively but in a few words and without surplus detail. Some specialists have difficulty in controlling their enthusiasm for the minutiae of their work: they may not find it easy to recognize let alone eliminate surplus detail. From the client's perspective, surplus detail is information that:

    - does nothing to support or strengthen the point being argued;

    - appears to have no relevance to the client's information needs; and so

    - has no practical application in helping to achieve the client's objectives.

- **Continuity** is about making sure that points are set out in logical order, without gaps, breaks in sequence or sudden changes of subject, and that links and connections between the requirements of the contract and the content of the bid are brought out clearly.

- **Coordination** – an aspect of version control that is an essential part of the management of technical documentation, particularly if several people are involved in writing the text and perhaps working on a section of the bid at the same time. The version control approach advocated in Chapter 8 will enable sections to be edited in phase, so as to preclude the introduction of changes that produce inconsistencies or conflicts.

Once the text is drafted, read it through carefully to spot omissions, repetitions, contradictions, non sequiturs, rash assumptions and plain careless errors. One type of mistake that is easy to make is the inaccurate numbering of items in a list. You may say, 'there are five key factors', and probably there were at one stage of writing, but when counted on the printed page they add up to four or six. That suggests a hasty and superficial presentation – not a good advertisement.

When the editing is completed, ask the specialist who produced the initial draft to read the text through. Issues raised by specialists at this stage and questions about why certain points were reworded or omitted will often help to clarify important aspects of the text.

A plea for paragraph numbering

If contractors make it easy to identify and locate specific points of information, they show they understand the practical needs of clients and are demonstrating the kind of helpful and methodical approach that marks them as good people to work with. If they make clients count paragraphs and lines to track down information and even omit page numbers, they may look as if they are ignoring the needs of their customers ('If these contractors can't even organize the bid efficiently, how would they ever manage the project?').

The basic unit of text in a bid is the individual paragraph. Ideally, each paragraph should be labelled with a unique reference number: it is this that provides the means of immediate access to detailed information. The use of paragraph numbering has two further advantages: 1) it minimizes the possibility of information not being recognized through inadequate referencing; 2) it displays the logical structure and progression of the text.

For most bids a simple two-level numbering system identifying sections and paragraphs will be adequate. Where sections cover a range of topics, three levels may be useful, identifying sections, subsections and paragraphs respectively. If you number subsections, it is advisable to number their component paragraphs, even though some of the examples in the book do not follow this principle. Avoid having more than three levels in a numbering hierarchy: references such as 'paragraph 3.4.1.1' are just too unwieldy. Restructure the text into more manageable parts, or remove the item causing the problem (the sub-subsection number) from the referencing system. Before the text is printed out, check it through for numberless paragraphs and duplicated paragraph numbers among other items.

James Brown
Deputy General Manager
Western Health Authority
Deliverance Hospital
Maintown

02 December 2004

Dear Mr Brown

Public consultation on management strategy

When we met on 15 November, you asked me to indicate how I might be able to assist your Authority in undertaking a consultation exercise related to its management strategy. This letter outlines my ideas on the scope and programme of the work and sets out an estimate of the costs involved.

1   Purpose of the consultation
1.1   The purpose of the consultation will be to assess local attitudes to the management strategy outlined in the Policy Committee report of October 2004, with particular reference to local access to health care and the implications for facilities at Deliverance Hospital. The results of the consultation will enable the Authority to determine the degree of local support for the strategy.

1.2   The public consultation will have two main elements:
- a local exhibition of the strategy
- a self-completion questionnaire.

Figure 12.4 _Example of a bid letter_

2 Exhibition

2.1   My initial view is that the exhibition should take the form of about ten modular panels, each focusing on a key aspect of the strategy. The presentation will aim to offer a straightforward and non-technical statement of the issues and options underlying the strategy.

2.2   The text and graphic material will be developed in liaison with your Authority. You have indicated that the Authority will produce enlargements of the charts included in the strategy report, together with such additional display material as resources may permit. I understand that the Authority can also make available a modular display system to accommodate the exhibition panels.

2.3   I suggest that the exhibition should be advertised primarily through a leaflet postal-dropped to each household within an agreed catchment area. The leaflet will explain the purpose of the exhibition, indicate its location and times of opening, and ask people to come and give their views.

2.4   An illustrated pamphlet reproducing the exhibition material will be made available on site, at surgeries and clinics, libraries, Council offices and other locations in the town. This pamphlet will contain the self-completion questionnaire. Material about the strategy and exhibition will also feature on the Authority's website.

2.5   The work that I will undertake in connection with the exhibition will include the following tasks:

(i)   analysis of ongoing consultation, as scheduled in the Appendix to the Policy Committee report;
(ii)   subcontracting of exhibition designer and supervision of design;
(iii)   preparation of exhibition concept and production of exhibition text and graphic material in the form of display panels;
(iv)   production of postal drop leaflet and exhibition pamphlet;
(v)   transport of display panels to the exhibition location;
(vi)   organization, signing, setting up, staffing and taking down of exhibition.

3 Exhibition design

3.1   To assist with the graphic design of the exhibition, I propose to subcontract a specialist designer, Janet Smith, who has worked as a colleague on numerous health sector consultation exercises and exhibitions. The Appendix to this letter gives a summary of her experience.

4 Self-completion questionnaire

4.1   The questionnaire will be brief and easy to complete, so as to encourage a high response rate. The questions will focus on key aspects of the management strategy. There will be a minimum of open-ended questions: most questions will be pre-coded

Figure 12.4 *continued*

as 'yes/no/don't know' or involve attitudinal scores and rankings. Space will be provided at the end of the questionnaire for further comments.

4.2   Respondents will be asked to indicate their address or the postcode of the locality where they live.

4.3   Responses will be coded and checked before inputting and computer processing. On submission of the final report of the consultation, the completed questionnaires will be transferred to the Authority.

4.4   Work in connection with the questionnaire will include the following tasks:

(i)   questionnaire design, finalizing in liaison with the Authority, production and printing;
(ii)   distribution, administration and collection;
(iii)   data analysis, inputting, computer processing and reporting.

5   Programme of work

5.1   I understand that the Authority has made a provisional booking for the exhibition at the Maintown Library from 9 to 13 May 2005 inclusive.

5.2   The bar chart (Figure A) shows the proposed programme of work. My aim will be to submit a full report on the consultation by the end of June. On the assumption that a decision to go ahead is agreed early in February, the key dates are as follows:

mid-February to mid-March	Preparation of exhibition concept and text, in liaison with your Authority
21 March	Draft of exhibition/pamphlet text available
28 March–18 April	Production of exhibition panels, leaflet and pamphlet
8 April	Draft questionnaire available
22 April	Distribution of postal drop leaflet
25 April	Finalized questionnaire printed
9–13 May	Exhibition
24 May	Closing date for postal responses
17 June	Questionnaire analysis completed
1 July	Report of consultation submitted

6   Costs

6.1   There are several cost elements, particularly on the exhibition production side, that are difficult to define precisely before the start of design work. To arrive at a budget figure for the consultation exercise, I have tried to base the cost estimates on reasonable assumptions about the standard of presentation required, bearing in mind the need for economy and value for money.

Figure 12.4 *continued*

6.2   My estimate of costs is as follows:

Ian Johnson: professional time:

	days	
• preparation of text and material for exhibition	7.0	
• exhibition pamphlet, postal drop leaflet	2.0	
• supervision and management of designer's work	2.5	
• design, administration and analysis of questionnaire	15.0	
• organization of exhibition	2.0	
• attendance at exhibition	3.0	
• meetings with your Authority	3.0	
• travelling time	1.5	
• preparation of final Report	7.0	
	43.0	
43 days @ £500/day		£21,500

Janet Smith: professional time:

	days	
• design of exhibition display (assuming 10 panels)	9.0	
• exhibition pamphlet, postal drop leaflet	2.5	
• layout and artwork for questionnaire	2.0	
• meetings with your Authority	1.5	
15 days @ £450/day		£6,750

Production of exhibition display panels (assuming 10 panels, with text screen-printed)	£4,500
Production of exhibition pamphlet (assuming 4pp A4 and 2-colour printing) and self-completion questionnaire (print order 2,500)	£2,500
Production of postal drop leaflet (assuming print order of 3,000)	£1,000
Report printing costs (assuming submission of 5 copies)	£50
Transport and travel costs	£450
Total estimated costs (net of VAT)	£ 36,750

6.3   I trust these total estimated costs are acceptable as a budget indication and as an initial basis for discussion. I assume that the Authority would wish to agree a contract on the basis of a budget ceiling for undertaking the work set out in this letter.

6.4   In a proposal of this nature, there are bound to be matters which need detailed discussion and clarification. Please let me know if you wish me to provide more information on any point, or if you would like to have a further meeting at this stage.

Figure 12.4 *continued*

7 Appendix

7.1 I am appending to this letter a summary of my experience and that of the designer in the field of health sector consultation.

I hope that the terms of this submission will be acceptable, and I look forward to the possibility of assisting your Authority by undertaking this important consultation exercise.

Yours sincerely

Figure 12.4 *continued*

13

Explaining approach and methodology

SHAPING THE ARGUMENT

Fulfilling a contract in a manner that represents value to the client is seldom just a matter of activating systems and applying procedures. Having better systems and procedures than your competitors will never harm your chances of winning a contract, but in most cases it is people that make the difference – their insight into the client's business needs and concerns, the ideas that inform their approach and the energies they bring to the work. These factors give the client the return on its investment in the contract. Don't neglect this aspect of the bid. In writing about your approach and methodology, the task is to show that you understand the objectives and priorities of the contract, are able to respond to them with a businesslike plan of work and can get to the heart of the matter more directly and dependably than any of your competitors. You need to convince the client that your approach has been thought through accurately and in detail as the most sensible and efficient means of delivering the outputs required.

The bid specification may outline the methods and procedures that successful tenderers will be expected to apply. Generally, these will be indicated only in broad terms, not so much to point contractors in the right direction as to give them a measure of the professional effort that the work will need. Unless you have a good and convincing reason for proposing an alternative, the methodology outlined in the specification should be adhered to.

Take care not to dissect the details of your work methods and processes to a level that presents the client with a template for the job. That would be rash in any competitive situation; and in some circumstances you may be competing not just with other consultants, whom the client might choose in preference to you and then ask to implement your ideas, but with the client organization itself, which may see in your proposal a free blueprint that its in-house resources can exploit.

COMMENTING ON THE BID SPECIFICATION

Clients may invite comments on the bid specification. Why? They are not fishing for compliments or platitudes, though that is often the only response they get. The real purpose is to give bidders an opportunity to do several things:

- make practical observations that tell the client they have done the job before and know the logistic essentials for achieving the contract successfully;

- put forward ideas that reflect their experience and perhaps point to approaches that can help meet the client's objectives more efficiently;

- indicate any points in the scope of work, schedule of deliverables or other items that have had a particularly formative influence on their response;

- declare any assumptions that have had to be made about points not specified by the client.

In some instances the client may appear to have misunderstood the technical demands of the contract, the time and other resources needed to undertake the work successfully or the results that the contract can achieve. The bid specification may contain inconsistencies; the data offered to bidders may appear dubious; there may be a bias toward a particular approach that restricts the scope for innovation, or a misplaced emphasis on methods and technologies that fails to take account of new developments in your field. How should you deal with this type of situation?

The thing not to do is to comment in a critical or patronizing way: you have nothing to gain by implying that the bid specification is unclear or inadequate. It is better to express your reservations as matters that you would like to have the opportunity to discuss further at the stage of negotiating and agreeing a contract. Take a diplomatic and tactful approach. And don't feel you are obliged to comment. It is worth doing so only if you have points to communicate that can help reinforce your bid.

You have to rely on your professional judgement since some clients may not appreciate having their ideas questioned in any form. Others may be worried about the risk of losing ownership of the project; so you must avoid giving the impression that it is you rather than the client who knows what is best for them. If you have the option to put forward a variant solution and decide to do so, it has to be one that you believe offers the best solution for the client's needs – which does not necessarily mean the one that will make life easiest either for the client or for yourself.

Unless the client requires comments to form a distinct section of the bid, there is no need to concentrate them under a separate heading. If there is a case for considering a different way of going about a task or activity, the best place to argue this case is in the main body of the bid.

WRITING ABOUT METHODOLOGY

No contract emerges from the void. It will always be set in a broader context such as a business strategy, a research programme, a development framework, an economic or environmental policy or a response to a difficulty or emergency. This context gives rise to the client's perception of needs and objectives. Meeting these objectives is the purpose of the contract, and this will in turn raise issues and set guidelines for your technical approach. We have here the basis of a simple but useful structure, outlined in Figure 13.1.

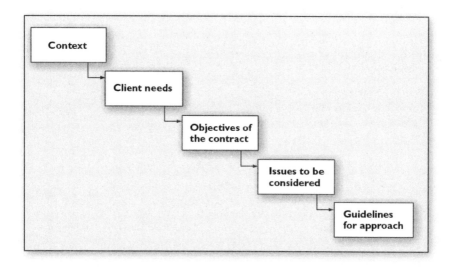

Figure 13.1 _Example of a structural basis for a technical approach section_

None of this material should simply repeat the wording of the bid specification, quote back to clients points made in their own documents or offer information about their organization or business that they obviously know already. When clients open your bid, it is your thoughts, your insights they want to find, not theirs! As an example of an effective treatment, Figure 13.2 reproduces the start of the technical approach section of a successful bid.

If current or recent contracts for the client have given you an in-depth knowledge of its working environment and business objectives, cite this as a factor that can ensure the budget is applied as productively as possible, without incurring the costs of learning curves or taking the work up blind alleys. If, on the other hand, you are unfamiliar with the detail of the client's business operations, you will need to set out your approach convincingly enough to reassure the client that you can rapidly get up to speed in understanding the context of your work.

What you write about methodology tells clients whether you have thought sufficiently about:

- the most direct, practical and cost-effective route to meeting their requirements;

- whether your plan of work or service delivery is consistent with their deadlines and robust in terms of timescale and cost;

2 Approach to the study

Our technical approach derives its thrust from four related elements:

- the structure of the project;
- the economic and social priorities that give the project its justification;
- the planning horizon of the project;
- the opportunity that the project offers to examine investment policies critical to tourism planning.

2.1 Structure of the project

We have treated the two phases of the study as separate streams of work:

- Phase I focuses on the design of an overall plan for the tourism sector;
- Phase II is concerned with the basic feasibility of individual projects, and is intended to provide the technical collateral on which the Department can gain funding for necessary improvements in social and physical infrastructure and for initiatives in tourism expansion.

The two phases complement each other and have a mutually supportive part to play in optimizing the benefits of growth. The study has to respond with an approach that is fully alert to the objectives of each phase and that can secure a sound and consistent basis for the attraction of investment. The intended result is a plan of action robust enough to yield practical benefits in the short term and to adapt successfully to the evolving tourism market over the long term.

The impact of the plan will depend as much on the imagination and vision of the agencies that seek to implement it as on the degree of skill and perception which the consultants bring to its formulation. For this reason we attach particular importance to the institutional aspects of the study and to the opportunity for collaboration with the counterpart personnel of the Department and other agencies that have a contributory role in the study.

We have interpreted the institutional analyses as directly related to (i) the requirements of project preparation and implementation, and (ii) the objective of achieving further improvement and diversification in tourism products within the region and a more emphatic participation of local skills in the senior management of one of the nation's major economic sectors. Institutional strength is especially needed in a situation of dynamic growth, where the aim must be to retain command of the development field and ensure the effective coordination of public and private sector initiatives.

2.2 Economic and social priorities

It is the massive contribution of tourism to the regional economy and its unparalleled role as a stimulus to development that make the analysis of inter-sectoral linkages so important within the study. The policy of steering tourism growth to island locations has an obvious part to play in the Department's efforts to improve the balance of development and the distribution of employment opportunities within the region as a whole, reducing the drift of working-age population to the urban centres and relieving the pressures on essential urban services. The planned expansion of tourism offers a greater prospect of integrating island communities within the regional economy and ensuring that they can participate equitably in the benefits of growth.

Figure 13.2 *Example of opening paragraphs of a technical approach section*

- the professional effort that you need to put into the assignment.

You have to ensure that:

- the methodology is technically sound and realistic in terms of inputs of time and other resources;

- the work plan includes all the tasks needed to achieve the intended results;

- it is structured into clearly defined and manageable components;

- the completion of each part of the work is marked by specified outputs and deliverables;

- the sequence of tasks is logical and consistent;

- the level and intensity of your inputs match the expectations of the client as well as the technical demands of the contract.

The professional effort you put into a contract has to be sufficient to get the work done properly in the available time, but it must also allow you to keep your price for the work competitive and within the limits of the client's budget. In some instances the bid specification may declare the funds available for the work and the client may ask bidders to show what they can provide for that amount. In most cases this information will not be explicit: one of the key tasks of client research will then be to try to identify the budget and develop a work programme that is achievable within its constraints.

In evaluating your bid, the client is looking for a realistic plan of work, not one that is over-ambitious. You certainly do not want to promise either a schedule of professional inputs you cannot deliver or a timetable of outputs you cannot sustain. Many of the key factors in a contract become much clearer once the work has started: at the bid stage it simply is not possible to foresee all the relationships between activities or the extent to which additional work may be necessary. So while it is right to avoid being vague or imprecise, it is important not to over-specify the work programme or to imply that the bar chart is definitive.

Describing the work plan

The first points to be explained are the structure of the plan, the main steps in the methodology and the objectives and outputs of each step. Start with the broad picture, the work plan at the macro level, before writing about activities in detail (Figure 13.3).

Structure denotes organization. All technical procedures have a structure even if it consists simply of a beginning, a middle and an end. The work with which the contract starts might at the simplest level of analysis be termed Stage 1, the activities that follow on from that Stage 2 and the work that concludes the contract Stage 3. These stages might themselves be organizations of smaller components – Stage 1A, Stage 1B and so forth – formed in turn by aggregates of tasks or activities, each with its own resource needs. The view of the project resulting from this analysis is called in project management terminology a work breakdown structure. The more complex the assignment, the more important it is to convey the underlying structural logic governing the way your work plan is organized.

Macro level – showing the broad picture

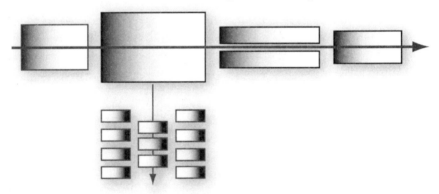

Micro level – detailing individual tasks

Figure 13.3 *Principle of a work plan analysis*

The division into stages, related to key outputs, may be suggested in the bid specification; it may be linked to 'yes/no' decision milestones for the client or to targets and breakpoints in the work; it may be derived from your past experience of similar jobs, or just from common sense; or it may require an iterative process of analysis to decide the best form of structuring the work.

Plan this part of your response by sketching out the components of the job in a **flow diagram**, starting with the activities that get the work moving and showing how they lead on to other activities in a sequence directed toward the final deliverable. If there is any degree of complexity about the contract, the diagram will need to show dependencies or links between tasks, and relationships between sets of parallel or converging activities or between clusters of tasks. The sketch will then be described more accurately as a logic network or PERT (project evaluation and review technique) chart, giving an overview of the challenges of the contract, illustrating the connections between tasks and showing how they affect the critical path through the contract.

You do not have to get the sequence or the relationships right immediately. The process will often require a series of drafts, each of which is improved and fine-tuned to get closer to the desired result. The initial flow diagram is very much a working draft to help you sort out the logic of your method and to decide:

- the identity and interlinking of component activities and the order in which they need to be undertaken;

- the most sensible division of the job into its main structural blocks – in relation to the client's decision points, your ability to manage the flow of work and the results each stage or block of work will produce;

- the level of detail to which the work plan needs to be analysed in the bid.

Including a final version of the diagram in the bid will help the client understand the route you propose to take in your methodology, as well as providing a reference map for your detailed analyses of individual tasks. A thumbnail sketch in the page margin, on the lines of Figure 19.1, can be a useful means of reminding the client where they are in the process.

If the technical method is particularly intricate – for example, in bids for contracts where work in several fields of expertise is taken forward in parallel through successive stages of design and implementation – you will need to produce a separate flow diagram for each stage or component, or even for each professional resource that you propose to use in the contract.

One point that generally will not be defined is the time within which client managers can be expected to review the drafts of reports and other deliverables and return their comments to you. The scheduling of activities in the work plan will need to include an allowance for review periods, particularly at key milestones. Make clear your assumptions on this point and the degree of flexibility built into the work plan. You do not want to find yourself in a situation where time constraints require you to start work on new activities that are contingent in terms of their detail on the client's response to the previous phase, though it may be practicable to bridge the review period with other tasks.

Itemizing activities

After explaining the broad structure of the work plan, the text can move on to an itemized and sequential account of its component tasks and activities. Clients may sometimes indicate that tasks do not have to be set out in detail, but they will always need sufficient information to allow them to assess the technical content of the bid against their evaluation criteria.

Tasks and activities should be discussed in order of their proposed start dates, either as a single list or by stream of activity. Give each activity a reference number related to the structural division of the work (eg Activity 1a or Task 1A.3) and a title (eg Task 1A: Economic evaluation).

For each activity the points to communicate include:

- the objectives of the task, expressed in terms of its contribution to the outputs of the contract;

- its technical content, identifying components or sub-tasks, outlining the proposed procedure, indicating any methodological options to be considered and explaining your choice of option;

- data requirements;

- issues to be taken into account, items to be analysed, trends and relationships to be examined, criteria to be applied and so forth;

- estimated start and completion dates – which must be consistent with the timings indicated on charts and diagrams;

■ resource commitment, indicating the personnel who would undertake the activity and the time they would spend in terms of staff-months, days or hours, together with other inputs;

■ consultation and liaison with the client and other bodies;

■ inputs from other activities that are part of the contract;

■ the intended outputs and deliverables of the activity (Chapter 15).

While recognizing that task descriptions can only be given in outline at this stage, take care not to portray activities in generalized terms. Explain how you propose to go about the activity, what procedures you intend to follow, what form the analysis will take, why you are going about it in that way, and how your approach will secure the desired results. Be as specific as is practicable; but don't fall into the trap of appearing to start work on the contract or use the bid to put forward solutions based on premature assumptions about the information to hand or the conditions in which the work will have to be done.

The bid may have to be read not just by managers familiar with its technical background. Your account of the methodology needs to have substance, but it should not be impenetrable to non-experts. In some instances there may be a case for including a simplified précis.

If there are alternative ways of going about the work, say what they are, outline the factors influencing your choice of option and justify your decision. There may be advantages in spelling out the implications of each option in terms of resources and outcomes, since this shows you have thought through the practical details of the work. If you are reluctant to commit yourself at the bid stage, explain the reason why. Remember that an inception report provides the opportunity to define tasks and activities in more confident detail (Chapter 15).

The itemized account of activities should be accompanied by a bar chart setting out a **time analysis of the work plan**, indicating the estimated start and completion dates of activities and their correlation with project milestones and decision points, including the schedule of deliverables.

'What if' questions

Project management software will allow you to test the effects of changes in schedules, adjustments in sequences and the addition and subtraction of resources, as well as providing information on resource loading and enabling you to maintain resources in consistent use throughout the work programme. The software will also generate a variety of reports and charts that can be used as graphic material in this part of the bid.

Scheduling time inputs

The section should include also a **Gantt chart of staff inputs**, indicating:

- the time scheduled to be spent on each activity by each individual or team;

- the total amount of time proposed for each individual or team in terms of staff-months, days or hours, depending on the length of the assignment;

- the sum total of the time chargeable to the assignment.

This information will be used to develop cost figures for the price information in the bid. Most project management applications will produce input data graphically as a matter of routine. Complex assignments may require separate bar charts for particular groups of staff or for individuals. As noted above, you need to allow sufficient time for the client's review and approval of deliverables and for consultation at decisive points in the work programme.

If the proposed staff have not been introduced earlier in the bid – for example, in the introductory section – the time input bar chart should be accompanied by: 1) a statement of the basis on which the team has been structured; 2) an outline of their roles in the contract (Figure 13.4); and 3) résumés for key personnel, with a forward reference to their full CVs. If the client has defined a starting date or mobilization date when team members are required to be ready for work, confirm that each individual or team will be available to provide the inputs marked on the bar chart and will not be committed to other work, assuming that the date indicated by the client holds good.

Aside from people and their time, the inputs you can bring to the contract may include items that have a high value for the client in terms of their contribution to performance and delivery, such as information systems, databases and database management systems, software, project management tools, quality auditing procedures and so forth. Don't just mention these inputs in passing or leave it to the client to

Public Utilities Engineer: Norman Johnson
The Public Utilities Engineer will have the following responsibilities:

- advising on the relationship of the proposed development to the existing utility networks and the means of achieving the most cost-effective integration of systems and services;
- assisting in evaluating strategic options for the development from the standpoint of infrastructure provision and utilities supply;
- estimating the total demand for public utilities (water supply; sewerage; sewage treatment; surface water drainage; waste collection and disposal; materials recycling and recovery; power; telecommunications; fire protection and other emergency services);
- preparing demand and capacity calculations as input to the phasing of the development programme;
- indicating techniques and engineering services needed to meet community requirements while safeguarding environmental quality;
- developing provisional cost estimates for utility networks and programmes, including support and maintenance needs.

Norman Johnson's qualifications for this role include 12 years' senior experience (1992–2004) as the firm's Senior Utilities Design Engineer, engaged on urban and industrial development contracts for the Department and on projects in comparable design environments within the region. In 2001 he was made an Honorary Member of the National Institute of Public Utility Engineers and Scientists. His fields of specialization are the cost-effective design of water supply, storage and irrigation systems and the application of computer techniques in demand/supply modelling. CV no.8 (Annex A) sets out his professional experience in detail.

Figure 13.4 _Team member: example of outline of technical responsibilities and résumé_

deduce their significance: explain the benefits they offer and include material that illustrates how they have been used in comparable work and how they can be applied to secure the success of this contract.

Advice on content and presentation

- Try to make the activity descriptions interesting to read. Communicate a sense of alertness and vitality in writing about your proposed methodology. Show that it offers innovative thinking while being founded on dependable techniques.

- Give each activity a strong practical slant, proving that you have thought the work programme through as a sequence of action.

- Check that your treatment of the work programme is balanced. Does each activity and field of expertise have the emphasis it deserves?

- Don't leave it to the client to piece together the logic of the work plan. Presenting this clearly can help you win the job. Clients will not feel happy with a bid if you make it hard for them to understand what methods you propose to use and why they offer the best approach.

- If you intend to entrust parts of the work programme to associates or subcontractors, make sure that the role you are expecting them to fulfil and the time inputs you are allocating to them match their resources and capabilities.

- Clients may ask for output such as data, plans or drawings to be supplied in specific formats. Confirm your compliance with this requirement.

14

Focusing on contract management

There are situations in which it may suit a client to say, 'You know what I want. I'll leave you to get on with it. Let me know when the job is done.' This may be a good enough approach where the work is straightforward, where the level of risk is low and where the client has reason to trust the contractors and is confident about the quality and commitment of their performance. By and large, though, clients will want to make sure that the work stays on track throughout the contract to achieve its intended results and that they obtain best value from the fees they are paying. In most sectors of procurement, client managers have standard procedures for maintaining an overview of the work, monitoring its progress and delivery and checking budget expenditure against outputs. In other areas, particularly service delivery contracts, it will normally be the contractors who are responsible for monitoring performance and the implementation of agreed management procedures.

Like other material in the bid, information about your contract management response needs to be project-specific, reflecting an awareness of the particular demands of the assignment and the priorities of the client's business environment. **The challenge you have to meet is to convince the client that you are able to organize the work in a way that will deliver the most cost-effective, time-effective and quality-effective service.**

Some bids merely generalize about professional accountability, project management support or internal management structures. There is more to be gained by showing how your arrangements for managing the work will help to achieve particular results and benefits. Find out, if you don't already know, how the client likes to work and show how well you will fit in. Let the client see that awarding the contract to you will ensure an alert response to changes in requirements as the work takes shape.

Referring to the concept of contract management as a form of preventative maintenance, Chapter 11 outlines the controls that clients will recognize as evidence of a commitment to help protect the contract from the risk of failure. These controls and related procedures are key components of the management information that the client will expect to read in your bid.

This information may cover the following topics, as appropriate:

- team management and resources

    - team structure

    - team leader

    - team induction

    - head office involvement;

- management interface

    - contract responsibilities

    - change management

    - management communication

    - role of a steering group or technical committee

    - work location

    - project logistics and support;

■ quality control

    – progress measurement, performance monitoring and contract review

    – quality control procedures.

TEAM MANAGEMENT AND RESOURCES

Team structure

The bid specification may identify the range of skills and competencies that need to be represented in a contractor's team, its size and structure, the responsibilities of individual team members and the outputs required from them. The client may indicate how team resources should be allocated to the components of the contract, the inputs of time expected from individual members of the team and the particular tasks they are required to achieve; job profiles or formal job descriptions may be provided for key personnel. Where these points are not specified, use your past experience of comparable work and your background research to determine the resources needed for the contract and how they can best be structured to form a coherent and efficient team.

The team named in your bid must have the competencies to fulfil all the technical requirements of the contract, but there are also other considerations that influence the way it is structured. These can be brought out usefully by emphasizing, for example, your ability to provide the following benefits:

■ consistency and proportion in the team structure, applying a strong commitment of professional effort to the core activities of the contract and an effective response to highly specialized areas of work;

■ clear-cut lines of management and direction within the team and between team and client;

■ integration – a team that will work as a unit to the same service quality standards and that ideally has achieved success together on comparable assignments;

■ continuity – securing the necessary resources to meet peaks in work pressures throughout the contract.

Bidders may be required to explain how they propose to select individuals for key technical and management positions where these are not already confirmed. If the services for which they are tendering are such that staffing levels are likely to fluctuate in response to changes in business volume and demand, clients may ask for a resourcing plan spanning the lifetime of the contract.

Clients differ in their attitudes to the substitution of personnel named in the bid. Some public sector clients may refuse to accept any requests for substitutions once bids have been evaluated, unless they foresee a protracted delay before the work of the contract can start: the bid specification may indicate that in the event of substitution they reserve the right to turn to the next-ranked bidders. For other clients substitution is not normally a problem up to the stage of negotiation. Naming alternatives for a team position is not recommended (Chapter 17).

Team leader

Because the capability, personality and experience of the team leader can play so critical a part in shaping the performance of the work, bid evaluation systems normally attach considerable weight to the competencies and professional background of the person nominated for this role. The information presented in the team leader's CV and in the description of his or her responsibilities can have a forceful influence on the outcome of the bid. The role of the team leader may be defined in the bid in terms of several sectors of responsibility, which may include:

■ representing the contractor's interests in post-contract dealings and negotiations;

■ acting as a focus of accountability for the work of the contractor;

■ developing and confirming with the client a definitive work plan to achieve the intended outputs;

■ organizing and integrating contract resources and the inputs of individual members of the team;

- managing and coordinating the day-to-day work of the team;

- maintaining a process of liaison and contract review with the client;

- maintaining effective quality management and time and cost control;

- taking action to correct aspects of contract performance and delivery that may not match the client's expectations;

- coordinating the technical documentation of the contract and the production of technical and management deliverables (Chapter 15);

- communicating and maintaining liaison with third parties specified by the client;

- ensuring that the team's approach is at all times responsive to the views of the client.

Fulfilling these responsibilities calls for a blend of technical authority and management ability as well as good interpersonal and communication skills, adaptability and the capacity to cope with pressure. For this reason, clients like to see a reasonably experienced person occupying the role. The bid should indicate whether the team leader will have the full authority of his or her employers to control the conduct of the assignment – for example, to agree adjustments in work schedules – and to receive instructions directly from the client. If the team leader also has specialist inputs to contribute to the technical work of the contract, these should be itemized separately.

In complex and large-scale assignments, the team leader may require the full-time assistance of a deputy, who should be nominated as such in the bid. There may be justification for proposing a change of team leader between stages of a contract, eg when there is a significant switch of emphasis in the technical content of the work.

Team induction

Even if the bid specification does not require a team induction procedure, you may find it helpful to undertake to provide this, particularly in bids to large corporate clients. The purpose is to ensure that team members start their work with an understanding of the business issues associated with the contract and receive practical guidance about access to services and data within the client organization. Indicate that client managers would be invited to contribute to the induction procedure.

Head office involvement

Bids for large-scale contracts often include top-level management inputs by directors, partners and other executives in the form of a 'review board', 'policy coordination panel' or similarly titled unit. Your reasons for proposing their involvement should always be made clear in the bid – eg 'to secure agreement on matters related to compliance with the terms of contract'. Clients will generally need to be assured that principals will make a technical contribution to the contract, especially if their names and experience are used to help win it. But they are unlikely to be impressed by bland remarks about headquarters managers 'supporting the project' or 'backstopping'. Tell the client exactly what these managers will do and explain how their participation will add value to the contract.

Bidders sometimes make the mistake of describing multiple layers of responsibility in which the team leader is overseen by project coordinators who in turn are answerable to project directors. Encircling the team with a profusion of 'advisory panels' or 'specialist resource groups' is another fault along the same lines. This approach may be intended to convince clients that you care about quality and are safeguarding their interests; but the client may see it as confusing, defensive and, worst of all, damaging to the credibility of the team actually doing the work. Whatever role you give top-level management, it ought not to detract from the authority of the people leading the team.

MANAGEMENT INTERFACE

The central aim of contract management is to obtain the services as agreed in the contract and achieve value for money. This means optimizing the efficiency, effectiveness and economy of the service or relationship described by the contract, balancing costs against risks and actively managing the customer–provider relationship.

The foundations for contract management are laid in the stages before contract award, including the procurement process. The terms of the contract should set out an agreed level of service, pricing mechanisms, provider incentives, contract timetable, means to measure performance, communication routes, escalation procedures, change control procedures and all the other formal mechanisms that enable a contract to function. These formal contract aspects form the framework around which a good relationship can grow. If the contract was poorly constructed, it will be much more difficult to make the relationship a success.

Increasingly, public sector organizations are moving away from traditional formal methods of contract management (which tended to keep the provider at arm's length and could become adversarial) and towards building constructive relationships with suppliers. The management of such a contract, in which the specification may have been for a relationship rather than a particular service, requires a range of 'soft' skills in both the customer and the provider. A key concept is the relationship, not just the mechanics of the contract. Agreements, models and processes form a useful starting point for assessing whether the contract is underperforming, but communication, trust, flexibility and diplomacy are the key means through which it can be brought back into line.

(*Contract Management Guidelines*, Office of Government Commerce, draft version April 2002)

Contract responsibilities

If the bid specification includes a draft form of contract, this will indicate the respective responsibilities of client and contractor. Confirm your understanding on these matters, and identify in the bid aspects of the contract where there may appear to be uncertainties, gaps or overlaps. A clear statement of responsibilities is particularly critical in contracts that integrate client and contractor personnel within a joint team: the technical and managerial control of the work has to be proof against misunderstanding.

In addition to the professional and technical responsibilities of the contract, there may be a substantial burden of administration and document management, particularly on complex projects involving large teams. Check whether the bid specification makes it clear how the client expects this to be handled – by its own staff or by administrative personnel in the contractor's team?

Where a contract involves the participation of several client organizations or interested parties – for instance, a number of public sector authorities, different units within a business group or even other contractors working on related projects – or where it combines the efforts of separate professional teams, it can be helpful to include a diagram showing how you envisage the proposed structure of management relationships for the assignment. Management diagrams should be drawn in a form that makes relationships appear direct and uncomplicated, with a balanced structure.

Change management

Project requirements will inevitably change during the course of the work, not least because there are matters that neither the client nor the contractor is able to define in precise detail at the procurement stage. New ideas may come to light that benefit the performance of the contract, and other circumstances may suggest the need for departures from an initially agreed specification. These changes may make an impact on the budget and the completion date, requiring a flexible and pragmatic approach on the part of both client and contractor. Clients may recognize this point by asking bidders to submit proposals for change management – covering matters such as the costing, scheduling, resourcing and documenting of change, and processes for assessing the impacts of change and translating the results of the assessment into action to minimize risk to the contract.

Management communication

Contractors who choose to keep at a distance from their clients cannot expect a long working life. Maintaining a continuous, close and transparent process of dialogue is a principle that clients view as critical to the success of the client/contractor relationship. It means that potential roadblocks can be flagged up early: if problems emerge they can be nipped in the bud before they begin to threaten the performance of the contract; and if there are differences of approach between you and client managers, they can be resolved quickly in a spirit of cooperation. It will pay you to underline your commitment to a relationship based on mutual understanding, respect and trust.

The more complex the assignment, the more important it becomes to present a direct channel of accountability for its performance and to ensure that communication is consistent at every level in the management structure of the contract. If you are proposing to use subcontractors on a significant proportion of the work, emphasize that it is your practice to maintain consistent and efficient communication with them.

Unless the point is covered in the bid specification, indicate that you would expect the client to nominate a counterpart manager to your team leader who would be the point of contact for both formal coordination and informal liaison. You will need the assistance of this manager in making the necessary introductions, obtaining internal data and ensuring that you are received helpfully throughout the client organization.

If the assignment is in a country where English is not the first language, what will be the language in which technical meetings with client personnel are conducted? You will be at a disadvantage if difficulties arise and you are unable to communicate your viewpoint effectively. Indicate in the bid your understanding or assumptions on this point.

Role of a steering group or technical committee

In managing large-scale contracts, clients may choose to set up a supervisory steering group, responsible for monitoring the direction of the work at a strategic level and providing policy guidance, or a technical committee acting as a forum for the discussion of findings, issues and recommendations and possibly exercising a measure of technical and financial control over the contract. Meeting at intervals related to progress reports and the production of other deliverables, both these management bodies may include representatives of the contractor as well as client interests. Where this form of management coordination is not indicated in the bid specification, it may nonetheless be appropriate to suggest its adoption, since a steering group offers a useful means of managing changes in the project design and resolving conflicts of priorities within the work programme.

Project logistics and support

The bid specification will normally indicate when the contractor is required to start work or to have staff at the project location: this is normally expressed as within a certain number of days after signature of the contract or agreement. Confirm your ability to fulfil this requirement.

If the specification does not identify the services and facilities to be provided by the client, you should indicate the level of client support that you regard as necessary or would reasonably expect to be provided. In certain contexts, it may be useful to itemize the minimum facilities that you will need in order to start constructive work as early as possible.

The main categories of **client support** that may be covered in a contract are as follows:

- administrative, secretarial and other support staff;

- working space and office equipment;

- telecommunications equipment and facilities, including internet links and fax lines;

- data, plans, maps, reports and other documentation;

- liaison with third parties;

- computer facilities and access to databases, management information systems, data communications networks and in-house IT support;

- technical and scientific equipment;

- laboratory facilities;

- training premises, materials and equipment;

- word processing, copying, scanning and document production services for project material;

- the use of cars and other forms of local transport for contract purposes;

- (on contracts overseas) assistance with visas and permits.

Does the specification indicate whether the contractor is expected to work in the client's offices or in separate office accommodation? There are advantages to be gained from having dedicated and suitably equipped office space on the client's premises: access to client information, ideas and feedback is easier and working relationships with client personnel are strengthened. But there may also be drawbacks such as security formalities, difficulties in gaining entry outside normal working hours and problems in keeping papers, phone calls and discussions confidential. And you are certain to face problems if you use the client's office as a base for your own marketing activity.

QUALITY MANAGEMENT

Progress measurement, performance monitoring, schedule and cost control

Corporate clients, particularly in the public sector, will expect you to set work targets, measure progress and help them monitor performance and the control of work schedules and costs throughout the contract. You may be required to deliver services against performance indicators and outcome measures defined in the bid specification. Explain the procedures you will adopt to meet these requirements, the performance measures and quality criteria that will be applied, the process you will follow to secure continuous improvement in delivery and value for money, your policy on technical audit and so forth.

Do not talk just in generalities about 'commitment to the highest professional standards', 'completion within time and budget' or 'maintaining a quality management system'. Clients want more solid material on which to judge the practicality of your intentions, particularly if they have in mind a joint approach to the management of performance and delivery. Write about this topic in a positive and confident tone: the message to convey is that progress measurement and performance monitoring are part of the 'best practice' approach that you bring to every contract you undertake. Indicate the measures you will adopt to ensure that any untoward delays in the phasing of the work programme or divergences from the agreed cost structure are resolved without prejudicing the objectives of the contract. If possible, support this material with examples of quality management procedures applied on comparable assignments.

The potential risks attached to the use of subcontractors were outlined in Chapter 11. It may be useful to include confirmation that their engagement will be on the basis of back-to-back contracts, and to indicate the quality management procedures that will be applied to ensure their performance and output are up to standard.

Clients may require bidders to submit a project-specific quality plan as part of their bids, indicating their approach to quality in each element of the contract, detailing the resources needed to achieve the quality objectives of the project and identifying any formal or proprietary methodologies they use. Supporting documentation may need to be included as evidence of quality assurance accreditation – for example, to the ISO 9000 family of quality management standards – and implementation of the principles of project-related quality management defined in ISO 10006, together with samples of inspection and report forms. The quality plan should be consistent with whatever quality management procedures the client organization itself may have in place.

A contract is being managed successfully if the following conditions are met:

- the arrangements for service delivery continue to be satisfactory to both customer and provider;

- expected business benefits and value for money are being realized;

- the provider is cooperative and responsive;

- the customer knows its obligations under the contract;

- absence of dispute;

- no surprises.

(from the Office of Government Commerce briefing, *Managing Contracts and Service Performance* (Business Change Lifecycle), April 2002 version)

15

Defining outputs and deliverables

There is a useful distinction to be made between the outputs and the deliverables of a contract. Outputs are the results the client wants to achieve – the outcome of the time, skills, energy and other resources put into the assignment. Deliverables are the items or services the bidder undertakes or is required to produce at a specified time and place, rather as a supplier delivers goods to a buyer. For example, advice on business strategy is a typical output of management consultancy: the corresponding deliverables will be either tangible items, such as reports and other documents that communicate the means of putting the strategy into effect, or demonstrable services such as management seminars.

Experienced clients know the importance of producing bid specifications that are output-based – focused on the requirements they are aiming to satisfy and the benefits the contract is meant to yield. They are looking for responses that recognize the intended outputs of the contract and demonstrate an informed understanding of their priorities. This means, among other matters, explaining how the way you work will obtain results that meet the client's targets and expectations. It also means making down-to-earth, practical points that tell the client you understand the logistic essentials for fulfilling the contract successfully.

CONTRACT DELIVERABLES

The bid documentation will normally make clear what the client requires by way of deliverables. These requirements may be set out in the form of a **schedule of deliverables** that reflects stages in the contract, the completion of particular activities or key decision points. Each date in the schedule sets a performance target for the team undertaking the work, enabling the client to check the direction and progress of the contract and to assess whether or not it is yielding its intended benefits. If the client includes a schedule of deliverables, you should either confirm adherence to it or explain the reasons for wanting to change it.

If the client has set no explicit schedule, it is important to indicate as precisely as possible what deliverables you are proposing to produce and when they will be submitted. This information has to be consistent with your work plan and methodology (Chapter 13). Include the schedule of deliverables on the work programme bar chart. Make sure the schedule is realistic: colleagues will not thank you for committing them to impossible deadlines, or for imposing an undue burden of document management on top of their technical responsibilities. Indicate specific quality management procedures that you apply to particular types of deliverable. The content, timing and sequence of deliverables may warrant a separate section of the bid – particularly if their early or prompt delivery can offer a competitive advantage.

One point that should be defined in the bid specification is the **final deliverable** that will allow the work to be signed off, marking the satisfactory completion of the contract. In many areas of procurement this takes the form of a completion report that the client will need to approve (see below). It may also be a presentation to interests such as directors, committee members, stakeholders or community groups, or a technical workshop at which findings are explained and their implications debated. If the identity of this deliverable is not made clear in the specification, you will need to indicate your assumptions about the matter.

There is a vast diversity of items and services that may be required as contract deliverables. One category of deliverable common to almost all consultancy and service contracts is management documentation such as progress and monitoring reports. Technical reports and other project-related documents often form the principal deliverables of consultancy assignments. But documentation is far from the whole story. Service contracts in particular are associated with a huge range of deliverables reflecting the products and characteristics of each sector of activity.

Management documentation

Progress reports

Except when the assignment is short, clients will normally wish to receive progress reports either at regular intervals – say, monthly or quarterly – or on a schedule related to contract review meetings or technical and financial auditing regimes. There may be a requirement to submit the reports as hard copy, in electronic format or online. In writing about progress reports in the bid, you may wish to set out your understanding of their function, which is to:

- record the status of work and progress toward meeting targets;

- review the performance of components of the work programme;

- list the deliverables produced during the reporting period;

- identify items needing to be discussed – for example, deviations from the work plan, constraints on progress or possible causes of delay;

- define recovery actions and procedures, where necessary to bring the work back on track;

- provide data on resources consumed during the reporting period, project costs and productivity, together with financial estimates for budget control;

- outline the work scheduled for the following reporting period.

171

Inception reports

As the term implies, an inception report is produced at or near the start of the contract: on long-term assignments, it is normal for clients to require an inception report within one to three months of the start date or the date of contract signature. Its purpose is to set out a finalized and agreed programme for achieving each component task, developed in the light of discussions with the client and the availability of data. Only when you have actually got down to work will you be in a position to check the assumptions made in your bid, to see the needs of the client in a fully informed perspective, to gauge the exact demands of the contract, and to develop a work plan and implementation schedule to the level of detail needed for effective management control. Requirements for additional items of work or additional staff inputs can be identified in this report.

An inception report typically contains the following information:

- a summary of initial meetings and discussions with the client and other parties;

- an analysis of issues raised in the course of discussions;

- a detailed work programme, perhaps with method statements and a critical path network;

- an indication of the scope and timing of additional technical input or other items that may be necessary or advisable;

- where appropriate, arrangements for liaison and consultation with other bodies such as community and interest groups;

- a statement of technical or management points that remain to be resolved.

Completion report

If a formal completion report is required for close-out and processing of the final payment, this normally has to be submitted no later than one month after the end of the contract. The report may include the following management-related material:

- an overview of the contract, commenting on the course of the work and the extent to which its objectives and outputs have been achieved;

- an explanation of problems encountered and corrective action undertaken;

- a financial analysis of the contract;

- recommendations for further action.

Technical documentation

Technical notes and topic reports

It can be useful to indicate your readiness to provide notes and memoranda, topic reports and so forth explaining technical analyses and procedures, and the bid specification may identify a requirement for supporting material; but avoid committing yourself to an open-ended sequence of background documentation. Make the point that the extent of the requirement for this form of deliverable will need to be the subject of agreement between the client and yourself.

Interim or mid-term reports

These are normally timed to coincide with events such as the completion of a stage in the contract or a decision point or project milestone. They explain the work done so far, set out preliminary results, indicate alternatives or options to be examined and draw guidelines for subsequent work.

Final reports

A final report may need to take the form of an extensive set of documents. It is essential to submit the report first in draft so that the client can review it, correct inaccuracies, request amendments on points that may conflict with technical, political or cultural sensitivities, and in due course give approval to the report – particularly when the document will carry the client's name.

Summary reports

These provide concise versions of the technical documentation, principally in the form of 'executive' summaries, intended to give managers, investors and other decision-makers an immediate and sharply focused view of the key results of the work. A summary may be included in the body of a report, but it may also be useful for it to be printed as a separate document that can be circulated more widely and cost-effectively than the report itself. If the contract is concerned with matters that are to be the subject of public consultation or community involvement, a consultation summary written especially to communicate the issues in non-technical language should be listed among the deliverables.

Tender and contract documentation

Where the work is one part or phase of a programme or sequence of contracts, the deliverables may include items such as the drafting of terms of reference and tender documents for subsequent phases or for related projects, guidelines for contractors or consultants, calculation of works, bills of quantities and cost estimates.

Other forms of technical deliverable

From drawings, plans and design guides to digital video and website content, there are innumerable kinds of technical deliverable that may need to be produced as part of a contract. Check the bid specification carefully for any detailed requirements the client may have defined in respect of format, presentation, conformity to standards and so forth.

Report production

Clients may specify the number of hard copies of each document they will need, the arrangements for review and approval, the preferred document layout and requirements for documents to be produced in electronic form as well as on paper. Formatting requirements also may be identified in terms of operating systems and software. When these details are not indicated in the bid specification, try to discover the characteristics of the client's operating environment and, if possible, refer in the bid to the fact that your output will be compatible.

Usually the client will expect to have ownership of the physical 'original' from which a report was printed and the computer disks holding the document files. Indicate your understanding on this point. If the final or interim report is to be published for a broader readership than the client's staff, you will need to find out whether it is to appear as a report presenting the views of the client or as a report from an independent source of professional opinion. When contractors' reports are published, it is normally under the imprint of the client that paid for the work, though in some circumstances it may be appropriate to opt for a more detached presentation, while there are clients who may feel uncomfortable about publishing a document reflecting an independent viewpoint rather than corporate policy. Some clients believe that requiring contractors to produce a report destined for a wide public is likely to secure higher-quality results and a more considered presentation.

16

Communicating added value

Adding value means bringing something to the arrangement that is genuinely beyond the (client) organization's capability or capacity; something that it could not source internally, even if it wished to. Contractual arrangements that add value can be highly beneficial to the organization.

Added value can occur at three levels:

- **business benefit:** identifying new opportunities for ways to benefit the customer's business

- **capacity/capability:** infusing new skills, methodologies and capabilities in the service delivery

- **economy:** better, more efficient and cheaper services through economy of scale or rationalization.

> A (service) provider's contribution to all three should be readily capable
> of identification throughout the deal either at the outset, on an ongoing
> basis or for individual programmes. This might also form a useful
> measure with which to assess their performance.
>
> (_Contract Management Guidelines_, Office of Government Commerce,
> draft version April 2002)

There is no purpose in submitting a bid unless it is as competitive as you can make it in terms of technical quality and value for money. You will not necessarily win just by showing that you have sound expertise, adequate professional resources, a solid record of experience and are competent to provide the services the client wants. Each of your competitors may be able to say the same. To defeat them on quality, your bid has to possess an extra dimension that sets you apart from them, a distinctive edge that represents the benefits you are uniquely placed to offer the client. **Offering more at no extra cost – this is what is meant by adding value to your bid.** Communicating added value means emphasizing those benefits and projecting the difference they can make to the success of the contract.

Remember that it is the client, not you, who decides what gives a bid added value. To get on the right track, you have to start from an analysis of the bid documentation, looking for signals about factors that really matter to the client. In some cases the specification may make these factors explicit; in others you may have to rely on your insight into the background of the contract. Keep in mind that one purpose of the bid process is to see whether any of the bidders can bring original and productive ideas to their work.

If you have been able to identify factors that have key importance for the client, respond directly and convincingly to those priorities. Depending on the subject of the contract, your bid can gain added value in various ways, as outlined here.

Protecting the contract

Many clients identify added value with reduced risk – a point that reinforces the need to make it clear in your bid that you understand the risks inherent in the contract and share the client's concern to see risks managed. A constructive response on your part, showing how you will secure efficient delivery and explaining the mechanisms you can apply to the task of risk management, will win you marks. You have everything to gain by demonstrating that you have thought about what could go wrong and have taken measures to protect the client's interests (Chapter 11).

People

Each individual named in a bid – for example, as a team member, manager or adviser – is a resource of skills and expertise that is (or should be) accessible to the client only through that bid and not through others. Your competitors may have people with comparable backgrounds, but they cannot replicate the precise blend of knowledge, energies and experience offered in your bid. These professional strengths can be rich in value for the client, particularly when the quality of the people proposed for the work is an important criterion in the contract award.

Processes

You may have devised methodologies, systems, procedures, computer models and other analytical or predictive techniques from which the work of the client organization can benefit, and that are not available from other bidders; or you may have developed specialist equipment and forms of technology in fields related to the contract. These can be presented as opportunities for the client to achieve improved value for money, generate efficiencies and savings or gain business advantages and new sources of revenue.

Professionalism

There may be aspects of your approach that the client will see as representing particular benefits: for example, an emphasis on innovation – pushing boundaries forward in a way that is informed and reliable; responsiveness and flexibility to changing requirements; partnering and sharing information; concern for the efficient control of budgets and work plans; helping the client unlock new potential and move in new directions.

For some clients the added value of consultants is measured in terms of the extent to which their presence and intervention make life easier. The consultants they want to use are those who understand what their clients expect and know the right things to do without having to be told, and who are prepared to put an extra effort into the work and go that bit further to ensure a satisfactory result.

Promising and providing more

Good ideas that no one else may have thought of, ideas that go further than the basic services all bidders are required to deliver and that show the extra benefits **you** will provide: these can have a decisive impact on the way your bid is received. Examples include starting the contract with an immediate action programme to deliver high-yield results; running workshops and seminars to extend and strengthen the competencies of client personnel; arranging secondments and placements for them; enabling them to share your research facilities; communicating the outputs of the work through newsletters and community media; setting up and maintaining a project website. Not all of these ideas will be appropriate for every type of contract, but each is a real example taken from a successful bid. And in most cases the bid was for a fixed price contract: the contractors were able to absorb the costs of these initiatives through efficiency improvements in other contract services.

Bidding for repeat business

Conveying a sense of added value can be critically important when you are bidding for further work from a client. Unless you have been able to build a sustained professional relationship through quality, performance and value for money, clients may feel they have already seen what you can do and conclude they are likely to obtain a fresher and more energetic response from a new contractor – particularly if your last contract ran into problems of resourcing or delivery.

To remain competitive, your bid has to take full advantage of the points in your favour. You should be able to show insights that only someone who has worked with the client can possess. Your price will be expected to reflect productivity savings through your knowledge of the client's business environment. If there were mistakes on a previous contract, do not ignore them – address them directly and honestly in the bid. The client will look for evidence that you have learnt from experience, that you have taken steps to ensure mistakes will not be repeated, and so present less exposure to risk than your competitors.

One thing your bid must do is put forward new ideas showing creativity, drive and innovation and offering clear and definite benefits to the client. As well as outflanking the competition, you need to convince the client that there is nothing stale about your approach. **Stay in front by offering and delivering more.**

VIEWPOINT

We have used consultants fairly regularly, mainly in fields such as survey design, statistical analysis, management training and marketing. The results have been variable. One factor that makes a big difference is the background of the consultancy firm and the attitudes that its personnel bring to their work. I suppose this can be described as the ethos or culture of the firm.

I can cite some examples. One group of consultants we used had started life as an internal consultancy unit in a local authority, part of the policy of compulsory competitive tendering in the mid-1990s. They were quite competent technically, and their local authority knowledge was relevant to the particular assignment, but they lacked any real understanding of business. Their output was not as useful as we had hoped. It focused on their technical procedures instead of our commercial priorities. We had the impression that they had thought they could turn themselves into a consultancy overnight, simply by replacing the 'Design Department' sign above their door by one that read 'Design Associates'.

We were disappointed also by a university group that we contracted to help us with some statistical work. The problem was that they did not seem to be sure what business they were in. Their first priority was not our needs as a client but their own research programmes. We took second place and our work was fitted in when it suited their timetable. We were also unhappy about having research students undertaking aspects of the work that we believed to need analysis at a more senior level. There was no sense of urgency or responsive management on their part. Cynically one might say they

---

had the advantage of being cheap, because they charged at uncommercial rates. But a more professional outfit would have been a better buy.

Not surprisingly, we have achieved the best results and the best value when we have used firms that started life as consultancies and that have proved themselves through genuine professionalism. The quality of their work is consistently dependable; they have some first-class people; they keep on their toes and care about getting things right. There is a sense that they are putting us first, thinking about our business needs, supporting our objectives and developing perceptive solutions specifically for us. Their professionalism means that we enjoy working with them; they appreciate being valued; and the result is a relationship that we are happy to maintain.

(Director, train operating company)

17

Presenting CVs

Clients normally require bidders to identify the people they propose to assign to the work, and to supply information that will allow a person's competencies to be assessed against his or her intended responsibilities. The managers evaluating the bid want to judge how closely the qualifications and experience of the individual match the competencies they regard as essential to the success of the work. When they read CVs, they are looking for evidence not just that the person possesses these competencies, but that the competencies have been applied successfully in comparable assignments to achieve benefits for clients.

They may ask for this information to be provided in the form of a full CV or as a résumé summarizing an individual's professional experience. In some contexts – for example, where the contract involves a large contingent of teams and units – you may not be asked to include individual CVs or you may be required to identify only core personnel; in other contexts, the tender may have to include a CV for each person engaged in the work. Whatever the scale of the contract, whether it is just you that is named or a team of people, the information given in a CV and the way it is presented can determine the fate of a bid.

It may be tempting for firms to include the same names and staff inputs at the same time in bids for different clients in the hope that at least one bid will turn out successful. Clients are well aware of the practice of 'double-booking'. As part of a strategy to counter the risk of selecting a bid on the basis of resources that are committed elsewhere, they may require CVs to be accompanied by a statement from the bidders promising that the persons nominated as team members will be available on time to fulfil the inputs shown against their names in the work programme. They may also require individuals to provide commitment letters to this effect and to sign and date their CVs, certifying that the content is correct.

Putting alternative CVs in a bid is not recommended. In scoring CVs as part of the bid evaluation, clients will usually take account only of the weaker alternative.

MANAGEMENT OF CVS

Most organizations that bid for work will recognize the importance of a structured and systematic approach to CV preparation. The pressures of producing an efficient tender, often within desperately tight deadlines, mean that no one can afford to waste time hunting for copies of CVs, trying to piece together information about a person's experience or having to reconstruct other people's CVs to make them presentable. Even when a CV is in reasonable shape to begin with, getting it right for the bid in hand can take several hours' work.

The management of CVs has three main elements:

- **compiling the material;**
- **applying procedures that enable CVs to be rapidly edited and fine-tuned;**
- **maintaining CV material in a form that keeps it up to date.**

Compiling the material involves holding in a database details of the professional background, competencies and experience of the individual, together with information on matters such as language capability, publications, training achievements and so forth. This material should include CVs produced as part of bids and proposals. The task of compilation is best undertaken within the technical unit with which the person works, not by a personnel department or staff records office. A large firm can derive significant benefits from a unified system of CV preparation, storage and maintenance; but it is generally preferable to have the system managed on a divisional basis rather than centralized.

Editing and fine-tuning means generating a CV that offers the best possible match to the requirements of the work, omitting material peripheral or inappropriate to those requirements. There are professional contexts – for example, in some European countries – where convention dictates that an expert's strengths have to be portrayed through a single, unvarying CV registered with the governing body of a profession; but this practice is the exception. In most areas of professional services procurement, clients do not expect to be presented with what is patently a stock, all-purpose CV, which they are likely to regard as evidence of a lack of effort and interest on the part of the bidder.

Shape the detailed content of the CV to focus on directly relevant experience and bring out positive features that reinforce its competitiveness. For example, the individual may have fulfilled comparable roles in previous contracts or worked in a similar business environment or project location. Clients sometimes include job profiles for key personnel in the bid specification, outlining the role the person is expected to perform, the responsibilities of the position and the competencies required. They will look for people who match these requirements.

The task of editing has to be done carefully and truthfully, without massaging, exaggerating or departing from the facts, and without making claims that may embarrass both your firm and the individual at a later date. You must be able to support every claim made in a CV. It is important in particular when outlining the role that a person played in an assignment to define precisely the extent of the responsibilities credited to him or her. Asserting just that an individual had 'responsibilities' or has 'proven experience' is uninformative and likely to win few marks. Substantiate the point with facts and details.

Maintaining CV material involves systematic review and updating on a routine basis. There are three main parts to the task: adding new information on people's assignments and career developments; revising material about current work – for example, ensuring that contracts that have been completed are written about in the past tense, not the present; and holding in the database those edited CVs that are likely to have further useful applications.

The information should be updated at intervals of not more than six months – perhaps quarterly if the person undertakes a large number of short-term contracts. Work done during the past year or so is often the most influential part of the person's record of experience. If you are a bid manager, you cannot rely on individuals to supply the relevant information without prompting and progress-chasing on your part. Your management system has to ensure that all CVs are kept in good order and ready for use. If you work on your own, you have to approach this maintenance task as you would the keeping of accounts and business records: if you don't tackle the job methodically, you are likely to face a huge burden at the last minute. Routine maintenance is the only way to make sure that up-to-date CVs are available to meet short-notice requirements.

STANDARDIZING CV FORMAT AND STRUCTURE

All CVs included in a bid should have the same format and structure. This is especially important in bids from consortia and multi-professional groups. Standardizing these features has a number of advantages:

- Consistent presentation builds an image of integration and competent organization.
- CVs can be prepared more quickly and cost-effectively.
- The task of regular and systematic updating is made easier.
- Consistency helps in assessing the relative strengths of possible team members and selecting the individuals best suited to an assignment.

If there are external specialists or other firms associating with you in a bid, their CVs should – after consultation – be redrafted to secure consistency with whatever instructions the client may have given and uniformity with your own CVs. You may find that the external CVs offered to you lack an appropriately organized or focused structure. If so, do not use them just as they are: make sure you obtain the necessary information to bring them up to standard. It is in your interests to help improve the CV presentation of those professional colleagues who regularly associate with you in bids. At the same time, be careful not to straitjacket CVs into a structure that may not be the most effective presentation for a particular bid.

Name:		
Profession:		
Fields of specialization:		
Proposed role / position:		
Year of birth:	Years with firm:	Nationality:

Key qualifications:
(Give a summary of professional strengths – outlining experience, extent of responsibilities, professional achievements, expertise in specialized fields, knowledge of a particular technology or environment.)

Education and professional status:
(List professional affiliations, diplomas, degrees, scholarships, awards and distinctions, vocational certificates, specialized courses and training.)

Record of recent experience:
(In reverse chronological order, list recent experience relevant to the contract, indicating the employment held, activities undertaken and responsibilities fulfilled.)

Computer experience (where appropriate):
(Indicate knowledge of operating systems, applications, databases, programming, software development and experience of a support environment.)

Language ability (where appropriate):
(Indicate grades of proficiency in speaking, reading and writing.)

Publications (where appropriate):

(Other categories of information relevant to specialized fields)

Certification:
I, the undersigned, certify that to the best of my knowledge and belief the data given here correctly describe myself, my qualifications and my experience.
Signature .... Date ....

Figure 17.1 *Example of a client template for CV information*

JOHN SMITH   CV no. 7

Proposed position in team:	Power Engineer
Nationality:	British
Fields of specialization:	Modelling and control of power plant; energy management systems; application of expert systems in power systems
Year of birth:	1968

Key qualifications

- Over 10 years' experience in power plant modelling and performance optimization, particularly in relation to the improved control of generating plant, grid connections and transmission networks and the minimization of system operation and maintenance costs.
- Recent experience includes direction of the Northern Power Plant Modelling Research Programme (2001–04); leadership of the Power Systems Operations Team, Eastern Power (1999–2001); specialist input to teams undertaking EC-funded system optimization projects and whole plant modelling of thermal performance...
- Expert knowledge of energy management systems and the application of expert systems for fault analysis in transmission and bulk power systems and system restoration.
- Specialist adviser (1996–98) to the NESA Directorate on the formulation of a national strategy for long-term coordination in energy planning and development, to meet the policy objectives of the National Energy Efficiency Programme. Responsibility for guidance on the analysis of energy saving potential and energy efficiency policy elaboration.
- Systems experience of conventional thermal power plant, gas-fired generating plant, combined heat and power and energy-from-waste.

Education and professional status

BSc (Hons) Electrical Engineering, University of Leeds
PhD in Electrical Engineering, Imperial College, London
Chartered Engineer
Member, Institution of Electrical Engineers
Member, European Advisory Panel on Power System Measurement

Recent experience

2001–04   **Northern Power: Project Director, Power Plant Modelling Research Programme:** Responsible for the technical direction and coordination of a series of research projects involving the detailed modelling of generators, turbines and boilers by computer simulation, laboratory models and tests on plant in power stations. The programme provided the basis for the investigation and experimental evaluation of advanced computer control systems, including multivariable adaptive and self-tuning controllers, with associated expert systems and parallel processing seeking to integrate plant control with power system control.

1999–2001   **Eastern Power: Principal Engineer, Power Systems Operations:** Team Leader of unit responsible for the minimization of system operation costs through the use of computer-aided plant loading and load management and related security constraints. Key areas of responsibility included short-term load forecasting; economic loading and load management; emergency control of frequency. . .

Figure 17.2 _First page of a CV showing recommended style_

BASIC STRUCTURE FOR CVS

Clients may specify how they want CVs to be structured and may include a template or standard format in the bid specification, as exemplified in Figure 17.1. When they do, you have no choice but to follow their instructions if you want to keep your bid compliant. But in most instances the choice of structure will be left to you. The guiding principle is to set out as clearly as you can the information that the client will use to judge the competencies of the persons for whose time, energies and efforts they are being asked to pay money. Your task is to communicate this information efficiently and convincingly: the structure should make it easy for you to highlight the distinctive strengths of the individual and easy for the client to recognize them.

Figure 17.2 shows the first page of a CV structured along lines used by most international financing institutions for key staff named in proposals. It is applicable to all sectors of consultancy and professional services tendering – not just international development – and it can be adapted for use by anyone, whatever his or her field of activity. Among its advantages are the clarity of its style and a pattern of organization that assists the process of CV evaluation in competitive bids.

The structure has four main components:

- **personal data;**

- **key qualifications;**

- **education and professional status;**

- **experience record.**

Further optional components may be appropriate in certain contexts – for example:

- **computer experience;**

- **language ability;**

- **publications.**

This structure is recommended as a basic model: other categories of information can, of course, be added to serve requirements in specialized fields.

Where a CV is more than one page in length, devote the initial page to the first three of the main components – ie personal data, key qualifications, education and professional status. The aim is to give the client an immediate, at-a-glance outline of the person's background, one page that holds the client's attention and highlights the credentials that match the person to the work requirement.

Personal data

Include name, nationality, profession and field(s) of specialization. Other data that may be appropriate include year of birth, position in the firm and proposed position in a team.

Under this heading, clients may ask for details about the number of years the person has worked with the firm submitting or associating in the bid. They often give higher marks to people who are permanent staff members than to individuals brought in from outside on contract assignments. There are several reasons for this preference:

- If they have maintained a place on the firm's payroll, they may seem to offer an assurance of quality.

- The management and coordination of their inputs may appear more secure.

- They may ensure a closer match to the client's competence requirements: a firm can be expected to be familiar with the temperament and aptitudes of staff members and should know how well they would fit into a particular work environment.

- They may be better motivated than freelance staff and less inclined to set their own priorities in terms of working hours and commitment, as well as less likely to depart to other employment.

On the other hand, there are many firms that operate with only a small body of full-time personnel and rely on outside advisers to staff their projects. Some highly specialized areas of knowledge may be accessible only through experts working on their own account. One way of acknowledging these characteristics is to describe an external expert as having an 'established working relationship' with the firm, emphasizing the mechanisms you apply to secure team integration and the delivery of results on time. Never give the impression that someone who is a consultant to your firm is one of your employees – he or she may also be a consultant to a competitor; and do not use the term 'part-time' in describing a person's post or status.

It may be useful to provide data on marital status and the number and age of any children if the CV is being prepared for an assignment where the person would be resident overseas for longer than, say, six months, and likely to be accompanied by his or her family. Do not include information on health or interests, address and contact details or names of referees.

Key qualifications

This part of the CV gives a synopsis of the person's professional strengths. The term 'qualifications' is used here to denote the attributes that fit the individual for the proposed assignment – factors such as extent of experience; breadth of responsibilities; professional achievements; expertise in specialized fields; knowledge of a particular technology, country or environment; and, above all, the benefits that the person has helped clients achieve.

Key qualifications are best set out as a series of bullet points: five or six should be adequate for most individuals, but no one should be given less than three key qualifications. If you cannot marshal at least three useful things to say about a person, think again about putting him or her in the bid! The points need to be oriented to match each contract, communicating strengths assertively without making exaggerated claims. Remember that these key qualifications have to be substantiated in the body of the CV.

The way the key qualifications are phrased can help to ensure that the individual's experience is seen to best advantage. For instance, if a large part of his or her career has been characterized by short-term assignments and rapid moves from one field of activity to another, this can be presented as a valuable credential by pointing out the diversity of experience gained and the hands-on familiarity with a broad range of work environments and management functions. The person may in the past have been employed by a similar organization or even by the same client: if so, bring this point out strongly to indicate that he or she knows how the client likes to operate and understands the client's side of the working relationship. Through attention to detail, each point in the key qualifications can build up a winning margin over the competition.

Education and professional status

List here professional affiliations, diplomas, degrees, scholarships, awards and distinctions, vocational certificates, specialized courses and training. Some clients require the names of colleges, dates attended and graduation years.

If the person does not have a professional affiliation or technical qualification, it is better to omit this section and allow his or her experience to speak for itself than to insert school attainments, which are more appropriate to job applications. Not having a 'professional status' does not necessarily mean that a person cannot contribute effectively to the work or fulfil a demanding assignment: if the individual's practical experience is strong and relevant and is set out clearly, the client will recognize his or her suitability.

Experience record

This is the meat of the CV. In developing this material, there are important guidelines to follow:

- **Focus on recent, relevant experience** – during, say, the last three or four years and in fields that have a direct bearing on the work of the contract. Clients want to know what people are achieving here and now, and they need to see evidence not just that they are up to speed with ideas and developments, but that they offer a stronger and more resourceful blend of competencies than any competitors. This is critical in sectors where techniques and applications are moving ahead fast.

- Set out experience **in reverse chronological order**. If the record for a particular year appears thin, it is worth prodding the person's memory for more information: short assignments are easily forgotten.

- Detail the **activities undertaken by the individual** rather than describing the assignment, project or organization.

- Specify the **actual responsibilities** that the person fulfilled, including (if appropriate) the numbers of staff under his or her charge or supervision, the values of contracts for which he or she was responsible and the turnover of any businesses managed.

- Pay particular attention to **comparable assignments** and work for similar clients. Look carefully through previous experience for signs of comparability. We sometimes categorize our experience narrowly and fail to appreciate that work we are accustomed to see in one light may equally well and truthfully be viewed from a different angle that brings out its relevance to the bid.

- For many individuals a single **listing of experience** will work perfectly well. For others, it may be more effective to structure the presentation into types of work, areas of experience or sectors of expertise, reflecting the focus of the contract.

- **Write in the third person and in note form, not continuous prose**. Do not use the person's name in the body of the CV: ie phrases like 'Mr Johnson managed a specialized archive of books and periodicals' should be avoided. Some firms of consultants affect an informal, chatty style in an attempt to look 'client-friendly' – 'Bill was responsible for all plant examination procedures'. Steer clear of this approach – after all, the person is being put forward as a professional adviser, not a personal friend.

Computer experience

Include – to a level of detail appropriate to the contract – information on knowledge of operating systems, applications, databases, programming, software development and experience of a support environment.

Language ability

Where this information is relevant, it should normally be stated in terms of grades of proficiency in speaking, reading and writing – ie 'excellent' or 'fluent', 'good' and 'fair'. If knowledge of a language is only poor, it should not be listed.

The language of the project location takes precedence in the listing. The language of the person's nationality should be indicated as 'mother tongue'.

Publications

There are sectors of consultancy and professional services procurement in which particular weight is attached to publications: research and education are obvious examples. In certain overseas markets, the strength of a person's expertise may be measured by the quantity of their publications: if necessary, check this point as part of your research for the bid. The listing of publications should follow the standard style for bibliographical entries and may include unpublished theses, research documents and conference papers.

Using an experience matrix

A matrix on the lines of Figure 17.3, setting out fields of expertise, activities, responsibilities, project locations and so forth, can be an effective means of highlighting the relevant features of an individual's experience. Bid evaluators find this form of presentation helpful, since it allows them to assess experience directly against the competencies required for a particular function. If an individual is known to the client from previous successful work, bring this point out in the matrix.

Deciding the length of a CV

Clients may set a maximum length for a CV, commonly two or four pages. Material beyond this limit is likely to be ignored. Where these constraints apply, it is vital that every phrase pulls its weight, which reinforces the need for detailed, bid-specific editing.

If no limit is set, you should still aim for brevity and conciseness while doing justice to the individual's experience. **As a general rule, try not to let any CV exceed four pages:** this length should normally be sufficient for a senior professional with about 20 years' career experience.

If you are bidding with local associates for an overseas contract, they can advise on the length and level of detail appropriate in the context. Staff in local firms may also hold teaching posts and have advisory roles in government departments as well as other professional functions, so that their CVs can easily run to 10 or more pages. You will need to agree a compromise target length with your associates and may have to expand the content of your CVs to achieve consistency.

CV presentation

Subject to whatever requirements the client may have indicated, you may choose to locate CVs in the part of the bid that deals with staffing

John Wilson: **Feature writer and editor**

	Corporate communications	Business publications	National press	PR consultancy	Media advertising
Feature writing	☐	☐	☐	☐	☐
Researching	☐	☐	☐	☐	
Editing	☐	☐	☐	☐	☐
Briefing and commissioning	☐	☐	☐	☐	☐
Contract negotiation	☐	☐		☐	☐
Document management	☐	☐	☐	☐	☐
Database experience	☐	☐		☐	☐
Press relations	☐	☐	☐	☐	☐

Figure 17.3 *Example of an experience matrix*

and resources, in a separate section or in an appendix. The number of CVs that need to be included should be one of the factors governing this decision: if there are a large number, it is best to place them where they will not disrupt the flow of the text. It is helpful also to give each one a serial number and to include an index at the start of the CVs. The order in which they appear may reflect the team structure, the array of disciplines required for the contract or considerations of professional seniority. The important point is to reinforce an image of the bid as an integrated effort.

A CV will have a stronger impact and its content will be more readily absorbed if it is laid out as a two (or two-by-two) page spread, starting on a left-hand not a right-hand page. Each page should be numbered and carry the name of the individual in either a header or a footer.

RÉSUMÉS

Instead of requiring a full CV for each person named in the bid, clients may ask just for résumés summarizing the person's professional experience and career achievements. A résumé should normally be no longer than about 150 words. It can be prepared from the material used to develop the full CV: if the 'key qualifications' capture the person's competencies adequately, they will supply the necessary basis. The text of a résumé needs to be edited and maintained in the same way as the full CV.

Résumés should not appear alongside full CVs. It is better to locate them in a different part of the bid – for example, in the section that introduces the team and its responsibilities (Figure 13.4). The aim is to offer a concise statement of the professional resources that can be applied to the work.

As noted in discussing Figure 12.4, it can be useful to attach résumés when you are responding to an informal approach from an existing client, even though there may be no explicit requirement to outline your experience or that of your team. Your ideas for the work may have to be reviewed and endorsed by managers who are unfamiliar with your professional strengths, and the appropriate information about your experience can help to disarm any suggestion that work is being put your way because of personal contacts rather than capability and experience. All that is needed is a paragraph or two summarizing your background and underlining the expertise that equips you to perform the work.

18

Describing professional experience

CLIENT REFERENCES

The bid specification may ask you to give contact information about existing and previous clients who have engaged you on comparable work and who can be approached to vouch for the quality and efficiency of your services. This is a sensible requirement, since it allows prospective new clients to discover what you are like to work with and how competently you have gone about similar assignments. You may be required also to supply site addresses where the client can view your work or see evidence of its implementation.

It is essential to respond accurately and conscientiously to this requirement: after all, if you don't have the experience or the confidence to name other clients who can provide references, what are you doing bidding for this contract? A key item of information is the identity and address of the client manager or unit responsible for

Name of assignment:	Client / Client organization:
Location and description of assignment:	
Description of actual services provided by your firm:	Name of client manager:
	Client address and contact data (phone/fax/e-mail):
Start date:	Completion date:
Key staff engaged on the assignment, indicating functions and responsibilities:	
Approx. value of services:	
Certification: I, the undersigned, certify that to the best of my knowledge and belief the data given here are correct. Signature .... Date .... Post	

Figure 18.1 *Example of a client template for project experience information*

employing your services. Do not make the mistake of phrasing the response in terms that are incomplete or vague, as if to impede the possibility of one client talking to another.

PROJECT SUMMARIES

'Project summaries' or 'contract histories' are a means of validating the claims made by bidders about the experience they can bring to an assignment. This information is normally the subject of a separate section of the bid; clients may require it to be set out on a standard form or template, as shown in Figure 18.1.

To pull their weight in a bid, projects have to be:

- **relevant – to the skills required to undertake the proposed services;**

- **recent – preferably undertaken within the past five years;**

- **related to the individuals or teams named in the bid.**

The last point is especially important. The experience of a firm resides principally in the people who performed the work. The experts who made a success of a comparable job three or four years ago may have moved on to other employment. But if they still work for you and are available to undertake the proposed contract, use the fact to your advantage by emphasizing it in this part of the bid.

If the bid is being submitted by a group or consortium and their record includes contracts on which they have worked together successfully, make a point of describing the results and present this experience as evidence of the benefits that the group can achieve for its clients.

People who have recently started in business may not yet have built up an independent record of experience. But their career backgrounds will probably include achievements and responsibilities that can be used to portray their professional strengths, as noted in the guidance on pre-qualification (Chapter 5).

The process of developing project summary material is similar to that outlined for CVs. Information about the work is held in a database and adapted for particular applications. To provide comprehensive data for use in pre-qualification material and bids, the material should include the following information:

- title of the contract, with a reference number for internal office use;

- name of the client and identity of client manager(s) responsible for the work;

- contract value;

- outline of scope of the contract;

- comments on its perceived degree of success in meeting the client's objectives;

- an itemized account of the services provided;

- start and completion dates;

- outputs and key deliverables, including reports;

- names of project director/team leader and other key team members;

- names of other firms or external consultants associated in the contract;

- any exceptional features of the work.

If a contract has involved more than one field of expertise or focus of interest, it is useful to have more than one summary available. The factual basis remains the same, but different aspects of the work can be brought into prominence in each version to suit the emphasis of the bid. For instance, a project to create a hotel and resort complex may be summarized from a planning and architectural standpoint, or in terms of tourism development, financial and investment analysis, hotel sector training and employment, engineering services, construction schedul-ing or project management, depending on the context.

Do not focus solely on the technical content of project experience. The management side of your contract record may be of equal importance to the client – particularly your ability to coordinate resources and deliver results to specification, on time and within budget.

There are sectors of business and government in which past and existing clients may not wish to have their identity made public or their need for specialist advice revealed. Respect their position and safe-guard your relationship with them; but you do not have to leave the assignments out of your statement of experience. It should be possible to describe the work and the features that make it relevant to the bid without disclosing the client's identity. For example, you can refer to a project for 'a multinational corporation', 'a leading European telecom-munications company', 'a government department', 'London-based timber importers', 'a UK defence contractor' and so forth.

Project summaries need to be maintained and kept up to date on a systematic basis in the same way as CVs. Contracts that have been completed should not be represented in a bid by summaries written while the work was still in progress. When a contract starts, it should immediately be entered into the database. When the work is completed, summaries should be updated with the aid of the final report and other project documents.

- Structure the summaries into **categories of experience**.

- Provide an **index** to this part of the bid, so that the client can easily access an individual summary. You can add impact to the index by presenting it graphically as a table or matrix.

- It is unreasonable to expect a client to trudge through 30 pages of lengthy project descriptions, however big and important the contracts. Do not overwhelm the client with verbiage – a clear signal of lack of self-confidence – or make reading your bid a tedious chore. It is far better to include a **careful selection** of experience, directly relevant to the subject of the bid, than to pile on masses of peripheral material.

- **An absolute limit of 20 lines** for each summary should give you enough space to communicate the essential features of an assignment without straying into excessive detail.

- Use **titles that are informative** about the scope of the work. 'Bridgewater Rehabilitation Phase II' may mean something to you and the client that commissioned the work, but a different client will need a more explanatory title.

BRINGING EXPERIENCE TO LIFE

Most bids go no further than setting out experience as a series of summaries and tables on the lines described above. This form of treatment can document your record in comparable work, but it does not show how you would put that experience to use in the proposed contract. **What you should be communicating to the client is 'We have fulfilled similar requirements for other clients; here is how we helped them resolve similar problems and issues, and this is how our experience can benefit you too.'**

Why not use project summaries as the framework for a more structured argument? For instance, your understanding of the contract may point to key issues that need to be faced or critical activities that have to be undertaken. Use the project experience part of the bid to explain how you approached those issues or activities in other contracts, the challenges or difficulties you overcame, what similarities and differences you expect to meet in the proposed work, and how your contract experience has equipped you to define the most direct means of achieving the client's objectives. In short, don't leave clients to draw their own conclusions about the relevance and value of your experience: make the point yourself, directly and convincingly.

A section developed in this way might have two main components:

- **information about comparable work, drawn from the material referred to earlier;**

- **a narrative pointing to the closeness of match between the requirements of the proposed contract and the results achieved in your previous and current assignments.**

The example that follows shows one style in which this material might be structured. When project summaries are dull and uninteresting – as is the case all too often – they are likely to be ineffectual. They earn their place in the bid only if they focus attention on the quality of your expertise and the distinctive value of your services. The best way to improve their presentation is to rewrite them to bring out the demanding or unusual features of the contract, the difference that your services made and your success in helping to resolve the client's problems.

Improving road safety, restoring the environment and moving underground utility lines are three technical challenges that the proposed contract shares with the A365 Improvement Scheme completed earlier this year for the Department of Roads. Our responsibilities included engineering design and construction supervision of a 30km section giving drivers a safer and smoother road surface on one of the region's busiest stretches of dual carriageway. Three of our team members played a key part in the scheme:

- John Brown, nominated as Project Manager, fulfilled the same role on the A365 scheme, overcoming problems caused by unfavourable weather in the early part of the construction period. His project supervision task was made all the more

---

demanding by the need to keep traffic moving during the roadworks. Nonetheless the work was completed substantially ahead of target and within the contract price.

- Jane Smith, Environmental Planner in our team, coordinated 100 volunteers in an ecological rescue operation to remove rare species of plants growing in areas at risk from the roadworks and to replant them in secure habitats. She also developed and supervised an extensive programme of screen planting, landscaping and hedgerow replacement.

- David Jones, nominated as Senior Utilities Engineer, had the task of locating and recording underground service ducts and utility cables and programming their diversion well ahead of construction. One of the problems he had to address was the fact that not all the utility authorities had exact information about where utilities were sited.

In the four months since the A365 Improvement opened, the number of reported accidents on this section of road fell to 40 per cent of the total for the corresponding period last year, despite a 12 per cent increase in traffic flows. The Department of Roads attributes a major part of the success of the scheme to the quality of our road design and the efficiency of our project management procedures.

These resources are benefits that we can apply in meeting the tight deadline of the proposed assignment, dealing with the complex pattern of services and utilities along the route of the highway, safeguarding its natural environment and developing a road scheme that will succeed in saving lives.

19

Making good use of graphics

Certain kinds of information are communicated more directly and powerfully by graphics than in words. This information principally concerns relationships – for example, the way a series of actions relate to form a process as in a network, and the way two variables relate as in graphs. Network diagrams communicate the logical relationships between project activities; the bar charts of team inputs portray the relationship between the use of resources (people) and the work calendar (time). These relationships could be expressed in words, but only at much greater length and with less likelihood of the message being absorbed and retained.

Even where the message is straightforward, graphics have an impact and an immediacy that words cannot always attain. They are more economical than text, allowing information to be condensed and punched home more directly. They are valuable also as design elements, adding interest and variety to the page and relieving an otherwise drab procession of paragraphs. Every part of a bid has material amenable to graphic presentation. Whether you are describing key credentials, patterns of cause and effect or the relationship of items and actions, think about a figure that can communicate these concepts clearly and directly.

TYPES OF BID GRAPHICS

The basic repertoire of bid graphics includes the following items:

- flow charts or network diagrams displaying the logic and structure of a work programme;

- Gantt charts and bar charts showing activities and professional inputs as horizontal bars against a calendar;

- work trees, illustrating the hierarchy of tasks in a project;

- matrices indicating, for example, skills and experience;

- plans and diagrams of systems, processes, mathematical modelling procedures, test procedures, design elements and other technical features of an assignment;

- maps, plans and layouts of sites, study areas, catchments and so forth;

- sections, elevations and profiles, etc;

- organization charts depicting the structure of teams, management hierarchies, institutions and other units;

- drawings, artist's impressions and thumbnail sketches (Figure 19.1).

This list can be supplemented by a host of items relevant to bids in specific sectors of work. Figures can be imported from business software, spreadsheets, project management packages and computer-aided design files, as well as from graphic design applications.

GUIDELINES FOR EFFECTIVE GRAPHICS

Whether bid graphics are generated on a computer, prepared by a technical designer or simply drawn freehand, there are practical guidelines to follow:

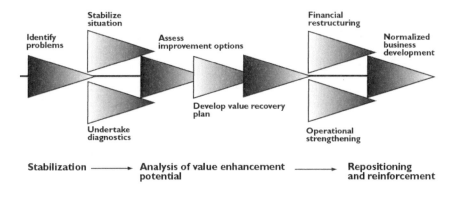

Thumbnail sketches in the page margin can help to guide the client through the description of a methodology.

Figure 19.1 _Use of thumbnail sketches_

References

- Give each figure a reference number and a brief title or caption summarizing its point. Avoid captions that state the obvious: use the opportunity to link the information in the figure to a message in your text.

- Captions should go alongside figures: do not use multiple captions that send clients on an orienteering exercise ('above far left, above left, centre left, below right. . .').

Content

- Make sure that what the figure shows is consistent with what is said in the text. But never repeat its detailed content in words.

- Overloading a figure with information will make its message hard to decipher. Think about legibility and impact. Take care not to cram different categories of information with competing graphic requirements on to the same base.

- Avoid figures that look undernourished. The size of a figure on the page should be in proportion to its information content.

Explanation

- If the figure contains symbols or various colours and shadings, it must have a legend explaining what they signify.

- Figures involving dimensions need a scale. Maps and site plans should show a north point.

- Graphs must have their axes labelled clearly and accurately.

- If you are using material from another source (eg government statistics, opinion surveys, study reports), indicate its origin.

Location

- Wherever possible, locate a figure next to or close to the relevant section of text. Try not to break the flow of the text with successive pages of figures.

- If you have figures such as network diagrams that may need to be read in conjunction with an entire section of the bid, consider having them printed as foldouts at the end of the section.

Legibility

- Avoid making the reader turn the document on its side. See if you can reduce the scale of the figure while maintaining legibility, so as to keep it upright.

- Bear in mind that figures need to remain legible if the client should want to photocopy them or transmit them by fax to another office.

- Another design point to remember is that figures should if necessary be suitable or adaptable for display if the client requires a presentation session (see Chapter 23).

Using photographs

- Photographs have their place in a bid if they are technically relevant and of high standard in terms of composition, print quality and visual interest. Don't forget that photographs can be cropped or enlarged: part of a dull picture can be turned into an interesting illustration if carefully selected, while image editing software will enable you to correct faults in photographs, apply special effects and transform virtually every characteristic of an image. If you are choosing illustrations on the basis of digital images, contact prints or 35 mm transparencies, examine them under at least five times magnification to verify their suitability for enlargement. Are they fuzzy at that degree of magnification? If so they will not be amenable to much enlargement.

Applying colour

■ Setting information off in a separate box or panel, perhaps in a second colour and with a light shading, can be an effective means of signposting material that illustrates or comments on points being made in the bid text. The technique is commonplace in most news publications and magazines, but is seen infrequently in bids. Underlining headings and highlighting columns with a bar or rule in a second colour can give a sense of focus and authority.

DESIGN SOFTWARE

If you use business software such as Microsoft Office, you may well find that it meets adequately your design requirements for documents that are essentially text-based such as bids. But if you want a system with the flexibility to produce other business material too – project sheets, brochures, newsletters and so forth – you should consider investing in graphic design, illustration and publishing software like Adobe Illustrator, CorelDRAW, QuarkXPress or InDesign.

There are basic rules to observe, whatever software you use:

■ Compare the presentation of your business documents against the standard of other material in your sector of work, including if possible the documents your competitors produce. Can you afford to look inferior?

■ Do not underestimate the time and patience it may take to learn to use graphic design and publishing applications.

■ Try not to be carried away by the luxuriant profusion of fonts, text sizes, line patterns, shapes, symbols, signs, shadings, colours, clipart images and other devices offered by graphics packages. About 99 per cent of these will be entirely inappropriate for bid documents.

■ Software may include specimen layouts, style sheets and templates, but it cannot supply you with an eye for good design.

THE BID COVER

The cover is the first the client will see of your bid: it is your first opportunity to project your identity and the quality of your offer. For the client too, the identity of the firm or group submitting the document is the key item of information on the cover. It should stand out more conspicuously than anything else on the cover by means of a logo or the use of effective typography.

Like other elements in the bid, requirements for cover information may be specified by the client. As well as the name of the bidder, they may include the heading used in the contract notice or invitation to tender, a reference number denoting the contract and the submission date.

When you are deciding on the design of the cover, avoid banal devices such as the client's logo or statements of the obvious (eg a picture of street lamps on a tender for street lighting services). Make the cover different and memorable – for the right reasons! Think about the attributes the client will expect to see in the winning bid. If creativity and innovation are important to the client, shouldn't the look of the bid have those qualities?

Any photograph used on the cover should be a powerful, high-quality image. There is much to be said for a straightforward, cleanly designed cover relying for its impact on an economical use of well-chosen typography and colour.

Remember that a bid can just as easily be laid on the client's desk face down as face up. Put your name or logo or both on the back cover too. If the bid is perfect bound, use the spine to indicate your identity and the subject of the bid.

BID DESIGN AND PAGE LAYOUT

Most publications on book design contain information and advice that will help you define an efficient and attractive design style for bids. In achieving this style, you have to balance a number of priorities:

- the client's requirement for direct access to information – which means that the design of the bid has to assist the clear and logical articulation of its content;

- the need to focus emphasis on points that play a key part in the message of the bid, using design to draw attention to items you do not want the client to miss;

- the importance of balance, discipline and a due measure of variety in the way text and graphics are deployed on the page.

The design quality of the bid makes a statement to the client about your professional ability. Do not neglect this aspect of the document. If your business has developed a corporate style for all its technical documents, with rules about typography, text areas, line spacing, margins, location of page numbers and so forth, you may need to adapt this style to take into account the specific considerations that influence good bid design. Bids are business offers not technical reports, and they should not look like technical reports. The difference in function between bids and reports needs to be reflected in their design treatment: both must centre on readability, but bids demand a more vigorous approach to grasp and maintain the reader's attention. There are particular design considerations that apply to bids submitted electronically: these are outlined in Chapter 21.

Design principles

Layout

- Use the page set-up and print layout options in your design software or word processor to define a consistent page grid and text area for the bid as a whole.

- Exploit the design value of white space, but use it in a consistent and disciplined way throughout the text.

- Unless you are quite certain which material will fall on left-hand and right-hand pages, use equal left and right margins on all pages: 25 mm to 30 mm margins should allow an adequate tolerance for binding. If in doubt, choose wide margins rather than narrow ones.

Typography

- Select a basic typeface for the bid and exploit the various fonts within its range, eg light, regular, bold. Consider using a contrasting typeface or a second colour for main headings. When you want to emphasize a word or phrase within a paragraph, avoid simple underlining (because it can look amateurish) and italics (because they tend to resist rather than attract attention): use a bold face instead.

- When you are choosing a type size, err on the side of generosity, which means using a larger point size and leaded rather than solid text.

Identity

- You may think it appropriate to impress your identity on every page by using pre-printed paper carrying your logo or a phrase or 'strapline' that expresses a key message. But using a client's logo in the same way can appear patronizing and presumptuous.

- Do not be tempted to mimic the appearance of the client's internal documents, to make it look as if you are already part of their team: this is a disingenuous device, and besides it is **your** distinctive qualities that interest the client.

- No amount of graphics can disguise a bid that is poor in technical content. A noisy design will simply draw attention to the bid's deficiencies.

20

Stating your price

Clients normally specify the price information to be included in the bid and the way they want it set out. This may range from tables of fees and expenses to cost schedules and standardized forms and templates. You may be asked to provide bankers' references, balance sheet summaries and other financial data in addition to contract-related price information. As with other categories of information, it is essential to follow meticulously the instructions in the bid specification.

By and large, the information requirements of clients are determined more by their need to be able to identify best value for money and obtain a consistent basis on which to assess the financial merits of individual bids than by the type of contract they intend to apply to the work. Value for money has been emphasized throughout this book as the prime consideration influencing decisions in services and consultancy procurement. Demonstrating the right quality of service is the function of the technical or 'non-financial' parts of the bid: the role of price information is to show that you can offer the right quality at the right price.

COMPONENTS OF PRICE INFORMATION

Whether the bid is for a fixed price contract, for work remunerated on a time charge plus expenses basis, or for some other type of contract combining fixed and variable cost elements, clients are likely to require a detailed breakdown of costs and an indication of how they were calculated. It is in the bidder's interest to provide a cost breakdown even when this requirement is not specified and particularly when bidding for a public sector contract, if only to demonstrate transparency and to show the factors that condition the price of the work. For some types of contract, bids may need to set out separately the costs of human resources – staff, management, administration and so forth – and physical resources such as IT systems, equipment and materials.

In addition to a statement of the total bid price, bidders may be required to provide information on the following items:

- the estimated costs of each stage or part of the work, or each field of activity, perhaps with an indication of the expected weekly, monthly or annual profile of cost accumulation;

- charge rates for the persons undertaking the work;

- a time charge multiplier;

- estimates of reimbursable expenses;

- estimates of subsistence allowances.

Total bid price

This should be stated in words as well as in figures – eg '45,000 (forty-five thousand) euros' or '£35,000 (thirty-five thousand pounds sterling)'. Identify the services and activities that are covered by the price – for example, by reference to the scope of work defined in the bid specification.

Make it clear whether the price excludes or includes VAT or whether the services are zero-rated. As a general rule, costs should always be expressed as net of VAT, partly because the net cost represents the true cost to a client organization that is itself registered for VAT, and partly because the tax rate may at any time be increased (or less likely reduced) by government.

In calculating the total bid price, you may wish to apply an across-the-board contingency margin to all categories of costs and expenses, particularly if the proposed duration of the contract is longer than, say, a year. Bear in mind that a contingency allowance normally reflects an element of risk to cover the cost of unexpected additional work, unforeseen circumstances or cost escalation. Clients are aware that if it is applied overall, particularly in an economic environment where the inflation rate is low, they will be paying it on conventional items of work that are relatively proof against exceptional risk. The most prudent course is to identify those parts of the work to which you would wish a contingency factor to apply, and explain why.

Charge rates

You may be asked to indicate the proposed charge rates for the persons involved in the work, calculated on an hourly, daily, weekly or monthly basis. In some contexts it may be appropriate to calculate a specific rate for each individual in a team; in others there may be advantages in grouping members by categories of responsibility or discipline that share a common charge rate. If the bid is submitted by a consortium or group of consultants, clients will expect to see a consistent set of charge rates applied by all its member firms.

The client may require rates to be analysed into their basic ingredients – payroll costs, overheads and profit:

- **Payroll costs** comprise: 1) the gross regular salary plus bonuses paid to the individual in the office where he or she normally works (or an equivalent target income if the person is self-employed); 2) the costs of the non-monetary or fringe benefits paid to staff, which normally include employers' statutory insurance, medical insurance and pension scheme contributions; 3) the costs to the employer of annual leave, sick leave and terminal leave (if taken at the end of an assignment); and 4) vouchers for meals or public transport and other similar items.

- **Overheads** are the business and premises costs not directly attributable to a specific contract and not reimbursable as distinct cost items under a contract. For example, the costs of maintaining a firm's quality management system and quality accreditation would normally be considered an overhead, whereas the costs of project-specific quality control procedures would not.

- **Profit** (or return on chargeable time) is normally set out as a percentage of the sum of payroll costs and overheads, and geared to reflect factors such as the degree of exposure to commercial risk inherent in a contract and the value of the work to the client. As a guide, many consultancy firms would hope to achieve average net profit margins in the range of 10 to 15 per cent.

Time-based contracts normally provide for the contractor to be paid up to an agreed price ceiling at rates identified in the contract and calculated on the basis of the hours actually spent in performing the work. Clients may require these costs to be presented as a composite estimate or as a set of estimates related to individual parts of the work or to the proposed inputs of individual personnel. If they are working within tight financial limits, they may ask bidders to cost individual parts of a contract as well as providing a total estimated fee, so that they can judge how the available budget might best be allocated.

Time spent on the work is usually interpreted to include, where appropriate:

- time incurred on professional work as defined in the contract;

- time spent on surveys or data processing;

- meetings with the client and with other contractors associated with the work;

- visits to work sites and other relevant locations;

- time spent travelling in connection with the work;

- preparation and production of deliverables;

- presentations of findings;

- follow-up work as agreed with the client.

Some clients have a policy of paying a reduced rate for travelling time incurred during the course of an assignment, for example 50 per cent of the rate payable for time spent on professional work. Other clients may not regard travelling time as chargeable at all. Where teams have to be mobilized and offices set up for contract work overseas or at locations remote from the home base, the time incurred on this activity is normally chargeable as part of the contract.

Time charge multiplier

The relationship of time charges to gross salary costs is sometimes expressed in terms of a time charge multiplier. The multiplier calculation works as follows. Gross salary costs are the basic unit (1.0). Three elements are added to this: 1) social costs and 2) overheads, both expressed as proportions of gross salary costs (say 0.5 and 1.3 respectively), and 3) profit, expressed as a proportion (say 10 per cent, or 0.28 in this example) of the gross salary costs plus social costs plus overheads. The multiplier is the sum of the calculation – in this case 3.08.

The values in the calculation will be different for each contractor and will be conditioned by a number of factors:

- the type of work that characterizes the contract;

- the probable duration of the contract;

- the form of fee payment proposed;

- the way the firm calculates overheads – for instance, in relation to time actually worked or potential workable time, which might include weekends and public holidays;

- the part of the world where the firm's office is based, since this influences salary levels.

Multipliers offer clients a means of gauging the degree of consistency in the pricing structure of the bids received from a contractor. Client sectors such as government departments and agencies may set a maximum acceptable level of multiplier. They may also request information about the average multiplier applied on similar contracts, and may wish to know how the multiplier proposed for the work has been derived – for instance, whether external consultants are included in the numbers of staff considered to be supported by a firm's administration, and if so how this affects the multiplier. Bidders may be required to state whether their overhead figures are audited, and if not to provide evidence of how the figures are determined.

By way of comparison, the Office of Government Commerce has defined a multiplier of 2 times salary as an alternative basis, if full costs are not available, for quantifying the costs of staff time in calculating the value for money benefits to government departments from an improved deal with a supplier (_Value for Money Measurement_, OGC Business Guidance, November 2000).

Estimates of reimbursable expenses

These are expenses directly and necessarily incurred on a contract and reimbursable either at cost or with a mark-up, management charge or handling fee. Clients will normally require bidders to tabulate individual groups of items separately, and may define budget ceilings for items that are hard to estimate reliably in advance of starting work.

The following are the most common categories of reimbursable expenses:

- **travel and transportation:** public sector clients normally apply distance-related allowances and cost limits for car travel and specify the use of economy or standard class for air and rail travel; some clients will reimburse air fares only when the relevant passenger tickets and boarding passes accompany the contractor's invoice;

- **office expenses** related specifically to the terms of the contract;

- **equipment, materials or supplies** purchased, leased or rented in connection with the contract, including for example the purchase and maintenance of vehicles: where it is expected that equipment purchased for the assignment will be traded in at the termination of the contract, it may be appropriate to include an estimate of depreciation;

- the costs of **support services** bought in from outside, such as project-related laboratory testing, surveys, field facilities, remote sensing, translation services, legal work and so forth;

- **communications** (phone, fax, internet connections and courier services), **IT and data system costs:** in certain types of project environment, an informed assessment of the level of IT support necessary for effective start-up and performance may be critical to the viability of your price;

- **printing and production**, including photocopying, scanning and conversion and the presentation of contract-related material in video, CD ROM or other forms;

- **documentation**, covering the purchase of any necessary documents that may not be supplied by the client;

- on overseas contracts, the costs of **local support staff** such as administrative managers, secretaries, translators, interpreters, accounts clerks, drivers and messengers, where these are not provided by the client and have to be hired by the contractor.

In certain contexts, such as EC-funded work, clients may stipulate that reimbursables are to be quoted free of taxes.

Subsistence allowances

When contractors have to work away from their home or office base, the client normally pays an allowance for living and accommodation expenses, calculated as a fixed amount per day for each individual. Clients in the public sector and corporate organizations may impose an upper limit on this amount, reflecting budget constraints or predetermined allowance levels.

On overseas contracts, subsistence allowances are normally paid in local currency and apply only to each day or night actually spent in the territory where the contract is being undertaken. They are generally not payable for periods of leave, save for local public holidays. Financing and development institutions such as the World Bank and UNDP as well as EC-funded programmes define standard terms and allowance rates for different countries.

COST ASSUMPTIONS

Though the bid specification will normally contain information about the financial basis of the contract, there may be points of detail on which you have to make assumptions when preparing the bid. If the format for this part of the bid allows it, you may find it useful to declare these assumptions as a means of safeguarding your position and reducing the possibility of misunderstanding. Points that might be covered, unless they have been specified by the client, include:

- the period for which the price and its component estimates will remain valid after the submission date;
- the assumed starting date of the contract;
- the values in which costs are expressed in the bid (eg January 2005 values);

- any index-linking of the estimates to allow for inflation;

- time – the definition of what is deemed to be a 'day' (how many hours of work), a 'week' (how many working days) and/or a 'month' (a calendar month or a set number of working days): in many sectors of business, the nominal working year is usually defined as about 210 potential working days, taking into account weekends, bank holidays, vacation time and an allowance for sickness leave;

- the applicability of subsistence allowances;

- assumptions about client inputs: ie what it is assumed the client will provide by way of logistical support, documentation and so forth;

- arrangements for the recruitment and payment of temporary personnel;

- arrangements for the appointment and payment of subcontractors;

- the extent of computing requirements and basis of computing costs;

- the treatment of travel expenses, including the applicability of any cost limits imposed by the client.

Defining the **period of validity** of your price is a point of key importance in bidding for overseas contracts, particularly when the work is to be undertaken on a fixed price basis. Contract negotiations may take longer than expected, while the start of work may be delayed because of political and economic considerations. Though costs may have soared in the intervening period, the client is likely to insist that you hold to the price stated in your bid unless there is a clear understanding about its validity.

Bids for contracts overseas may involve a further set of assumptions in addition to those listed above:

- the currency (or currencies) in which the contractor will be paid;

- the foreign exchange rates on which estimates of local costs are based;

- whether the cost estimates are exclusive of local taxes (value added, sales, corporate and personal income), customs duties and levies, fees and other impositions under existing and future legislation in the overseas territory;

- the extent of any participation in the technical work of the contract by counterpart personnel in the client organization;

- if appropriate, the allocation of a separate budget for training and transfer of expertise;

- reimbursement or defrayment of the costs of local technical documentation;

- the language to be used in reports and discussions, and the extent of any need for translation or interpretation.

The most prevalent financial hazard in overseas assignments is the **escalation of local costs** through inflation. In some countries it may be difficult to identify an appropriate retail price index to which local costs can acceptably be linked or even, in the case of government clients, to gain recognition that the problem of inflation exists. Commercial banks may be able to act as an authoritative source of reference in these situations. The financial part of your bid should emphasize the need for an eventual contract to include a mechanism that takes account of cost escalation. Matters such as the applicability of withholding taxes and the provisions of double taxation agreements will need to be covered in the terms of a draft contract at the stage of negotiation. The extent to which it may be advisable to address these points in your price information will depend on the particular circumstances of the contract.

PAYMENT

The bid specification may define the schedule on which payments will be made to the contractor. On fixed price contracts, payments are normally linked to the submission and approval by the client of agreed deliverables and the achievement of performance targets or project milestones. On relatively short time-based contracts, invoices are normally submitted immediately on completion of the work, in the case of assignments of less than one month's duration, or at regular intervals in arrears, eg on the last working day of each calendar month.

Advance payment

Contractors may regard an advance payment as necessary on contracts where the initial costs of setting up the project and starting work are likely to be substantial – for example, assignments that require the contractors to buy in special equipment, or work undertaken in remote locations or overseas. The precise amount of an advance will depend on the contractual arrangements to be agreed during negotiations and need not be defined in the bid, which might seek only to posit a requirement for an advance payment and place it on the agenda for negotiation.

Clients are often reluctant to agree the need for an advance payment. When they do they will generally require the contractor to provide an advance payment security or guarantee, which will have to be arranged through a bank or an export credit guarantee scheme. Overseas clients may stipulate that guarantees have to be obtained through a nominated bank in their country. The effect of the guarantee can be to tie up a large amount of a contractor's working capital or substantially increase its indebtedness to banks, while the time and effort needed to organize a guarantee and obtain the advance payment on time may offset any benefits. Moreover, an advance payment may not in itself be adequate to secure a positive cash flow at the start of a contract, and the contractor may still need either to commit the firm's own resources or to increase its borrowings. These practical difficulties are often compounded by delays in the reduction or release of guarantees by clients.

SEPARATE FINANCIAL PROPOSALS

In certain sectors of procurement such as contracts for EC-funded work and projects financed by international or regional development institutions, it is standard practice for clients to require bids to be submitted in two parts: 1) a technical proposal, which has to contain no financial information; and 2) a separate financial proposal, which is opened only after the technical proposal has been evaluated. This is the 'double envelope' or 'two-stage' procedure, which considers technical quality first and then cost (Chapters 21 and 22). Figure 20.1 reproduces a typical introduction to a financial proposal.

The reason for separating financial information is to try to ensure that the client's technical evaluation of the bid is not influenced by

Newstyle Consultants submit this financial proposal to undertake consultancy services for the Southern Region Health Authority, in response to the letter of invitation dated 12 July 2004 from the Director, External Services Office (ref. MC/GCL-02/15). The proposal is to be read in conjunction with the accompanying technical proposal (forwarded under separate cover) which sets out in detail the proposed technical method and work programme, staffing schedule and relevant capabilities and experience of the consultant team.

The cost estimates presented in this proposal are based on a set of assumptions itemized and described in Section 2. The assumptions are consistent with the information provided by the Authority in its terms of reference and its supplementary information for consultants.

Estimates are set out under the four main headings specified by the Authority:

- fees for professional services
- reimbursable travel and subsistence expenses
- survey and computing costs
- other specific expenses.

Table 1.1 provides a summary of the estimated costs for Phases I and II of the work respectively. The total estimated costs of consultancy services and all related expenses for Phase I are £65,000 (sixty-five thousand pounds) and for Phase II £117,500 (one hundred and seventeen thousand five hundred pounds) net of VAT.

Figure 20.1 _Example of the introductory paragraphs of a separate financial proposal_

considerations of price. If an assignment is simple, capable of precise definition and subject to a fixed budget, the bid specification may declare the size of the budget and bidders will be instructed not to exceed it in their financial proposals.

Collusive tendering certificate

In some areas of public sector procurement, bids may have to be accompanied by a collusive tendering certificate. This is a document in which bidders declare that they have not come to an understanding with another person to fix or adjust the amount of the tender, and undertake among other matters not to disclose the amount of the tender to any unauthorized person before the contract is awarded or to arrange that another person either should not put in a tender or should pitch a tender at a certain price.

BEST PRACTICE IN DEALING WITH PRICE

- **Keep price information concise, direct and businesslike.** If the work is a relatively small-scale and straightforward assignment, there may be no requirement for detailed tables. A single summary table may be perfectly adequate.

- It is essential to **confirm that price information is consistent**: where costs are set out in detailed tables, they must match correctly the amounts shown in a summary table.

- Check that you have not omitted **cost items** or accounted for them more than once.

- The importance of **conforming fully and precisely with any schedule or template** the client may have provided for financial information was emphasized at the start of this chapter. Your accounts people will probably have a standard way of setting out costs and this may tempt them to use cost headings that differ from the client's instructions. Do not make that mistake. It may be inconvenient to have to adapt your calculations to the client's pricing schedule but failing to do so can turn out expensive.

- Make sure there is **no vagueness or room for misunderstanding** in the financial terms of your bid. Remember that in law if any term in a contract is ambiguous or unclear, it will be interpreted against the party that drafted it.

- Avoid **unexplained terms** such as 'other administrative costs' or 'general expenses', unless the client has used those headings.

- Take care not to appear to be hedging your price with **niggling conditions and exceptions**. If you do, the client may conclude that you will be troublesome to work with.

- **Develop the financial and technical sides of the bid together.** They have to reinforce each other if both the bid and the work that results from it are to succeed. This principle is particularly important when relating price to the levels of risk that you are accepting in the contract. You may win the contract, but it is likely to go wrong if your price does not properly match the requirements of the work or the scale of its risks.

- **Getting the price right is at least as important as making the right technical response.** If the competition is fair, a bid that succeeds in combining the highest technical quality with the lowest price should always win. In most sectors of procurement such bids are rarities, and most contract awards involve a balance of technical and financial considerations.

  Your prime objective in bid development must be to make both your technical approach and your price as sharply competitive as possible: in other words, to be perceived as offering **better value for money** than other bidders. The client needs to be convinced that you have thought out properly the cost aspects of the work and that you are able to apply a standard of professional effort that justifies your price.

- In analysing the bid specification, you will have made provisional estimates of project costs. Develop and refine these estimates as you firm up your ideas on the work programme and inputs. Spreadsheets and accounting programs can help you model the effects of changes in the size and composition of the work team, the scale of time inputs, charge rates and the levels of other costs.

- If the deliverables of the contract are products that you offer to a variety of clients and involve well-defined procedures and standard tasks – for example, in certain areas of financial consultancy, statistical analysis or legal work – you may find it appropriate to quote on the basis of your average charging rates for that sector of activity. Where the work does not involve a set product, the prices you quote must be project-specific.

  In developing price bids for this type of work, you will need to form a reliable estimate of the direct costs likely to be incurred both in obtaining the work and in performing the contract. You will have to consider the likely impact of the contract on your variable overheads and its implications for cash flow. Your normal practice may be to price work on a cost-plus or percentage mark-up basis, ie aiming to make a target contribution to fixed costs and profit after covering your direct costs and variable overheads. A depressed market or the particular circumstances of the contract may make it necessary to move the target and bid at a lower price, so as to compete more effectively.

  But remember that **while you can always reduce your price for the work when negotiating a contract, you cannot increase the**

price if you started by pitching it too low. Moreover, a price that is clearly too uneconomic to allow the required depth and quality of work is likely to put you out of the running.

■ Clients sometimes underestimate the work needed to produce the results they want and as a consequence set budgets that are not fully in scale with the requirements of the work. If the client's figures seem wrong, try to find out how they were arrived at – which means understanding the financial constraints within which the client has to operate. Contracts may have to be channelled through plans and programmes with predetermined spending limits: it is often difficult to extend the budget or arrange for an increase in expenditure to cover any additional work that a contractor may think necessary.

■ **Fixed prices** are tricky to calculate. If the price on which you win a contract is based on a misinterpretation of the client's expectations, if you underestimate the effort and resources needed to deliver the required outputs, or fail to allow for possible changes of priority within the scope of the work, you may well find that your profit on the contract is wiped out. To avoid this situation, make sure you gauge accurately the demands of the contract; build appropriate contingencies into the bid price without inflating it uncompetitively; and identify clearly and precisely the services and activities that are covered by your price.

If the scope of your contracting activity means that you tender for work from parts of a large organization that share a common procurement and purchasing arm – for example, divisions within a business conglomerate or government departments and agencies – you will need to explain any variations or inconsistencies in the basis of your pricing.

■ **Aim to minimize your exposure to financial risk.** This is particularly important in estimating for contracts that involve long-term horizons or large-scale commitments of staff. Risks may include cost escalation as a result of inflation, rises in interest rates and unfavourable exchange rates; delays in receiving payment; changes in tax liability; the adverse consequences of political changes or reversals in management policy; or planning and programming errors on the part of the client. Many of these risk factors represent contingencies with impacts that can be critical to the financial outcome of a contract.

■ **Think in terms of the price the client is prepared to pay for the right outcome, rather than the price at which you are prepared to sell your services.** In other words, **the value of your work to the client**, not its cost.

What evidence do you have about the client's perception of value for money in your sector of activity? Do your clients associate your work with distinctive, high-value skills? Some clients regard contractors as agency staff or temporary extensions of their in-house personnel and may want to minimize the differential be-tween payroll costs and contract payments by setting fee rate ceilings that bear no relation to market conditions and would be acceptable only if there were a secure promise of continuity in the engagement. Pitching your price at the right level means being aware of these considerations.

■ If you work on your own and are new to contracting, deciding what price to put forward in a bid can be a difficult task. The price has to be competitive in terms of the market for your services while providing you with a reasonable level of profit. New contractors are liable to undercharge for their services, either out of fear of los-ing opportunities for work or through a lack of reliable information about market rates. You must be wary of bidding initially at marginal prices in the expectation of entrenching a position with a new client and capturing a source of further profitable work: you may find it hard to negotiate upward the rates you accepted at the start, and the expected stream of work may never rise to the surface.

■ Some clients adopt a policy of continually taking on different contractors rather than giving repeat work, since they reckon that new people will charge lower rates to secure the work but still deliver a good quality of service in the hope of more contracts coming their way. Never let a client persuade you to accept a rate you know is uneconomic by holding out the promise of more work in the future. **What matters is your cash flow here and now!**

FINANCIAL INFORMATION IN RESEARCH BIDS

Proposals for research funds and applications for project funding from government departments need to include estimates of the total costs for which support is sought. For long-term funding, detailed cost profiles for each project year may be required. Costs are normally disaggregated into the following items:

- salary costs of the personnel who will be working directly on the project;

- consumables such as scientific laboratory supplies;

- capital equipment, which may be defined as fixed assets exceeding a specified threshold cost;

- overheads, ie costs that support research activities but cannot readily be attributed to a particular project;

- subcontractors' and consultants' fees;

- travel and subsistence expenses;

- other miscellaneous items such as the costs of equipment servicing, computer software, recruitment and financial services: these may be categorized as indirect costs by the funding body.

EC research contracts use a range of cost bases. Participants may identify all the direct and indirect costs incurred on a project, provided they have an accounting system that allows this to be done with sufficient accuracy; or they may identify their direct costs and charge overheads as a flat rate percentage of their direct personnel costs; or opt for an additional cost basis as defined by the Commission.

Research clients will require information also about the amount of funding secured or expected from other sources. As part of the Small Business Research Initiative (Chapter 4), government departments in the UK may ask for information about the amount of funded work that might be subcontracted to small businesses.

21

Producing and submitting the bid

Every seasoned bid writer will recall emergencies when it seemed touch-and-go whether the bid would ever see the light of day let alone the client's office. Missing the deadline means losing the contract, no matter how good the bid. If only for this reason, try not to leave things until the last minute. Problems and glitches may occur, but you can minimize the damage if you **plan and think ahead**. Make sure every part of the production process is covered, from the safe back-up of files to maintenance checks on copiers and other equipment.

ELECTRONIC SUBMISSION

Clients may require or permit bids to be submitted electronically as well as in written form. This point will normally be made clear in the bid specification. Electronic procurement is steadily gaining ground in the public sector: the EC Communication on Public Procurement (March 1998) set a target of having 25 per cent of all public procurement in EU member countries handled electronically by 2003, and the EC intends to move toward full electronic proposal submission. Reinforcing the use of e-procurement is one of the aims of the new consolidated public sector procurement directive (Chapter 2). The wider use of electronic media is reflected in the delivery of pre-qualification documents and tenders as well as through the publication of standardized contract documentation via the internet. Within Europe, national legislation is being amended to permit the submission of tenders other than in writing. For instance, the Utilities Contracts (Amendment) Regulations 2001 allow this option provided that the means of submission enables each tender to contain all the information needed for its evaluation, maintains the confidentiality of tenders pending their evaluation and enables tenders to be opened only after the time limit for their submission has expired. Where an electronic submission is allowed, an authority is able to require either that the submission of the tender is confirmed in writing or that a hard copy of the tender is delivered to it in person or by post, in either case as soon as possible after the submission of the electronic version.

In some cases, bidders may be asked to submit electronically data such as detailed cost information, which would otherwise have to be keyed manually into the client's computer system, and to produce the rest of the bid as hard copy. Check whether the format for electronic documents is indicated in the bid specification; generally it will be MS Word, though clients may ask for a PDF document.

If it is your own idea to submit material electronically, confirm that this is acceptable to the client. In preparing the material there are key practical considerations to bear in mind:

- Because of issues of resolution, the page size for a screen-based document will be smaller than for a printed document. Though the person viewing the bid on the screen will be able to scroll vertically and horizontally and zoom in and out, it will not be so comfortable or convenient to read as a paper copy, and it will be less easy to maintain a sense of where one is in the document.

- To accommodate the needs of clients who may be using older displays, it is advisable to adopt a design basis that enables a page to be viewed in its entirety on a standard VGA resolution display (640×480 pixels) without recourse to a zoom facility.

■ Electronic documentation imposes constraints on the text area, typography and inclusion of graphic objects. For good legibility, it is advisable to leave at least 45 per cent of the screen page as white space. Two-column layouts may cause problems. The most readable font is a sans serif typeface such as Arial, Gill Sans or Helvetica, with an average size of 12pt for body text. At certain screen resolutions and settings, a bold face may not appear bold, and the screen display may be limited to 16 colours. If your bids normally include your corporate logo on each page, the size of the file may become hugely inflated.

■ Apply a minimum of formatting and use tables not tabs.

■ Flow charts, spreadsheets and forms may be unwieldy to read, particularly if they extend to numerous rows and columns spanning more than one page. Unless you have carefully thought through the design of a worksheet, printing it from a file may give the client more work than you would wish.

■ Preview the electronic version before sending it to the client, so that you have if necessary the chance to correct errors in spacing, formatting, margins and pagination.

In short, supplying an electronic version is not just a matter of scanning the bid into a computer. You are likely to have to design the document twice – once for a conventional hard copy and again for its electronic counterpart. And even where you do provide both, the client will probably find the one on paper more useful when it comes to examining and evaluating the bid.

It is now quite common for clients to require bids to be submitted both as hard copy and on CD. Make sure your CDs are properly identified: if you are not able to print directly on to them, use CD labelling software or at least a CD marker pen.

SIZE AND PRESENTATION

Though clients like bids to be concise and to the point, large-scale contracts that involve complex work programmes and multiple teams of experts can require a sizeable body of documentation. Should the material be kept in one large volume or split into a number of smaller ones? In deciding this question you have to find a balance between two priorities: first, the client's need to be able to read and examine the document conveniently; second, your need to safeguard the physical integrity of the bid. The advantage of having one volume is that all the relevant information is to hand within a single cover. The drawback is that the bid may be unwieldy and hard to navigate.

You may choose to resolve the problem by setting a limit beyond which the bid, with all its detailed material, will not be allowed to grow, and then applying the necessary editing skills to contain the document within this limit by pruning down the material. In instances where a mass of information has to be supplied, dividing it into multiple volumes may be an appropriate answer, particularly if there is essential or highly relevant appendix material that resists editing or condensing. If resources extend to the multiple option, the use of a slip case housing the complete set of volumes is recommended.

The majority of bids are produced in an A4 portrait orientation. A4 documents are conveniently shaped for shelf storage, but it is worth considering the use both of a landscape orientation and of alternative sizes and shapes. Bids by their nature are ephemeral documents, not intended to have a long shelf life. Their format can play a part in building an image of creativity: **a bid that looks different may project a message about being not only different but better**. The important point is to present the bid in a format that makes it easy for the client to recognize and assimilate the value of your expertise.

The style of presentation must be geared to the client's expectations of professional quality. Your bid may be addressed to a middle manager in the client organization but may well find its way to the desk of the chief executive or the boardroom table before a decision is made. Think about the impression the bid is likely to make at top management level. The style of the document has to be efficient and business-like: above all, it must strengthen your image as the right source of specialist advice for that client and for that job. Bids that are overloud or overdressed in terms of word processing and graphic presentation may look as if they are trying to compensate for a lack of confidence and content. **Where professional services are concerned, a restrained design is better than overstatement.**

■ Check the client documentation for instructions about the number of copies you have to submit. Clients may require a 'top copy' of the bid to be identified as the 'original' and the others to be marked with the word 'copy'.

- Check that every part or page of the document that needs to have your signature has in fact been signed.

- Some clients may require every page of the bid to be initialled by an authorized representative of the contractor, and even to have the representative's authorization confirmed by a written power of attorney accompanying the bid.

- Keep at least three hard copies of the bid documents for future reference. Make sure the computer files and artwork from which the bid was printed are backed up and retained for at least a year after the selection decision, even when a contract has been lost.

- There are particular production issues such as questions of translation that may need to be addressed when the bid is for a client overseas. These issues are best resolved before the bid is written not afterwards. They are outlined briefly in Chapter 10.

PACKAGING AND DELIVERY

It is vital to follow precisely the instructions for submitting and delivering the bid – the deadline for submission, the address where the bid must be sent, the number of copies required and the form in which the bid has to be packaged. This latter point is critical when technical information and price information are to be presented separately: usually the technical and financial proposals have to be submitted in separate sealed envelopes, which are in turn placed within a sealed outer package.

In public sector procurement clients have to apply deadlines scrupulously for reasons of even-handedness. If you fail to meet the deadline, and there are no extenuating circumstances, you cannot reasonably complain if your bid is rejected unread.

The client may specify in detail how bids are to be identified. You may be required to leave envelopes unmarked, to use pre-addressed labels included with the bid documentation or to use identification codes. Failure to mark the bid packaging correctly is likely to invalidate a bid.

Delivering the bid may be a matter of simply handing the copies in to an office in the next street or of flying them out to the other side of the world. In every case the most dependable method is to have either yourself, a member of your organization or someone else committed to the success of your bid (for example, a reliable local associate) take the bid personally to the client's address and obtain an official form of receipt recording the date and time of delivery. If you entrust bids to the mail within the UK, use the Special Delivery service, which guarantees delivery by 1.00 pm on the next working day. When you need to use an express courier service, make sure you know the range of services they offer and the respective costs; check their estimated delivery times carefully and add a contingency margin.

If a bid has a long-haul overseas destination, plan for delivery two full days ahead of the submission deadline. International express courier services may sometimes fail to meet quoted delivery dates through a lack of urgency on the part of local agents: in the world's largest cities, their agents may have a schedule that takes them only once a week to the district where the client's offices are located. If you have kept in touch with your embassy, you may find that the staff there can help with the delivery of the bid. Should your delivery plans go wrong, it may be possible to retrieve the situation and meet the deadline by e-mailing the text of the bid, if the client accepts this procedure. It is not unusual though for clients explicitly to rule out the submission of bids by fax, to avoid having their phone lines permanently engaged.

22

Understanding how clients evaluate tenders

EVALUATION CRITERIA IN PUBLIC SECTOR PROCUREMENT

Contract award on the basis of the most economically advantageous tender was discussed in Chapter 2. Identifying this tender involves the use of multiple evaluation criteria. The public sector procurement regulations give examples of criteria that may be applied – including quality, technical merit, aesthetic and functional characteristics, delivery date or period for completion, running costs, cost-effectiveness and so forth, as well as price. But they make it clear that this list is far from exhaustive and that an authority is able to make its own choice of criteria to suit the particular requirements of a contract, provided the criteria used are free from bias or discrimination, permit objective assessment, are related to the essential features of the contract in question and generate an economic advantage for the contracting authority.

It is evident also that terms such as 'quality' and 'technical merit' allow ample scope for interpretation through sub-criteria. For instance, an authority may assess 'technical merit' in terms of the structure and components of the work programme, the credentials of the people named in the bid, the extent to which the bid shows an innovative approach or addresses priority issues, the scope it offers for team working and partnering, its approach to managing the work and the risks inherent in the contract and its proposals for controlling and coordinating the input of subcontractors, among other factors. It is up to the authority to judge if it will obtain a better response by setting these factors out explicitly in the bid specification than by writing simply 'technical merit'. This point underlines how important it is for contractors to pay close attention to the detailed information in the bid specification and to research as thoroughly as possible the considerations that will shape the client's view of the practicality and value for money of a bid.

Whatever criteria are used to identify the most economically advantageous tender, they must be the same as those indicated in the contract notice or bid specification: as noted in Chapter 2, they have to be stated so far as possible in descending order of importance. Changes in the list of criteria or in their relative importance may indicate that the authority favours a particular bidder: they can be grounds for questioning the fairness of the award procedure. The bid specification will normally have included a warning to the effect that the authority will consider only bids that fully meet the evaluation criteria.

Generally the detailed evaluation will be preceded by a **compliance check** to verify that each bid conforms with the requirements set out in the bid specification. Points that may be covered in this check include:

- consistency with the authority's instructions about the submission and delivery of bids;

- presence of all the required categories of information;

- confirmation either that the bid offers a conforming solution (where variant solutions are not allowed) or that a variant solution is accompanied by a conforming solution (where this requirement was indicated);

■ conformity with instructions about structure, use of templates, signing of documents, initialling of pages or CVs, etc;

■ inclusion of formal statements, for example on legal, environmental or health and safety policies;

■ confirmation that the contractor's participation in the contract would not raise a conflict of interest or the possibility that its judgement in performing the work might be biased;

■ (where the bidder is a consortium) inclusion of letters confirming the association and designation of a lead company signed by all consortium members;

■ (where subcontracting is involved) inclusion of a statement from the bidder about the content and extent of the proposed sub-contracting;

■ inclusion of a signed statement of availability from each expert proposed.

Tenders that are incomplete or that substantially fail to meet formal requirements are normally rejected at this stage. In some circumstances, a client may give bidders an opportunity to correct minor errors or to supply material that was missing from their documentation. It is, of course, always open to a client to seek clarification or additional information from bidders during the course of the evaluation.

METHODS OF EVALUATING BIDS

Because the process that leads to identification of the most economic-ally advantageous tender needs to be auditable and objective, most public sector authorities employ a form of **marking scheme** in which each bid is scored against the defined criteria, which are weighted to reflect their degree of priority. Evaluators normally use scoring sheets or evaluation matrices (Figure 22.1) and may also prepare written statements of the strengths and weaknesses of each bid. They seek to establish a consensus about the merits of the competing bids, discus-sing any major discrepancies in assessments or scores. The bids are then ranked in the order of their total scores. Either the bid with the highest score is selected as the winning bid, or – if the evaluation is in two parts, the first concerned with technical merit and the second with price –

those bids with total scores at or above a pre-set threshold (say 65 or 70 points out of a maximum 100) go forward to a financial evaluation before being given a final rank on the basis of their combined and weighted technical and financial scores. This final rank identifies the most economically advantageous tender.

	Weight	Firm 1	Firm 2	Firm 3	Firm 4	Firm 5
A Experts proposed	**40**					
A1 Competencies and qualifications of seminar personnel:						
• Experience in financial aspects of transport development	12					
• Experience in transport-related training	10					
• Experience in C and E Europe	8					
Additionally for Seminar Leader:						
• Leadership, coordination and management of comparable seminars	10					
B Experience of the firm	**10**					
B1 General experience in financial analysis of infrastructure projects and transport schemes	4					
B2 Practical experience of training event implementation in C and E Europe	4					
B3 Experience of providing training seminars related to the transport sector	2					
C Organization and methods	**50**					
C1 Logic and organization of proposal	3					
C2 Understanding the project objectives	3					
C3 Appropriateness of seminar team:						
• Size of team	3					
• Structure of team	3					
C4 Programming of seminar preparation	3					
C5 Proposed work plans for seminar components	8					
C6 Appropriateness and blend of proposed training methods	3					
C7 Timetables and time inputs	3					
C8 Proposed seminar materials	3					
C9 Integration of local counterpart support	3					
C10 Multiplier benefits and added value of proposal	4					
C11 Choice of seminar location	4					
C12 Proposed seminar timing	4					
C13 Logistical arrangements	3					
TOTAL (maximum points available = 100)	**100**					
All firms scoring over 65 points qualify for financial evaluation						

This example is drawn from the technical evaluation of proposals for an EC-funded training project.

Figure 22.1 *Example of a technical evaluation matrix*

The relative weight given to the technical and financial scores in this calculation (the **quality:price ratio**) may follow a set formula (eg 70 per cent quality, 30 per cent price) or it may be decided on a case-by-case basis. As a general principle, the more a contract for services or consultancy demands complex analytical work or innovative thinking, the greater the weight attached to quality in the bid evaluation: so, for example, the quality:price ratio for a strategic planning contract or a feasibility study might be set at 80:20. These values are likely to be reversed for what may be considered routine, straightforward work or repeat projects, where the emphasis will be predominantly on price.

The structure of the marking scheme will be conditioned by the nature of the contract. In cases where the standard of contract performance appears likely to be determined by the calibre of the key people undertaking the work, 50 to 60 per cent of the technical evaluation marks may be awarded in respect of personnel, while the proposed methodology may carry 30 to 40 per cent and the qualifications and experience of the contractor 10 per cent. If the bid names a team leader or project director, this individual's competence, suitability and experience can have a critical bearing on the marks awarded for personnel. Methodology may have more importance in the marking where the contract involves intricate processes of technical analysis.

Clients may base the **financial evaluation** on a comparison of total bid prices, unit prices (for example, fees and direct costs divided by the number of staff-days or staff-months) or the overall costs of the required services over the life of the contract (whole life costs). In public sector procurement the recommended policy is to judge best value for money on the basis of whole life costs. Various formulas may be applied in scoring price. For example, where a quality:price ratio of 70:30 is used, the lowest-priced bid may automatically be awarded the full 30 points available and the other bids marked by dividing their prices into the lowest price and multiplying the result of the division by 30; or the mean price of, say, the three lowest-priced bids may be given a value of 30 points, and one point may then be deducted from the score of each bidder for each percentage point above the mean, while one point is added to the score of each bidder for each percentage point below the mean.

In those contexts where it is standard practice to accept the lowest-priced responsive tender and variant solutions are permitted, clients will normally apply specific procedures for dealing with variations so as to ensure a fair basis of comparison. These procedures may be identified in the bid specification.

Where a contract is subject to public sector procurement procedures, a bid with a price that is **abnormally low** cannot be rejected out of hand. The bidder has to be given an opportunity to explain and justify the price, which may, for example, reflect the use of particularly economical procedures and novel solutions or other factors allowing the required services to be delivered for a cost that competitors cannot match. The authority may still turn the bid down as unreliable, but only after it has reconsidered its content against the bidder's explanation.

For large-scale and high-value contracts, the client may undertake **tender evaluation in two or more stages**. The first stage may use the process of technical and financial evaluation described here to identify, say, two or three shortlisted bidders who are asked in the second stage to refine their bids and develop further their proposed solutions to the client's requirements. Commercial negotiations may start during this second stage. The shortlisted bidders will be evaluated on their final responses and the client will then select a preferred bidder for detailed negotiations.

In a different form of multi-stage procedure, the client may perform an initial evaluation against a specific part of the bid; only those bids gaining scores above a defined threshold will go on to receive a full evaluation. This type of procedure is hazardous for bidders, since material in other parts of the bid – which might well be a substantial document – will be ignored in the initial evaluation. If you are facing this procedure, the safest course is to make sure that the text that is the subject of the initial evaluation contains all the salient points of your bid, even at the cost of repeating material elsewhere. You have to get through that initial barrier, and your response to it must demonstrate the full value of the bid as a whole.

The evaluation process may include interviews and presentations (Chapter 23). Before formally awarding a contract, clients may wish to refer their selection decision to an independent expert for endorsement, for example on the value-for-money aspects of a bid.

Main steps in a typical evaluation process – public sector

- Commercial and financial analysis by procurement managers.

- Technical analysis by task managers, focusing on:
  - conformity with specification, technical requirements and programme;
  - technical alternatives, where these are permitted;
  - quality of resources;
  - practicality of methodology.

- Review of safety and quality aspects of the tender, including:
  - quality plans;
  - contractors' documented quality and safety system;
  - compliance with health and safety, equality of opportunity, environmental and other regulations.

- Review of proposed subcontracting arrangements, where appropriate.

- Value-for-money assessment.

- Recommendations on contract award.

QUESTIONS CLIENTS ASK

Though there is room for choice in the criteria on which the evaluation is structured, the questions that matter to clients when judging the responses of bidders will in many contexts be broadly similar.

Background and experience of contractors

- Do the contractors have a sound record of achievement in comparable work?

- Are claims about experience backed up by facts and evidence, with client references and contract details?

- Was the experience we are reading about gained by the people who would be working for us?

- Do we have past experience of working with these contractors? If so, what do we know about their attitudes to performance and delivery?

- Do the contractors have available the facilities to perform the contract effectively and manage it competently?

- Do they have quality accreditation?

- Does the bid make sensible and constructive points about their contract management responsibilities and their working relationship with our technical and management staff?

Personnel

- Does the bid offer the scale of resources appropriate to the work?

- Is the bid precise about the availability of key personnel, scheduling of time inputs and delivery of outputs? Is it clear exactly who would do the work?

- Do they have the necessary competencies and levels of expertise?

- Are their work responsibilities clearly defined? Are they related appropriately to their competencies?

- What is their employment status with the contractor?

Approach, methodology and work programme

- Does the contractor appear to understand our objectives and the key issues to be addressed?

- Has the work been thought through in the necessary detail? Is there a work plan and a clear statement of the proposed methodology and technical procedures? How well are these related to the scope of services set out in the bid specification? How good is the methodology?

- Has the contractor explained why a particular method has been chosen and set out its advantages or limitations?

- If the methodology for achieving our objectives allows options and alternative approaches, have these been discussed in the bid?

- Does the bid give a balanced response to the work requirements of the contract?

- Does the work programme indicate a sensible and realistic input of time and effort, and is this likely to deliver results on target?

- Are the deliverables identified clearly? Is there an appropriate emphasis on output delivery and recognition of the need for performance monitoring?

- If there are aspects of the work about which the bid specification is prescriptive – in order, for example, to meet statutory requirements or reduce exposure to risk – has the contractor recognized the significance of these points?

- If the bid puts forward a variant solution, does it make a good case for this?

- How has the contractor dealt with responsibilities for the management and direction of the work? Is there a clear and direct line of accountability?

- Does the contractor appreciate the importance of problem-avoiding mechanisms and risk management? Is there an awareness that the work might not go according to plan, and an indication of how the contractor would deal with such situations?

- Does the bid offer added value and multiplier benefits?

- Does it show convincing evidence of professionalism and a sound basis for trust?

Price

- Is there a clear statement of the total estimated price and how it was arrived at?

- Are tables and cost schedules arithmetically correct?

- If price information is set out in several tables, are the sums consistent?

- Have any cost items been accounted for more than once or omitted?

- Is the price realistic and within our budget? Is there a convincing match between the price quoted and the scale and quality of the services offered?

- Does the price include items that were not asked for in our requirements? Do they strengthen or weaken the value for money of the proposal?

- Are there aspects of the price information that suggest economies of effort on the part of the contractor?

- Have the consultants applied a contingency margin across the board, even to items of work that carry no exceptional risk?

- Are there unexplained items in the schedules, such as 'other administrative costs'? Do we need to find out what these are?

- If the price seems unusually low, do we need to check out why?

Quality of bid presentation

The client's view of the quality and technical merit of a bid is influenced also by the way the document is written and presented and the efficiency with which it performs its function as a business offer:

- Does the quality of the bid suggest hasty preparation, or does it give an impression of professionalism and reliability?

- Does it offer a distinctive added value that sets it apart from other bids?

- Does it respond well on the points we consider important?

- Is reading the bid hard work or does it have interesting things to say?

- Are there ideas in the bid that are so good, we wish we had thought of them ourselves?

- Where we have tried to give bidders advice on the issues to address and factors to consider, have they paid attention to these points?

- Is there evidence of genuine commitment and involvement, or does the bid read like a routine exercise?

- Is the bid uncertain, confusing or evasive on any point?

- Have the contractors simply fed back the information we supplied and dressed it up to give the appearance that it is their own work, or have they applied it in ways that show insight and perception and tell us something new?

- Is the terminology in the bid consistent with our specification, or do the contractors use a vocabulary of their own? This may show they are focusing on their view of the project rather than seeing it from our perspective.

- Is the bid well organized? How easy is it to locate the information we are looking for?

- How competently is the bid written? Are there sentences that do not make sense?

These factors may or may not appear in a marking scheme, but they are important in communicating professionalism and they do influence the way evaluators respond to the bid. For example, clients often request that bids are kept concise. Though a bid may not be rejected if it is less brief than it need be, failure to understand the meaning of conciseness ('giving a lot of information clearly and in a few words') is likely to colour the client's reaction. Moreover, if the client has instructed that a particular part of a bid must be no more than five pages long, any text that runs over that limit is likely to go unread.

Keep in mind the advice in Chapter 16 about adding value to your bid. If you deal in a detailed and convincing way with a topic that is of particular concern to the client, or if yours is the only bid to offer a bid response matrix or to structure information helpfully, it will become the standard by which the rest are judged. Think of it as keeping up the pressure on your competitors. You do not know what good ideas they may put into their bids, so try to get the better of them with good ideas of your own.

How to annoy a bid evaluator

- Put the bid together in the way that suits you. 'Instructions to tenderers' can safely be discarded. 'Instructions' are just suggestions, aren't they? Anyway, no one really bothers about formalities.

- Don't worry if you have lost any forms that came from the client. Set things out as you choose to – isn't individuality supposed to be important in a bid?

- Leave out items that will take too much time and effort to prepare.

- Don't take seriously anything the client may say about wanting CVs to be just two pages long.

- Don't hesitate to insert marketing brochures into the bid – the more the better, since it may be read by someone who has never heard of you before, and brochures add weight to the document.

- Assume that the people evaluating your bid can be left to comb the text for key information without any guidance on your part.

- Don't bother to number paragraphs, or give titles to tables or figures, and don't even think of cross-referencing them in the text.

- Don't make any effort to be consistent with the phrasing of the bid specification: for example, write about 'the feasibility analysis stage' of the work, when the client talks about 'Phase 1', or call someone the 'project manager' when the client uses the term 'team leader'. While you're about it, why not give the same item of work two or more different titles?

- Ensure that information in tables and figures does not match information in the text.

- Test the evaluator's alertness by building arithmetical errors into tables, and decorating figures with unexplained splashes of colour.

- Avoid committing yourself to a precise statement of deliverables, a clear work programme or an explicit schedule of staff inputs.

- When writing about your team, take care not to specify the role for which each person is nominated or what exactly he or she would do in the assignment.

- Make liberal use of your organization's own internal management jargon.

- Ignore misspellings, incorrect grammar and faulty sentence construction.

- Give the evaluator an opportunity to take exercise by having to rotate the bid 90 degrees to read a table or diagram.

EVALUATION OF RESEARCH PROPOSALS

As observed in Chapter 4, the documentation sent to applicants for research funding normally includes detailed guidance on the structure of the evaluation process, the criteria that the funding organization proposes to apply in assessing bids and the weights attached to particular criteria. The FP6 _Guidelines on Proposal Evaluation and Selection Procedures_ cover every aspect of the process, as well as guidance on proposal submission.

The principles central to FP6 procedures are common to proposal evaluation in most areas of research:

- external peer review by independent experts;

- equal, impartial and transparent assessment of proposals;

- requirement to demonstrate scientific and technical excellence, relevance to the objectives of the research programme and management competence, expressed in a realistic plan for progressing the research;

- priority ranking of proposals in terms of merit and value;

- factors conducive to bidding success include:

  - strong support for the proposal from referees;

  - management competence;

  - composition, strength and credibility of the research partnership;

- sound methodology;
- clear identification of milestones and deliverables;
- exploitability of the research in terms of its downstream benefits;
- effective mechanisms for transmission and communication of project results;
- links with other research and development initiatives;
- access to secured complementary funding from other sources;
- added value and multiplier benefits that reinforce competencies and performance.

In each FP6 call for proposals, the criteria against which proposals are evaluated and the interpretation of those criteria reflect the type of funding instrument being used for the research (Chapter 4) and the characteristics of the work programme. The specific criteria to be applied in the evaluation are identified in the work programme documents. As noted in Chapter 4, some work programmes apply a two-stage evaluation procedure, first assessing short outline proposals against a number of core criteria and then examining detailed proposals against the full set of criteria.

Depending on the nature of the research, proposals may be subject to an ethical review. The purpose of this review is defined in the FP6 *Guidelines* as making sure that the EU does not support research that would be contrary to fundamental ethical principles: these concern, in particular, research in fields such as clinical trials; the use of human tissues and, in particular, foetal and/or embryonic tissues; and the use of animals, especially non-human primates and genetically modified animals.

Research councils and most of the UK government departments and agencies that fund research programmes publish information on evaluation procedures as part of their guidance for bidders. In assessing quality, expert panels consider principally the relevance of the proposal to the strategic objectives and requirements of the research programme, as well as scientific and technical merit. They look for the factors listed above – in particular a well-defined and competitively priced work plan, proven management ability and a viable method of disseminating the results of the research. The expertise and research infrastructure available to the applicant is taken into account, alongside whatever experience the department may have of previous research work from the same source.

23

Presentations to clients

Clients may call bidders to attend an interview and present their ideas about an assignment either in place of a written submission – for example, if the contract value does not warrant or require a formal tendering procedure – or as a follow-up to a tender or a step in a negotiation process. Presentations give clients an opportunity to judge face to face the quality and professionalism of the people competing for the work as well as enabling them to pursue questions that may have emerged from an examination of the tenders. In situations where the tenders reveal no clear winner, a presentation can have a decisive effect on the contract award.

PLANNING AND MAKING THE PRESENTATION

The interview commonly has three parts:

- an initial presentation by the bidder;

- a question-and-answer session in which each side may raise points it wishes to have clarified;

- a final statement by the bidder.

The detailed agenda of the meeting and the time available for the presentation will be set by the client: depending on the scale of the contract, an interview may take just a half-hour or last a large part of the day. Who attends the interview on the bidder's side is usually left open, though clients generally want to see the people scheduled to do the work or those who will be directly responsible for it. They may indicate that they expect to see key members of a proposed work team – especially the team leader and the partner or director who would be in charge of the work – and they may set a limit on the size of each bidder's delegation.

You risk losing the contract if you turn in a poor and indifferent performance. A competent presentation is not enough – it has to be a winning one! It is essential to plan and rehearse your side's part in the proceedings and prepare for the questions you are likely to be asked, so that you are in a position to answer them fully and directly. At the same time, you have to be sufficiently sharp and alert to respond confidently to any unexpected questions the client may raise.

Planning and preparation

Make sure that each area of the work and each aspect of the tender can be covered by one or other member of your presentation group. Nominate a presentation leader whose role will include developing the structure of the material, defining and coordinating the contributions of individual participants, deciding on the visual aids to be employed, setting up a pre-presentation planning meeting and rehearsal, managing the logistics of the presentation and introducing the members of the group to the client.

If you are competing for further work, think twice about including in your presentation team any individuals that you know have had a problematic working relationship with client managers. You cannot afford to have the presentation overshadowed by previous conflicts of personality: it must focus on what you can do in the future and on the new approach to performance and partnership that you will bring to the work.

When you rehearse the presentation, have at least one member of your team play the part of the client. This does not mean taking an adversarial role or asking awkward questions: it is more important to listen for inconsistencies or gaps in the material and points where the argument may not seem entirely convincing. You can then work out how to communicate these points more effectively. Spot and correct any distracting mannerisms, weak body language or a tendency to talk too fast or hesitantly.

Putting your message across

On the day itself, keep the initial presentation concise. You can use an executive summary of the bid as its basis, but do not simply repeat word for word what the client has read in the document. Develop the points outlined in the summary in a logical sequence to emphasize your businesslike approach to the work programme, the commitment of your team and your concern for value-for-money performance, delivery and reliability.

Signpost the route through your material and confirm whether the client wants to ask questions at the end of the whole presentation or after each part. Remember that it is open also to you to ask questions ('This is our understanding. . . is it correct?'). Try to open up a dialogue with the client about the issues inherent in the contract and the responsiveness of your approach.

If the presentation is the sequel to a tender submission, you will normally not be permitted to introduce new material at this stage; but the client may allow you the opportunity to expand on points made in the bid. A final statement should focus on the messages at the heart of the bid, but it should also refer to any comments voiced by the client and show how the approach you have proposed is robust and adaptable enough to accommodate the fine-tuning and amendment that invariably take place as requirements are defined more sharply.

Though you may not be able to do much about the seating, try to make sure your group can maintain eye contact during the interview. A chance comment by the client can occasion an urgent need to communicate with each other!

Remember that in addition to the technical messages in your bid, the presentation has to give a feel of the relationship you will develop with the client. Everyone taking part has to come across as confident, intelligent and enthusiastic to undertake the work. You should enjoy presenting your ideas, and the client should find listening to them enjoyable.

VISUAL AIDS

If practicable, arrange to see the room where the presentation will be made. Check that it has the necessary power sockets and other facilities. Can the lighting be adjusted? If you have to draw curtains and close blinds, will there still be enough light to allow people to write? Is a screen available or will you have to supply one? If you propose to use a portable screen, can it go in a place that is convenient both for the client and for yourselves? Confirm these matters with the client: don't just assume that everything you need will be in place. In any event, it would be prudent to bring your own projection equipment (hired for the occasion if necessary), fallback material (in case of a total power failure) and an emergency kit of cables, plugs, lamps, batteries, tools and other spares, since you cannot afford to have the presentation go wrong for lack of planning.

Many clients will expect bidders to deliver a PowerPoint or digital video presentation, using a laptop and a portable, lightweight projector: they may regard anything less – for example, OHP acetates or slides – as lacking the professional touch. Whatever form of technology you use, the logistics of the presentation have to be coordinated precisely, so that things happen in the right order – another reason why it is imperative to have a full rehearsal.

PITFALLS TO AVOID

■ Do not make the mistake of using just a single speaker for the entire presentation and leaving the rest of your group sitting there as mute observers, opening their mouths only if the client aims a question in their direction. Give each person a distinct role in the presentation. Back your people up by listening attentively when they are speaking rather than shuffling papers or holding whispered conversations.

- Ignoring the client's questions, side-stepping difficult points, failing to give straight answers or replying on impulse without thinking can be fatal to your chances of success.

- Don't spend the time talking about your own credentials. It's the client's requirements that should be the centre of attention.

- Don't be defensive or self-destruct by drawing attention to weaknesses the client may not have perceived.

- Do not overload the presentation with a mass of detailed material. Know how much information you can get across in the time available – visually as well as in words. Divide the presentation into easily digestible time slots and try to vary its pace and tone without wasting time.

- Make sure you do not overrun: keep a note of the rehearsal timing.

- Each slide should make a few well-chosen points, using no more than five or six lines of text.

- Visual aids that consist solely and uniformly of lists of bullet points can be tedious. Use graphics imaginatively to bring the presentation to life.

- If you use PowerPoint, take advantage of its features, but do not over-egg the presentation with an extravagance of animations and transitions. You are likely to irritate rather than impress the client.

- Unless you are really adept and practised in using the technology, avoid tricks and devices such as trying to control the sequence of slides by signals beamed from your mobile phone. If things go wrong, you will look foolish and the presentation will get off to an unconvincing start.

- Bids for contracts overseas may require you to give presentations to clients whose first language is not English. Like the text of the bid, the content of the presentation should be free of informal expressions and unexplained references – for example, to 'English Heritage', 'GPs', 'S levels', 'PFIs' – that may leave the client wondering what on earth you mean.

24

Do your own tender auditing

USING FEEDBACK FROM CLIENTS

Whatever its outcome, the tendering process is incomplete without an effort to understand the reasons for success or failure. If the tender was subject to public procurement rules and you were unsuccessful, you are normally entitled to ask the contracting authority to explain the grounds on which your bid failed and to indicate the advantages offered by the winning bid. The authority may decline to give this information if it judges that to do so would be prejudicial to the public interest or the maintenance of free competition.

Clients are sometimes helpful enough to volunteer information on why a bid has failed. Where they do not, make it your business to obtain feedback from them and encourage them to be frank in their assessment. There is no need to be apologetic about approaching them on this point, and clients ought not to react defensively: if your bid was technically deficient in some respect or fell short of the required standard, it is important for you to know the reasons so that you can redress the problem on a future occasion. Most clients will respect this as a professionally responsible attitude and recognize that it is in their own interests to encourage more efficient and competitive tenders.

Without this information you may be unable to analyse correctly the factors that have worked to your favour or disadvantage in particular sectors of the market. The analysis may involve criticism when a tender is lost, but its intention should be constructive not accusatory. Look on it as a positive exercise to improve the quality and force of your bids and draw lessons that can improve your response to future opportunities.

Learning from success and failure

Learn both from the bids that take you through to negotiation and from those that do not, and use the information to reinforce your tendering skills. Perhaps a key factor that brought success was your awareness of the complexity of a problem or willingness to tackle difficult issues; perhaps it was the innovative nature of your approach, the structure of the work programme, your ideas on managing the project, the competitive level of your price or the emphasis you placed on the quality of working relationships that convinced the client that you could provide the best value for money. These are winning elements you will want to develop further in other bids.

If the structure of your tender seemed unclear, the experience of your team inadequate or your level of costs too high, you need to reflect on your approach to bid development and put matters right. If you failed to appreciate the scale of the required technical commitment or the impression you conveyed at an interview was poor, you will wish not to repeat those mistakes. It is the bids that do not result in contracts that have the most to teach you: a bid can be said to have failed only when you learnt no lessons from its development.

THE AUDITING PROCEDURE

Whether or not your firm has quality accreditation, it is important to maintain a commitment to continuous improvement in the quality of bids and in the procedures for their development and production. Like all aspects of quality assurance, this commitment needs to be driven from the top down, encouraging a sense of ownership of the bid so that everyone who contributes to its preparation is aware of the relationship between quality and competitiveness and shares a personal responsibility for the standard of the document.

One of the most useful things you can do to strengthen your competitiveness is to adopt a systematic practice of auditing your bids. The procedure has of course to be fitted in with other work priorities, but it need not be an arduous task if you adopt a methodology like the one suggested in this chapter, and you will not regret the time you invest in it. The aim is not so much to determine whether the way you go about tendering conforms to defined standards and procedures – though it can be used for that purpose – as to look back at your bids from a client's viewpoint and ask: if you were a client receiving this bid, what impression would you get about its competitiveness and professionalism?

An auditing procedure as outlined here will provide a baseline for measuring improvements in bid quality by enabling you to:

- **assess the extent to which your bids are consistent in their approach;**

- **identify recurring problems and shortcomings that may be impairing their quality;**

- **measure the impact of your bids against the factors that represent added value in the eyes of your clients;**

- **gauge the overall scope for improvement in the development, content and presentation of bids.**

The auditing procedure, outlined in Figure 24.1, involves the following steps:

1. Choose a representative sample of bids, including some that won and others that lost.

2. Examine the bids as if you were the client, reviewing their content and presentation against a set of audit parameters that reflect client priorities rather than your own concerns. For each parameter, draw up a set of key questions. The list that follows sets out audit parameters and questions that will be common to most contexts and that mirror the concerns addressed in the quality management process advocated in Chapter 8, but they are viewed here in a broader perspective and from the client side of the bidding process.

3. Assess how well or badly each bid performs in response to these questions. You can do this on a subjective basis by judging

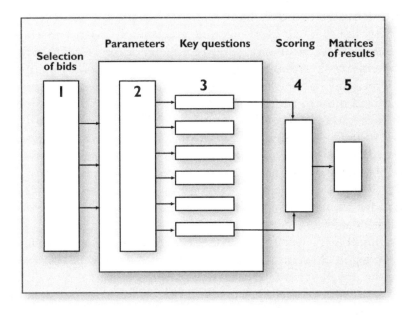

Figure 24.1 *Outline of auditing procedure*

Presentation

The assessment covered five bids, denoted here as a to e.

Item	High	Medium	Low
Overall appearance of bid			a b c d e
Binding		a b d	c e
Cover			a b c d e
Page layout		a b c d e	
Table layout			a b c d e
Font style			a b c d e
Typographical accuracy	b	a e	c d
Graphic content		a d	b c e
Consistency of graphic style	a e	b	c d
Balance of text and graphics		b	a c d e
Match between text and graphics	e	b c	a d
Distinction between tables and figures	d	c	a b e

Figure 24.2 *Example of audit parameter scoring*

performance as 'high', 'medium' or 'low' (Figure 24.2); or you may wish to develop a more objective and quantitative approach. For example, if each question allows a 'yes/no' response, you can mark the bids by awarding 1 point for a 'yes' response, and 0 points for a 'no' response.

To illustrate an objective method, let us consider the question 'Does the bid show empathy with client values and processes?', one of the points listed under 'Insight into client issues and requirements'. The way to convert this into an objective form is to decide what statements or other elements in the proposal would constitute showing empathy, and frame a series of more precise questions addressing these. For example, 'Is the proposed methodology described from the standpoint of the people who will use the outputs of the work, or from a narrowly technical point of view?'; 'Does the bid recognize the financial and operational constraints affecting the client?'; 'Does it refer explicitly to a key concern expressed by the client, namely the need to improve mechanisms for budgeting and financial accounting?'; 'Does it acknowledge that the survey findings from the concluding tasks in Phase 1 may lead to modifications in the Phase 2 programme?' Most of these questions should be amenable to 'yes/no' answers.

4. The ratings for each proposal can then be combined to arrive at an overall assessment of the scope for improvement (Figure 24.3). If a point-scoring method has been adopted, the marks can be summed and expressed as a percentage of the total possible points. The people undertaking this assessment need to agree the proportion of total points to be awarded to each parameter and the weighting to be assigned to particular factors.

Do not try to identify every possible item that might be considered under each parameter: the procedure would become over-complicated, impossibly time-consuming and unmanageable. The audit should instead focus on aspects that are likely to have had a critical impact on the success or failure of the bid.

The matrix shows the overall scope for improvement identified in bids a to e.

	Summary of parameter scores		
	High	Medium	Low
Matching the bid specification	b	e c	a d
Projection of value and benefit		b e	a c d
Strength of team/partnership	b	a c	d e
Client insight	b e	a c	d
Accessibility of information		a b c e	d
Communication style	b e	a	c d
Business thrust	b e		a c d
Management capacity	b	a d e	c
Presentation		a b	c d e
Technical:price relationship	b e	a d	c
Bid management	a b c	d e	

Figure 24.3 _Example of a summary of audit parameter scores_

AUDIT PARAMETERS IN DETAIL

Matching the bid specification

- Is the bid fully compliant? If not, how is it at variance?

- Is the document structured in a way that makes it easy for the client to check against the bid specification?

- Does it respond to points that the client had emphasized or specified precisely – for example, commitment to the availability of key personnel, competencies required of staff or the scheduling of time inputs and deliverables?

- Is it a complete response, in terms of its technical content and the breadth of its analysis?

- Does the bid focus sharply on the project and on the closeness of match between what the client requires and what your team can do?

- If the bid puts forward an alternative approach or a variation, have you presented a convincing argument for this? Is the variant solution accompanied by a conforming solution?

- If you were invited to comment on the bid specification or terms of reference, did you use the opportunity constructively?

Projection of value and benefit

- Does the bid put across the message that your response offers added value that clients would not be able to obtain from competitors?

- Are the outcomes of the work described in terms of the benefits intended by the client or just as services provided by your firm?

- Does the bid convey a sense of creativity and dependable innovation?

Emphasis on strength of team/partnership

- If a partnership, group or consortium is proposed, does the bid explain the rationale for its formation?

- Does the bid identify clearly the personnel forming the work team? Does it emphasize critical 'winning edge' points about the team, their experience and their knowledge?

- Do the CVs communicate the experts' professional and management strengths in ways that are particularly relevant to the requirements of the work?

- Does the bid provide supporting evidence that the nominated experts possess the required competencies?

- Is there an appropriate balance between information about the technical competencies of the team and information about your contract management skills?

- Is there evidence that team members have worked together successfully on comparable projects?

- Does the bid express a sense of team integration and commitment?

Insight into client issues and requirements

- How well are client issues and requirements analysed?

- Does the bid contain original material resulting from your own research and perceptions rather than repeating or paraphrasing data supplied by the client?

- Does the bid show empathy with client values and processes, and an understanding of the client's working environment?

- Does the bid ignore social or political issues that ought to have been recognized and discussed?

Accessibility of information in the bid

- Is the content of the bid structured efficiently in terms of its delivery of information?

- Does the bid possess a convincing logic?

- Are the parts of the bid signposted to assist navigation through the document?

- Is there a bid response matrix?

- How much cross-referencing is there from one part of the document to another?

- If there is a bid summary, is it used effectively?

- How are headings and sub-headings used? Do they highlight outputs and benefits or inputs and services? Is there a logical hierarchy in the use of headings?

Effectiveness of communication style

- Is phrasing consistent within the bid and with the client's documentation?

- Are key selling points placed up front and projected strongly and explicitly?

- Does the bid appear to have been written expressly for the occasion, rather than assembled by copy-and-paste methods?

- Are all technical points and issues adequately explained?

- Is the text free of errors in grammar, spelling, sentence construction and punctuation?

- If there are numbers in the text, do they add up correctly?

- Are appendices or annexes used appropriately for material such as extended CVs, summaries of experience and detailed statistics?

- If the bid is to be read by evaluators whose first language is not English, does the way it is written take this into account?

Business thrust

- Does the bid have a businesslike feel, as if you have done the job before?

- Do the logistics of the assignment, in terms of getting the work done efficiently, appear to have been thought through in detail?

- Is there a sense of looking ahead to problems and difficulties that might arise and building in the means to avoid or overcome them?

- Does the previous experience outlined in the bid focus on work that is recent, relevant and related to the subject of the bid?

Quality of methodology

- Are your work methods explained logically and comprehensibly?

- Is it evident how each component task and activity in the work programme will be addressed?

- Is there a direct relationship between activities and outputs?

- Are tasks itemized to an appropriate level of detail?

- Are options and alternatives analysed?

- Are innovative or challenging aspects of the methodology high-lighted?

- Does the bid avoid the temptation to include project solutions?

Projection of management capacity

- How well does the bid convey your strength in managing teams and contracts?

- Is there an appropriate emphasis on performance monitoring and progress measurement?

- Does the text refer effectively to mechanisms for quality assurance and risk management?

Quality of presentation

- Does the bid look a professionally produced document and a competent business offer?

- Is there evidence that someone has thought about the design of the document and its appearance?

- What is the quality of the page layout? Is there a balanced relationship between column width, font size and line spacing?

- Do tables have an efficient layout? Are they captioned and numbered consistently?

- Is there sufficient graphic content?

- Is the style of graphics competent and consistent throughout the document?

- Are text and figures well integrated? Or are there discrepancies between them?

Relationship between technical and price information

- Does the tender price match the technical content of the bid?

- If the client required separate technical and financial proposals, were these developed in tandem?

- Were any work components or inputs underpriced or overpriced?

- Were contingencies included for high-risk elements?

Bid management

- How efficiently were the development and production of the bid managed?

- How well had the context of the bid been researched?

- If there was specialist technical input to the bid, how effectively was it coordinated?

- Were there factors that caused difficulties or delays? Could these problems have been foreseen?

- Were any particular resources lacking or insufficient? If so, why?

Implementation

- How accurately was the bid translated into work on the ground?

- Were correct assumptions made about the project environment, work output, team competencies and so forth, when developing the bid?

- Did you recover the costs of your investment in the bid?

Client feedback

- What information came from the client about why the bid succeeded or failed?

- Have further invitations to bid been received from that client? If not, do you know why?

APPLYING THE RESULTS OF THE AUDIT

The audit will have little point unless its results are taken to heart and applied conscientiously to raise the standard of your bid documents. It is important to move the focus away from the particular bids examined in the audit to the broader canvas of your tendering activity overall. If you are a contractor working on your own, draw up a balance sheet of the points of strength and weakness in your bids, and think about how you can remedy any faults you have recognized.

Firms can use audit results as the background for internal workshops that form part of a feedback and learning strategy: the aim is to develop an approach to bid improvement that people can accept as sensible and manageable, and that helps apply the lessons of experience in specific client environments. A half-day workshop might be sufficient to explore the issues: if it were extended to a full day or more, the programme could include a hands-on case study, offering an opportunity to demonstrate ways in which ideas on bid improvement can be put into practice. The exercise might adopt the type of formula used in other quality improvement programmes: analysing how the job of preparing proposals is being done, deciding what can be done better so as to make the process more efficient and productive, and then implementing the agreed improvements.

25

Ten true stories

1

Companies seeking to pre-qualify for an EC-funded assignment were asked to include details of selected projects in their expressions of interest. One research unit sent in a form that surprisingly omitted their most relevant work. Dismayed by its failure to pre-qualify, the unit phoned the contracting authority to ask what the problem had been. The contracting authority explained that the procurement rules meant they could take into account only the information submitted in the expression of interest: it was unfortunate that the unit's selection of references had not included its key projects. 'But they are so well known we assumed you didn't need to be told about them' was the reply.

2

A consortium of UK and local contractors had been shortlisted for the preliminary design of a mass transit system in an overseas capital.

Representatives of the UK firms were helping to put the bid together in the offices of local associates. Its preparation was a complex task involving the coordination of a mass of specialist inputs, copious amounts of translation and intricate negotiations between the consortium members to meet a two-week deadline.

The design and appearance of the document received detailed attention: because of the importance of the project, the first-ranked bid would have to be placed on the desk of the president of the republic for his approval. As a consequence of all these pressures, the printing of the three-volume bid required an all-night session on the eve of the submission date. Waiting for the copies to emerge, the senior UK representative read through the text of the bid. No one had found time to do that properly before. At 4 am he discovered that the consortium was volunteering to produce full tender documentation for the next stage of system design, all within the same fixed price. After a brief explosion of anger and a hastily convened meeting, the text was revised and reprinted. The bid was delivered to the client with just half an hour to spare.

3

One bid that was not so lucky reached the offices of the client, a public sector authority in the UK, five minutes after the deadline. It was sent back unopened. The courier who brought it had been delayed in traffic and then found difficulty in locating the client's address. The authority considered it had no option but to apply the rules of the competition strictly.

4

The client had made it clear that only fully compliant bids would be considered. The contractor's management summary, the first item in the bid, included a formal statement to the effect that the bid was compliant in all respects. The credibility of this claim was undermined in the very next part of the bid, which introduced a series of conditions, variations and prevarications, partly as improvements to the scope of work and partly as reflections of the superior experience of the contractors. It was clear to any perceptive reader that the bid was not at all compliant. Despite the effort that the contractor had put into the bid, it did not progress far in the evaluation.

5

The structure of bids was left for contractors to decide. One firm started with eight pages of historical background about itself and its services: the first words were 'In 1864 when the firm's founding fathers first came together. . .'. This was for a contract due to start in 2002. The client was mentioned first on page 11 of the bid and then only in passing.

6

The client required bids to include the names of three previous clients who could be approached for references about the work done by the contractor. One bidder chose to name only the managers in its own organization who had been responsible for the contracts. When the suicidal nature of this approach was pointed out, its argument was that clients could not be expected to know the technical details of the work, and anyway its performance record was commercially confidential. Do you need to be told the result?

7

The pitfalls of repeating word for word what the client writes in the bid specification were brought home to one contractor who was unaware that the data given in the specification contained a factual error that had since proved particularly embarrassing to the client. The contractor might have been able to plead that it was misled by the client had it not presented the inaccurate information under the guise of its own research into the situation!

8

The bid specification had invited comments on the terms of reference. One of the competitors, a firm of consulting engineers, thought the invitation meant that they were expected to respond to every single clause in the client's document. The problem was that they had little to say about its content. As a result that section of their bid consisted mainly of lists of clauses with the comment, 'No comment'.

To make things worse, they called the section 'Qualification of the terms of reference'. The client regarded that as an unhelpful choice of wording. Some of its managers initially wanted to reject the bid, arguing that it was not open to bidders to qualify either the terms of reference or their response, since variant solutions were not allowed. Eventually they accepted that the firm's 'qualifications' were inconsequential matters of detail and the bid went through for evaluation. But the error cost the bid valuable marks.

9

Contractors often fail to project adequately the competitiveness of their response. For example, an expert named as a team member in one bid had worked a few years back on the client's staff, where he had done a successful job and still had many friends; but the only mention of this experience was buried deep within his CV.

While preparing the bid, the contractor had made a visit to the contract site; but few perceptions came through about what had been learnt from talking to people there, and the fact that there had actually been a visit was far from obvious. An important part of the work was a set of actions to improve the client's laboratory facilities. These were introduced one by one in a long sequence of paragraphs, whereas it would have been more effective to start the account with an overall statement of the improvement programme so that the client saw the broad picture before reading about the details.

10

The evaluation panel examining another bid found it not too far off the mark in terms of technical quality and price. But they were irritated by strange and unexplained inconsistencies. For example, the bid specification referred to a 'project manager' whereas the terms 'project director' and 'team leader' were used interchangeably by the contractor to denote the same role. The client had talked about 'tasks and activities': in the bid these became 'components and sub-components'. The bid specification required the successful contractor to set up a series of 'launch workshops'; in the text of the bid they were called 'inception workshops for senior management', while a related figure showed them as 'vision workshops'. Fertile ground for confusion.

AND THE MORAL OF THESE STORIES?

- **Follow the client's instructions.** If you choose to do something different, you have to justify it convincingly.

- **Keep bids direct and to the point.** The right choice of style will strengthen your image as the right source of professional advice.

- **Apply a structured approach to managing the development of the bid.** Remember, in asking you to prepare a bid the client is setting you a test: the quality of your response will be seen as a proxy for your performance of the work.

- **Don't feed clients data they have already.** It's your ideas and your insights that are important.

- **Recognize that the client sees your work as part of a process to be translated into action, not as an end-product in itself.**

- **Don't commit yourself to an unrealistic work plan or lead the client to expect results you cannot deliver.** Show you have thought through the work and its challenges in detail.

- **Put energy and enthusiasm into your writing.** The contract is important to the client and it has to be seen as important to you.

- **Keep a close eye on quality and compliance all the way through the development and writing of the bid.** Ensure that all the information the client has asked for is included in the bid and presented in the way the client requires.

- **Understand what the client values.** Make this a strong feature of your bid. Add value by offering more.

- **In competitions for service contracts and consultancy there is seldom a second prize.** The winner usually takes all. To write a winning tender it is not enough just to be the best value for money: you have to demonstrate your distinctive value throughout the bid and communicate it to the client emphatically and irresistibly.

Index